Teacher's Guide
Unit 1 Family

Opening the World of Learning™

A COMPREHENSIVE
EARLY LITERACY
PROGRAM

Judy Schickedanz, Ph.D.
David Dickinson, Ed.D.

in collaboration with
Charlotte-Mecklenburg Schools

PEARSON EARLY LEARNING
Pearson Learning Group

The following people have contributed to the development of this product:

Art and Design: Stephen Barth, Sherri Hieber-Day, David Mager, Judy Mahoney, Elbaliz Mendez, Jim O'Shea, Dan Trush, Jennifer Visco, Heather Wendt Kemp

Editorial: Diane Arnell, Danielle Camaleri, Teri Crawford Jones, Jaime Dritt, Deborah Eaton, Mary Lou Mackin, Susan Poskanzer

Marketing: Diane Bradley, Laura Egan

Production/Manufacturing: Karen Edmonds, Nathan Kinney, Jennifer McCormack

Publishing Operations: Carolyn Coyle, Richetta Lobban

Photo Credits:

All photography © Pearson Education, Inc. (PEI) unless otherwise specifically noted.
3: © EyeWire Collection/Getty Images, Inc. 5: *t.l.* Judy Schickedanz; *r.* Nancy Pearce/Charlotte-Mecklenburg Schools; *b.l.* Stephen Vedder, MTS, Boston College. 19, 25, 30, 31, 37, 42, 43, 46, 57, 63, 67, 68, 75, 82, 93, 98, 99, 103, 109, 113, 114, 131, 134, 135, 146, 153: *b.* © Steve Gorton/DK Images.

Acknowledgments:

In grateful acknowledgment to Alice Klein, Ph.D., and Prentice Starkey, Ph.D., who have selected activities from the Pre-K Mathematics Curriculum for use in *Opening the World of Learning*™. The Pre-K Mathematics Curriculum is scientifically research-based, and was developed and field-tested over eight years. Math Activity Aids previously published in PRE-K MATHEMATICS CURRICULUM by Klein, Starkey, and Ramirez, copyright © 2002 by Pearson Education, Inc.

Contributing Writer: Annmarie Blaney

"Clap Your Hands" Copyright © 1948 by Ruth Crawford Seeger. Used by permission.

Oonga Boonga by Frieda Wishinsky. Illustrated by Carol Thompson. Text © 1998 Frieda Wishinsky. Illustrations © 1998 Carol Thompson. Published by the Penguin Group.

Peter's Chair by Ezra Jack Keats. © 1967 Ezra Jack Keats. Published by the Penguin Group.

Noisy Nora by Rosemary Wells. Text © 1973 Rosemary Wells. Illustrations © 1997 Rosemary Wells. Published by the Penguin Group.

Whistle for Willie by Ezra Jack Keats. © 1964 Ezra Jack Keats. Published by the Penguin Group.

Corduroy by Don Freeman. © 1968 Don Freeman. Published by the Penguin Group.

Use of the trademarks and copyrights listed below implies no relationship, sponsorship, endorsement, sale, or promotion on the part of Pearson Education.

DUPLO™ is a trademark of the LEGO Group.

KAPLA © is copyrighted by Kapla World.

Lauri® is a registered trademark of Learning for All Ages.

ISBN 1-57212-747-3

Printed in the United States of America

6 7 8 9 10   V003   11 10

Opening the World of Learning™ is a trademark in the U.S. and/or in other countries of Pearson Education, Inc. or its affiliate(s).

Pearson
Early
Learning

Pearson Learning Group

1-800-321-3106
www.pearsonlearning.com
www.pearsonearlylearning.com

CONTENTS

UNIT 1 Introduction

A Comprehensive Program

Opening the World of Learning™ (*OWL*) is a comprehensive early literacy program designed for use with preschoolers. Teachers of young children have long known preschoolers are eager learners. Recent research has made abundantly clear that, for many children, these years hold the key to children's later academic success and social adjustment. *OWL* works to tap the learning capacities of all children during these critical early years.

Skills-Based Learning

OWL offers teachers the detailed guidance required to implement a comprehensive preschool program. The research-based activities contained in the Teacher's Guides foster children's learning in all content areas. The activities also build the personal and social skills required to function well in a classroom community and to establish positive relationships with peers and adults. *OWL* builds these early academic and social skills by

- enabling teachers to use strategies consistent with current research to teach all of the concepts and skills associated with oral language and literacy, including those that systematically support "code learning," such as alphabet knowledge, early writing, and phonemic awareness.

- supporting language skills throughout the day, as teachers are helped to identify and reinforce vocabulary and to strengthen conversation skills.

- building children's mathematical knowledge across the full range of concepts and skills identified by research as a foundation to later mathematical competence, including number concepts, basic computation, geometry, and measurement.

- addressing standards in a variety of content areas.

- providing a range of opportunities for children to develop the social skills required in a variety of settings.

- offering activities that help children become aware of their feelings and those of others.

- encouraging the practice of social skills and skills helpful for regulating behavior in the face of strong emotions.

- supporting children's sense of competence, curiosity, and creativity through experiences that involve creative exploration, discovery, and imaginative play.

- providing children with many opportunities to experience success as a consequence of individual effort and through guided practice in contexts where adults provide necessary scaffolding.

Effective teaching of young children is a highly complex activity, and teachers in most settings have far too little time to plan curriculum, think carefully about the intricacies of instruction, and gather and construct materials. *Opening the World of Learning* provides teachers with richly interconnected sets of experiences that appeal to children and ensure learning of the academic, personal, and interpersonal skills essential for school success.

4

Meet the Authors

Judy Schickedanz is a Professor of Literacy/Language and Cultural Studies in the School of Education at Boston University. She received her Ph.D. at the University of Illinois at Urbana-Champaign. She served as director of the Laboratory Preschool and coordinator of the early childhood program at Boston University. She has worked with a wide range of preschool programs. Dr. Schickedanz served as past president of the Literacy Development in Young Children Special Interest Group of the International Reading Association (IRA). She also served as a member of the Teaching Resources Team for NAEYC's accreditation standards revision in 2004. Dr. Schickedanz is the senior author of several books, including *Much More Than the ABCs, Understanding Children and Adolescents*, and *Writing in the Preschool: Orchestrating Meaning and Marks*.

David Dickinson is a Professor of Language and Literacy at the Lynch School of Education, Boston College. He received his doctoral training at Harvard's Graduate School of Education after working as an elementary school teacher in the Philadelphia area for five years. For twenty years he has studied language and early literacy development among low-income populations and developed and studied varied approaches to helping preschool teachers more effectively support children's language and literacy growth. He has served on many national advisory panels, including serving as a commissioner to NAEYC and helping it to revise its program accreditation standards. Dr. Dickinson is the author of numerous research articles and book chapters and has edited or co-edited four books: *The Handbook of Early Literacy Research* (Volumes I and II), *Beginning Literacy With Language*, and *Bridges to Literacy*.

The **Charlotte-Mecklenburg Schools**, Charlotte, North Carolina, are pioneers in the implementation of a literacy-based curriculum designed to lay the foundation for early school success. They continue to participate in the scientific research and assist in creating the professional development materials for *Opening the World of Learning*.

Charlotte-Mecklenburg Schools

UNIT 1 Overview

Theme: Family

In Unit 1, children will be exploring and talking about families and the many different ways family members relate to and help one another. Through the Story Time books, children will hear about a boy who helps his family take care of his baby sister, a boy who realizes how much he has grown when a new baby arrives, a girl who behaves badly when she wants attention, and a lonely stuffed bear who finds a new friend. Besides listening to stories, children will begin to recognize initial sounds in words and identify rhyming words as they build vocabulary and comprehension skills. They will also be participating in a variety of music, poetry, mathematics, science, and art activities during Center Time and in Small Groups.

Theme Concepts

* Family members have role names: mother, father, sister, and so
* Some family members live together; some live in other places b still family members.
* Grown-ups in a family take care of the children. Younger children need more care. Older children can help take care of younger brothers and sisters.
* Children sometimes get angry at parents and may feel that their parents don't love them as much as their siblings.
* Sometimes grown-ups in a family don't like things that children do and tell them to stop or be quiet.
* Families do things together that are fun.

UNIT SKILLS

Language and Literacy

* Uses language in play situations and to tell needs, wants, or thoughts; tells a personal narrative
* Responds to own name and requests for action; asks and answers questions and gives directions
* Listens with attention; follows directions
* Demonstrates increasing levels of sustained and focused engagement during read-aloud times
* Chooses to read or to pretend to read books; understands that pictures, print, and other symbols carry meaning; uses pictures to understand a book
* Indicates own writing conveys meaning
* Recognizes name; names all letters in own name
* Names the main characters and recalls some main events in stories
* Participates in dramatic play that is influenced by stories heard read aloud
* Experiments with letter forms
* Recites songs, rhymes, and poems, and engages in word play; produces words that rhyme

* Finds words with the same beginning sound

Social Studies

* Identifies similarities and differences in personal and family characteristics; begins to understand family needs, roles, jobs, and relationships
* Demonstrates awareness/respect for abilities
* Begins to understand consequences or cause and effect of personal actions or actions in stories
* Discusses valued qualities, such as honesty, courtesy, kindness, fairness, and self-control

Science

* Observes, explores, and asks questions about materials and objects in the environment
* Uses language to describe physical phenomena
* Displays familiarity with the properties and behaviors of many kinds of materials
* Observes and identifies the characteristics and basic requirements of living things

Mathematics

* Says number names at least to 20

* Counts accurately up to 10 objects in a set using one-to-one correspondence; knows that the last number in a set also names the total number
* Arranges sets in one-to-one correspondence
* Sorts objects by one or two attributes
* Recognizes and names basic geometric shapes
* Compares length and weight of objects

Social and Emotional Development

* Follows rules and routines
* Shows interest and curiosity in learning new concepts and trying new activities
* Shows empathy and understanding to others
* Participates in resolving disagreements

The Arts

* Plays simple musical instruments
* Experiments with wet/dry media to create art

Physical Development

* Uses equipment for physical development
* Uses tools and materials to strengthen hand grasp, flexibility, and coordination

Unit Components

Story Time Books

Predictable Books

Information Book

Songs and Poems CD

DVD

Language and Literacy Assessment Book

Family Connections

Adaptations Booklets

Poetry Posters

Picture Cards

OTHER THEME-RELATED BOOKS

Cox, Judy. *My Family Plays Music*. New York: Holiday House, 2003. A girl finds the perfect instrument to play along with each member of her musical family. The illustrations include pictures of string and percussion instruments.

Hoban, Russell. *A Baby Sister for Frances*. New York: Harper Trophy, 1964. The badger family has a new baby. Big sister Frances is upset about the attention her baby sister gets. She "runs away from home" by sitting under the dining room table.

Jennings, Sharon. *Into My Mother's Arms*. Ontario, Canada: Fitzhenry and Whiteside, 2003. A little girl and her mom spend their day together doing household chores, shopping for groceries, playing in the park, and so on. The little girl wants to be like her mom when she grows up.

Potter, Beatrix. *The Tale of Peter Rabbit*. New York: Penguin Putnam, 2004. Peter disobeys his mother by going into Mr. McGregor's garden and almost gets caught.

Scott, Ann Herbert. *On Mother's Lap*. New York: Clarion Books, 1992. A little boy discovers there's room enough for himself and his baby sister on their mother's lap.

Sendak, Maurice. *Where the Wild Things Are*. New York: Harper Trophy, 1998. A little boy makes a lot of noise in his house as he makes up games to have something to do. When he's sent to his room, he has an imaginary adventure.

Shea, Pegi Deitz. *New Moon*. Honesdale, PA: Boyds Mills Press, 2000. A big brother teaches his little sister to say *moon*, and to look for it in the sky.

UNIT 1 Materials and Resources

BASIC MATERIALS

To help you plan the unit on families, here is a list of the basic materials for Centers and Small Group activities. Many of these materials can be used for other units as well. You will often use these materials every day, and they can be recycled for use in the activities. If appropriate, you might want to involve families in helping you gather materials.

Beautiful Junk

Ask parents, friends, or local retail or business office staff to save materials for you.

Cardboard boxes (copy paper size)

Empty plastic squeeze top bottles (baby shampoo, baby oil, lotion)

Empty plastic pump type bottles (liquid hand soap)

Empty plastic spice-type bottles with lids (holes in lid for shaking out contents)

Newspapers

Old letterhead stationery (trim heading and use at writing center)

Old gift wrapping paper

Old paint cans (empty)

Paint can stirrers

Paint sample brochures

Paper towel cardboard tubes

Plastic baby food jars

Plastic buttons

Plastic tops from jugs of laundry detergent

Polystyrene foam plastic trays with and without divided sections

Shoeboxes with lids

Small metal cans

Small size yogurt containers

Smaller size plastic, soft drink, or water bottles

Paper, Tag Board, Stickers

Butcher block paper (white, 2 rolls, 1000', 36" wide)

Colored tissue paper

Construction paper (12" × 18" and 9" × 12"; 3 packages of each in primary colors, secondary colors, white and black)

Newsprint (for painting activities)

Tag board (manila or white; 9" × 12" and 12" × 18"; 2 packages of each)

Tissue paper (100-sheet package of 20" × 30")

Variety of self-adhesive stickers

White photocopy paper

White drawing paper (ream of printer paper)

Writing/Drawing/Painting/Collage Materials

Chalk (dust free)

Cotton swabs

Crayons, markers, pencils

Objects for printing (spools, cookie cutters, marker caps, short dowel rods, small wooden blocks or shapes)

Paint cups (for easel)

Paintbrushes for glue; wooden paintbrushes for easels (various widths)

Plastic paint palettes

Smocks

Sponges

Washable tempera paint, primary colors, white and black (4 one-gallon containers of each)

White glue

Water Table Supplies

Dishwashing detergent (for bubbles)

Duct tape

Plastic dishes, spoons, bowls, containers

Plastic dishwashing tubs to hold water in water table

Plastic funnels (various sizes)

Smocks

Sponges

Dramatic Play Area

Bars of mild baby soap

Burping cloths (cloth diapers, terry face cloths, small flannel towels)

Small size baby bibs (for dolls)

Terry bath towels, small size

Writing Center

Rings: metal rings (to make sets of name cards)

Metal cans to store sets of markers

Puzzles and Manipulatives Area

Lacing cards

Puzzles: simple wooden puzzles, alphabet puzzles

Self-fastening materials

Book Area

Alphabet books

Information books about animals, fruits and vegetables, clothing, vehicles

Simple storybooks

Simple predictable-text books

OTHER MATERIALS

The following materials are organized by week and are used with specific activities.

Week 1

Plastic baby feeding bottles

Plastic baby food jars

Small spice containers

Week 2

Cans: small coffee cans with snap-on lids

Newspaper and craft books (for making paper airplanes)

Objects: a variety including pebbles, popcorn kernels, kidney beans, paper clips, and so on

Paint chips from hardware or paint stores

Small dolls

Water play pumps

Week 3

Alphabet bingo materials

Baking props: muffin tins, small cookie sheets, small bread pans, spatulas, pastry crimpers, garlic presses

Boxes: bottoms of large greeting card boxes

Glass marbles with colors streaked through (about 24)

Magnifying glasses

Play dough (homemade recipe)

Week 4

KAPLA© blocks (or use small colored blocks)

Cafeteria-type trays, wooden bases, masonite bases (surfaces on which to build)

Dress up clothes (jackets, shirts, ties, purses, and so on)

Picks (to strum a guitar)

Water wheels

Variety of elastic bands

Variety of small boxes

SUGGESTED SUPPLIERS

Lakeshore Learning Materials, 800-778-4456

Discount School Supply, wooden doll families, 800-627-2829

Constructive Playthings, DUPLO™ people, 800-448-4115

Creative Educational Surplus, 800-886-6428

Lauri® Puzzles, 800-451-0520

Kaplaworld.com

Weekly Planner*

	Day 1	Day 2	Day 3
Start-the-Day Centers 30 Minutes	Greet children and open selected Centers.		
Morning Meeting 15 Minutes	Introduce Center Time activities.		
Center Time 60 Minutes pp. 12–14	**Sand and Water:** Exploring Water's Movement; **Book Area:** Exploring Books; **Art Area/Table:** Making Paper Collages; Printing With Objects; **Art Area/Easel:** Painting With Primary Colors; **Blocks:** Building With Blocks; **Puzzles and Manipulatives:** Constructing Puzzles, Sorting Buttons; **Dramatic Play:** Playing House; **Writing Center:** Writing My Name		
Toileting/Snack 15 Minutes			
Story Time 20 Minutes	**1st Reading** – *Oonga Boonga* pp. 19–21	**1st Reading** – *Peter's Chair* pp. 25–27	**2nd Reading** – *Oonga Boonga* pp. 31–33
Outdoor Play 35 Minutes	**Conversations:** Observe and talk with children about cooperative play in the sand box.	**Conversations:** Observe and talk with children about including others in play on the climber.	**Conversations:** Observe and talk with children about following the rule not to enter the safe zone around swings.
Songs, Word Play, Letters 20 Minutes	**Songs:** "If You're Happy"; "Eentsy, Weentsy Spider"; "Five Green and Speckled Frogs" **Poems:** "Ten Little Fingers"; "Stand Up" **Literacy Skills:** If Your Name Starts With [name a letter], Raise Your Hand pp. 22–23	**Songs:** "If You're Happy"; "Eentsy, Weentsy Spider"; "Down by the Bay" **Poems:** "Ten Little Fingers"; "Diddle, Diddle, Dumpling" **Literacy Skills:** Chiming In With Rhyming Words; Those Words Begin With the Same Sound pp. 28–29	**Songs:** "Open, Shut Them"; "Five Green and Speckled Frogs"; "Down by the Bay" **Predictable Book:** *Over in the Meadow* **Literacy Skills:** Chiming In With Rhyming Words; Let's Clap Our Names pp. 34–35
Handwashing/Toileting 10 Minutes			
Lunch/Quiet Time/ Center Time 90 Minutes	**Conversations:** *Do you have a baby in your house?* Learn their names and encourage stories about them.	**Conversations:** *What are we eating today?* Discuss names of food and familiarity to children.	**Conversations:** *Who is sitting at our table today?* Review names. Check which names children knew from before.
Small Groups 25 Minutes pp. 15–17	**Writing:** Storytelling Through Pictures and Words **Language and Print Manipulatives:** Alphabet Puzzles; Name Matching; Alphabet Letter Matching **Book Browsing:** Exploring Books	**Writing:** Storytelling Through Pictures and Words **Language and Print Manipulatives:** Alphabet Puzzles; Name Matching; Alphabet Letter Matching **Book Browsing:** Exploring Books	**Writing:** Storytelling Through Pictures and Words **Language and Print Manipulatives:** Alphabet Puzzles; Name Matching; Alphabet Letter Matching **Book Browsing:** Exploring Books
Let's Find Out About It/ Let's Talk About It 20 Minutes	**Showing Empathy and Understanding** p. 24	**Learning About the Care That Babies Need** p. 30	**Learning to Regulate Behavior** p. 36
End-the-Day Centers 20 Minutes	Open selected Centers and prepare children to go home.		

* This is a suggested schedule. Adapt to meet the needs of your program.

Day 4	Day 5
2nd Reading – *Peter's Chair* pp. 37–39	**3rd Reading** – *Oonga Boonga* p. 43
Conversations: Observe children's reactions to their own scrapes and bumps, and to the scrapes and bumps of others.	**Conversations:** Observe and talk with children about their persistence in trying to learn to pump on a swing.
Songs: "Old MacDonald Had a Farm"; "I'm a Little Teapot"; "If You're Happy" **Poems:** "Ten Little Fingers"; "Stand Up" **Literacy Skills:** Chiming In With Rhyming Words; If Your Name Starts With [name a letter], Raise Your Hand pp. 40–41	**Songs:** "Five Green and Speckled Frogs"; "Head and Shoulders, Knees and Toes" **Predictable Book:** *Over in the Meadow* **Literacy Skills:** Chiming In With Rhyming Words; If Your Name Starts With [name a sound], Raise Your Hand pp. 44–45
Conversations: *Have you helped someone feel better today?* Discuss helping and being helped.	**Conversations:** *How many spoons are on the table today?* Count and see if there is one per person.
Mathematics: Watch Me Count **Writing:** Draw and Label Pictures of Family **Book Browsing:** Exploring Books	**Mathematics:** Watch Me Count **Writing:** Draw and Label Pictures of Family **Book Browsing:** Exploring Books
The Harmonica and Other Musical Instruments p. 42	**Making Bottle Shakers** p. 46

Half-Day Program Schedule

2 hours 45 minutes
A half-day program includes two literacy circles.

10 min.	**Start-the-Day Centers** Writing Center, Book Area, Puzzles and Manipulatives
10 min.	**Morning Meeting**
60 min.	**Center Time** Incorporate some mathematics, science, and writing activities from Small Groups.
20 min.	**Story Time** Use discussion questions from Let's Talk About It to address social-emotional issues and topics from Let's Find Out About It to address concept development. Read *Let's Make Music* on Day 5 after reading *Oonga Boonga*.
35 min.	**Outdoor Play**
20 min.	**Songs, Word Play, Letters**
10 min.	**End-the-Day Centers** Writing Center, Book Area, Puzzles and Manipulatives

Connect With Families

- Help children learn about their world through information books. Encourage families to go to the library and find books about babies with lots of pictures and read-aloud text that children can understand easily. Suggest that parents look at the pictures and talk about what babies need. Families should share what children were like when they were babies.

- Encourage families to sing "If You're Happy" and "Head and Shoulders, Knees and Toes" if they know the tunes. Parents should ask children to chime in with the parts they know, or parents should chant the lyrics with children.

Start-the-Day Centers

- Open two to three Centers (e.g., Writing Center, Book Area, Puzzles and Manipulatives) for children to go to upon their arrival.

Morning Meeting

- Introduce children to Centers by showing some selected objects from each Center and briefly demonstrating activities to help them make a first choice.

- For example, on **Monday**: Show how to use squeeze bottles and funnels at the water table. Brush glue on construction paper and add pieces of tissue paper to demonstrate paper collages. **Tuesday**: Demonstrate printing with objects like blocks and forks using an inkpad soaked with tempera paint. Show name cards and writing/drawing tools from the Writing Center for writing their names. **Wednesday**: Demonstrate painting with primary colors at the easel. Show some objects from Puzzles and Manipulatives and talk about ways they can be sorted (by color, shape, etc.). On all mornings, introduce selected vocabulary books from the Book Area, show blocks from the Blocks area, and props from Dramatic Play to inspire play.

- Use the suggested vocabulary in a manner that makes their meanings clear as you demonstrate activities for each Center.

- You might want to modify or substitute an activity to meet your children's needs. For more information on organizing and adapting Center Time activities, see the Notes to Teachers on page 47.

▲ Making Paper Collages

SAND AND WATER

Exploring Water's Movement

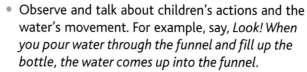
SCIENCE

Purposes: Uses simple tools in exploring water. Develops fine-motor skills.

Materials: funnels, small dipping containers, squeeze bottles, tubs of water

Suggested Vocabulary: air, bubbles, funnel, spout, top, tube; empty, full, narrow; aim, insert, pour, refill, squeeze, squirt, submerge

- Observe and talk about children's actions and the water's movement. For example, say, *Look! When you pour water through the funnel and fill up the bottle, the water comes up into the funnel.*

- Give suggestions such as, *After you squeeze the bottle, let go so air can get in. Then squeeze again and more water will squirt out.*

- Encourage experimentation, such as submerging the squeeze bottle to refill it and observing the bubbles.

BOOK AREA

Exploring Books

Purposes: Chooses independently to read or pretend to read books. Uses pictures to understand a book.

Materials: a variety of picture books—storybooks, information books, collections of nursery rhymes

- Provide eight to ten books for children to look at for the first few days.

- Encourage children to look at books together or independently.

- Join children when possible. If time permits, read aloud parts of books and talk with children about what they're reading. For example, *What kind of fish is that?* Or, *Yes, the starfish does look like a star.*

ART AREA: TABLE

Making Paper Collages

Purposes: Creates artwork to express thoughts, feelings, and energy. Uses a variety of tools and materials. Uses basic shapes and forms of different sizes to create artwork. Explores and experiments with concepts of pattern and symmetry.

Materials: construction paper, colored tissue paper cut into shapes (e.g. circles, squares), white glue, brushes, small containers, crayons, smocks

Preparation: Provide a sheet of construction paper for each child and place tissue paper shapes and glue within reach. Have children wear smocks.

Suggested Vocabulary: brush, circle, collage, construction paper, corner, glue, square, tissue paper; above, below, beside, middle, next to, on top of; spread

- Demonstrate how to brush glue on the construction paper and add tissue pieces. Talk as you demonstrate. For example, you could explain, *I'm going to use my brush to spread a little glue on my construction paper. Then I'll paste a round piece of yellow tissue on top of it.* Provide help as needed.

- Talk with children about their collages. You might say, *Oh, I see you put a big red rectangle in the middle of your paper.* Ask children to describe their work by saying, *Tell me about the colors and shapes in your collage.*

- Invite children to write their names with crayons on their pictures and display them in the center. Provide help if children request it.

Printing With Objects

Purposes: Develops understanding of 3-D objects and their surfaces. Explores and experiments with a process. Uses basic shapes and forms of different sizes to create artwork. Chooses artwork for display in the classroom.

Materials: liquid tempera paint (primary colors), markers, paper (11" × 18"), paper towels or sponges (for inking pads), polystyrene foam plastic trays, smocks, variety of objects (e.g., blocks, short dowel rods, spools, forks, cookie cutters)

Preparation: Put a sponge or layers of paper towels on trays to create ink pads (two colors for each pair of children). Soak the pads with liquid tempera paint. Place the ink pads and trays with objects within reach of children. Give each child a piece of paper and a smock to wear. Refresh inkpads as needed.

Suggested Vocabulary: block, bottom, circle, color names, corner, cube, dowel rod, edge, fork, ink, inkpad, line, side, square, top; press, print

- Encourage children to print with a variety of objects. Talk to children about their work. You might say, *What did you use to make those red lines? A fork? How interesting. Mmm . . . what other objects do you want to try?*

- Have children write their names with markers on their pictures. Provide help if children request it.

- Make a bulletin board with finished pictures.

ART AREA: EASEL

Painting With Primary Colors

Purposes: Creates artwork to express thoughts, feelings, and energy. Uses a variety of tools to explore properties of paint. Uses language to describe artwork and process.

Materials: easel, easel brushes, easel paper, newsprint, paint cups, smocks, liquid tempera paint (yellow, red, blue)

Suggested Vocabulary: bristles, color names, smock; drips, mix, spread

- Talk with children as they paint freely. You might comment, *Oh, look. I see a bit of orange where this red paint goes into the yellow. This big patch of yellow up here at the top of your painting is very interesting. Can you tell me about it?*

- Give markers to children to write their names on paintings. Provide help as needed.

BLOCKS

Building With Blocks

Purposes: Develops representational skills using 3-D objects. Interacts appropriately with others by cooperating, helping, sharing, and expressing interest. Uses language to develop and maintain relationships in play. Explores spatial relationships. Explores concept of balance.

Materials: basic collection of unit blocks

Suggested Vocabulary: balance, bridge, structure, tower; cylindrical, high, long/longer, on top of, rectangular, short/shorter, tall; build, connect, share, stack, topple

Continued on next page

- Observe children as they play and build with blocks. Encourage them to describe their buildings. Make comments on their actions such as, *That's a tall building! Tell me about it.* Or, *Oops! Sometimes it's hard to balance your blocks so they don't fall down.*

- Help children resolve conflicts and negotiate differences when they occur. You might address a problem by saying, *Oh, that was an accident. He didn't mean to bump the house. Here, I'll help you rebuild it.*

PUZZLES AND MANIPULATIVES

Constructing Puzzles, Sorting Buttons

Purposes: Develops spatial and observational skills. Uses language to describe objects.

Materials: collection of puzzles, buttons for sorting, small dishes for sorted groups of buttons

Suggested Vocabulary: buttons, corner, edge, holes, plastic, puzzles, side; big, next to, outside, part of, pointed, small, smooth, square, straight, triangular, wooden; sort

- **Constructing Puzzles:** Join children as time allows. Provide prompts to discuss the shapes and colors of puzzle pieces and discuss picture details. For example, *What color piece goes next to this one?* Or, *Does that look like part of the airplane's wing?*

- Help children identify corner and outside puzzle pieces and locate their correct positions. You might say, *The corner piece has a point, like this, and it has two straight sides, like this. There are four corner pieces altogether.*

- **Sorting Buttons:** Have children inspect the buttons and ask them to describe the buttons they are playing with. For example, *Tell me about that button. How many holes are in it? What color is it? Is it big or small?*

- Suggest that children sort buttons they think go together into dishes and ask them to explain their reasons. You might ask, *How are the buttons in this dish the same?*

DRAMATIC PLAY

Playing House

Purposes: Interacts with others by cooperating, helping, sharing, and expressing interest. Uses language to develop and maintain relationships in play. Begins to recognize and respond to the needs and emotions of others.

SOCIAL STUDIES

Materials: basic house play materials, baby bottles, baby food jars, bibs, burping cloths, dolls

Suggested Vocabulary: baby, bib, bottle, burping cloth, jar, lullaby, nipple; calm, soothe, upset; burp, feed, sleeping, whisper

- Observe children playing freely and listen to their dialogue. Comment on their actions. You might say, *It sounds like your baby is upset. Does she need burping? Maybe a lullaby would help your baby go to sleep.*

- Suggest that children act out behavior from *Oonga Boonga.* For example, *If your baby doll keeps crying, what else can you do to make her feel better? You could rock her gently, and say "oonga boonga" or "bunka wunka," just like Daniel did for Baby Louise in the story we read.*

WRITING CENTER

Writing My Name

Purposes: Uses a variety of writing and drawing tools. Experiments with letter forms. Explores the process of creating marks. Recognizes letters and names.

Materials: container for writing tools, crayons, drawing paper, markers, pencils, sets of cards with children's names printed on them, metal binder rings

Preparation: Write children's first names on tag board strips with standard form on one side (uppercase first letter, lowercase for others). On the other side, write the child's name in all uppercase. Secure the name cards with metal binder rings. Place writing tools in containers within easy reach of children.

Suggested Vocabulary: book, crayon, letter, line, marker, name card, paper; down, long, middle, short, up; draw, write

- Show children a set of name cards. Read a few names, and explain that everyone's name is on a card. Tell them they are going to practice writing their names like they appear on the cards. Allow each child to take his or her name card to use as a model.

- Prompt children to experiment with various writing materials. For example, *You might want to try a marker to draw a picture or write your name like you see on your name card.*

- Accept scribble marks and very rudimentary letters, if children are satisfied with them. Help with letter formation if children ask for it. You might say, *I see you are writing an* E *for the first letter in your name, Emily. I see one line that goes up and down. Now you need to add three lines that go across, like this.*

Overview of Small Groups

- Each day there are three different Small Groups activities. The same three activities are made available for three days, and each group of five or six children spends one of the three days in each activity. Small Groups work best when children are at tables.

- On Days 1, 2, and 3, children tell stories through pictures and words, work with a variety of language and print manipulatives, and browse information books.

- On Days 4 and 5, children count pictures, draw and label family pictures, and continue to browse information books. These Small Groups will continue on Day 1 of Week 2.

- Use the suggested vocabulary words in a manner so that their meanings are clear.

- For more information about managing Small Groups, refer to the Notes to Teachers on page 47.

Watch Me Count ▲

WRITING

High support

Storytelling Through Pictures and Words: Days 1, 2, 3

Purposes: Creates original artwork or imitates artwork from memory. Tells a personal narrative. Makes up stories that follow basic story structure.

Materials: blank books (4–5 half-sheets of white paper stapled together on the left side), markers, pencils, crayons

Procedure

- Have children draw freely in their blank books.

- Ask children about their drawings to encourage them to talk about their own experiences or stories—actual, or fictional. For instance, if a child draws a picture about a time he or she visited a park, you might ask, *What did you do there?*

- *EXTRA SUPPORT* Offer to write labels for pictures or take dictation for stories that children tell. Tell children that you have to write down their words, so they should speak slowly.

- *EXTENDING THE ACTIVITY* Ask questions that encourage children to reveal more details about their story. For example, *When did this happen? Where were you? Who else was there?*

- *ELL* Talk with children about their pictures. Repeat English words several times. Ask them to show their picture to a child sitting nearby.

- *SOCIAL-EMOTIONAL SUPPORT* Display children's books on a shelf or table. Tell them that their pictures make the classroom beautiful. Show the books to parents when they pick up or drop off their children.

LANGUAGE AND PRINT MANIPULATIVES

Medium support

Alphabet Puzzles: Days 1, 2, 3

Purposes: Associates the name of a letter with its shape. Names many uppercase letters. Names all the letters in his or her own name. Uses eye-hand coordination to perform fine-motor tasks.

Materials: collection of simple (5–7 piece) wooden jigsaw puzzles

Procedure

- Have children work with alphabet puzzles.

- *SOCIAL-EMOTIONAL SUPPORT* Before passing out alphabet puzzles, demonstrate how to care for puzzles by removing pieces one at a time, rather than dumping them out in a pile.

- *EXTRA SUPPORT* Help children find puzzle pieces and the spaces where they belong. Provide prompts such as, *Do you think* C *would fit right here?* Comment about attempts to place wrong letters in spaces, if a child does this repeatedly. You might say, *Yes, the* E *looks like it might fit there, but there is no room for the bottom part. Maybe* F *would fit better. Where's* F?

Continued on next page

Small Groups (continued)

- *Extending the Activity* Comment about the first letter in a child's name. For children who are ready, comment about letters that are at the end or in the middle of their name. For example, *Oh, your name has T at the end—Brent /t/. There's a /t/ sound. We spell that sound with T.*

- *Extra Support* Encourage two children to do a puzzle together, taking turns adding pieces. Suggest that both children look for the needed piece. This helps integrate shy children.

- *Social-Emotional Support* Praise children for their efforts.

Name Matching: Days 1, 2, 3

Medium support

Materials: tag board or poster board, marker, tray

Preparation: Make two copies of children's names on tag or poster board strips. Make several sets with 4–5 names in each set. If names begin with the same letter, put them in the same set. Put a set of them on a tray and mix them up.

Procedure

- Demonstrate the activity. You might say, *Look at the name cards on the tray. Can you help me find two names that match? That's right. These two cards say "Matthew" so let's put them on the table.*

- Have children find the matching name cards and place them on the table. Ask them to identify the names, point out the letters in names, and/or differences among names. For example, *Look! Both* John *and* Jacob *begin with the letter* J.

- *ELL* Read the names and pronounce them clearly. Encourage children to repeat the names several times.

- *Extending the Activity* Point out the first letters in names a child has matched. Tie letter and sound together. For example, *The first letter in* Hannah *is H, which sounds like /h/. Can you think of another word that begins with /h/, like* house?

Alphabet Letter Matching: Days 1, 2, 3

Medium support

Materials: tag board or poster board, letter tiles, double-sided tape or other self-fastening material, laminating machine (optional)

Preparation: Mount 6 letters in the left column of a piece of tag board or poster board. Make 3–4 posters this way, with a different collection of letters on each. Create individual letter tiles of the same letters from tag board. Laminate poster and letter tiles if possible. Use double-sided tape or other self-fastening material on backs of letter tiles to stick to tag board.

Procedure

- Demonstrate and describe activity. You might say, *Pick a letter on the poster. Try to find a letter tile that matches it. If you do, stick it on the poster next to it.*

- *ELL* Say the names of the letters as much as possible.

- *Extra Support* When children do not match letters correctly, point to a unique feature of the letter. Ask them to look closely at the letter. You might say, *Did you notice that a B has two parts on this side, and a P has just one? That's the difference between* B *and* P.

BOOK BROWSING

Exploring Books: Days 1, 2, 3, and Days 4, 5

Low support

Purposes: Chooses independently to read or pretend to read books in the book area and other settings. Reads or pretends to read information books.

Materials: collection of at least eight picture information books about animals, fruits and vegetables, clothing, and vehicles; collection of simple jigsaw puzzles, Picture Cards 1–17

Suggested Vocabulary: names of animals, clothing items, fruits, vegetables, vehicles

Procedure

- Have children look at books in pairs or individually. Encourage children to swap books.

- *Extra Support* Ask children questions about the books they are reading. For example, *What animals are in that book?* Provide names when children do not know them and label items as you talk about them. You might say, *That apple is so bright and red that it makes me hungry. Do you like apples?* Note each child's vocabulary.

- *ELL* Have children repeat the names of pictured items after you've said them several times. Face the children, so that they can watch your mouth movements.

- *Extending the Activity* When children already know basic names for things, focus on names of parts (e.g., roots, leaves, truck bed, cab tires).

- Have pairs of children look at the Picture Cards and then find the same or similar pictures in the book illustrations. Provide puzzles as an additional alternative to Book Browsing.

MATHEMATICS

Watch Me Count: Days 4, 5

High support

Purposes: Counts increasingly larger sets of objects. Counts sets of objects by using a stable sequence of number names, establishing one-to-one correspondence between the number names and objects counted, and stating the cardinal number name for the sets of objects counted.

Materials: Activity Aids 1–3; strips of paper representing sets of objects to count; *alternative:* strips of paper or tagboard, markers

Preparation: Make two photocopies of each Activity Aid. Cut along the dotted lines so that each child has a 3-object strip (3 elephants), 7-object strip, and 15-object strip. The 30-object strips should only be given to children who are ready to count beyond 15. Alternative: Make strips by dividing strips of paper or tagboard into equal cells in the following quantities: three each of 3-person and 5-person strips; two 7-person strips; one each of the 10-, 15-, and 30-person strips. Draw smiley faces in each cell.

Suggested Vocabulary: how many, one, two, three, etc; count

Procedure

- Tell children that today they are going to count the pictures on counting strips.

- Place a 3-object strip in front of the first child and ask, for example, *How many elephants are in this family?* Encourage the child to count the pictures on the strip. If the child says, "1, 2, 3," but does not immediately state the cardinal number name for the set, ask, *How many elephants are there?* If the child makes errors but self-corrects, have him or her recount the strip.

- Give a 7-object strip to children who counted the 3-object strip correctly. Give a 3-object picture strip again to children who did not count it correctly. Continue in this fashion so children do not move on to larger strips if they count incorrectly.

- *EXTRA SUPPORT* If the child makes an error and does not self-correct, provide extra support. You might say, *Let's count again. I'll count with you this time.* Then count with the child.

- *EXTENDING THE ACTIVITY* If time permits, as an extension give a 30-object strip to children who counted the 15-object strip correctly.

Progress Monitoring

You may copy and use pages 155–156 to keep notes on your observations. Note which sets (e.g., 3, 7, 15, 30) the child correctly counted. Record types of errors the child made: number word error (e.g., does not know number words beyond ten), one-to-one correspondence error (e.g., skipped objects), cardinal number error (e.g., re-counted instead of stating the cardinal number of the set). See page 47 for more information on Progress Monitoring.

WRITING

Draw and Label Pictures of Family:
Medium support

Days 4, 5

Purposes: Creates artwork to express thoughts, feelings, and energy. Shares ideas about personal creative work. Talks about their understanding of relationships among people and animals.

Materials: paper, markers, pencils

Procedure

- Explain to children that *Oonga Boonga* and *Peter's Chair* are stories about families. Tell them that mothers, fathers, grandmothers, grandfathers, aunts, uncles, and children make up families.

- Invite children to draw families. Ask them to name the people or animals in their picture. Children may write the names if they wish.

- *ELL* Use children's drawings to aid their understanding of family words. Ask them to point to and name different family members, such as *mother* or *brother,* in both English and their first language.

- *SOCIAL-EMOTIONAL SUPPORT* Some children choose not to draw and say that they can't. Talk to them about what they want to draw. Help them decide whom to draw first. Then, point to your head and suggest they start there. For example, *You can draw a circle for the mother's head. You could draw this part of her body next, from the shoulders to the waist.*

- *EXTENDING THE ACTIVITY* Ask questions to prompt children who are ready to add details to their drawings. For example, *Does the grandmother wear glasses? How many fingers do you have?*

SUGGESTED RESOURCES

Books

De Bourgoing, Pascale and Gallimard Jeunesse. *Fruit: A First Discovery Book.* New York: Scholastic, 1989.

Royston, Angela. *Eye Openers: Sea Animals.* New York: Simon and Schuster, 1992.

Royston, Angela. *Eye Openers: Trucks.* New York: Simon and Schuster, 1992.

Developing Children's Language Through Conversation

One of the best ways to form a relationship with children is to talk with them about their families, their home experiences, and their feelings. Talking with children also helps them master new words, develop concepts, and learn to think about things. For these reasons, it is very important to have conversations with all the children in your

Families

In the first weeks of school, it is important to have conversations that help you get to know each child. The topic for the first unit is Family. Invite children to talk about experiences or people in their families that are like events or characters from the books. Encourage them to use names for different kinds of relatives *(cousin, sister, uncle)* and help clarify the person's relationship to the child. For example:

Teacher: *Is Carla a child or a grown-up?*

Child: A grown-up.

Teacher: *Is she your aunt, your mommy's sister?*

Mealtime

Use Oonga Boonga to Talk About Families

After you've read *Oonga Boonga*, sit at a table with several children as they eat snacks or lunch. Listen to what they are talking about. Join in by asking them to say more or to clarify their ideas. If the children are quiet, start a conversation about one of the characters or events in the book. See the model conversation for examples of questions and prompts.

A Model for Conversation

Mealtime: Conversation About Families

Teacher: *In* Oonga Boonga, *Baby Louise cried very loudly. Do you remember how she wailed and sobbed?*

Child: Yeah. The pictures fell!

Teacher: *That's right. She wailed so loudly that the pictures fell off the wall. Do you have any younger brothers or sisters who cry?*

Child: No, but I got a baby cousin, Tanika.

Teacher: *Does she ever get upset and cry?*

Child: Yeah. She can cry real loud.

Teacher: *Uh-oh! It sounds like maybe she can wail, too! Have you ever helped her stop crying?*

Child: Yes. I make faces and sometimes she laughs.

Teacher: *Yes, babies do like it when we make silly faces for them and talk to them. Is there anything else you have tried that works?*

Child: Yes, sometimes I sing to her.

Teacher: *Wonderful! It must feel good to know that you are making Tanika feel better. And I bet her mother likes that too.*

Child: Yeah, she wants me to come over all the time!

Good Conversations

Help clarify the ideas the child is trying to communicate. Do not pretend you understand. Instead, listen carefully and ask questions to help the child express his or her ideas.

18

▶ **Start-the-Day Centers** (see pages 12–14)
Make available two or three Centers as you greet children and their families.

▶ **Morning Meeting** (see page 12)
Gather children and review plans for the day. Orient children to center activities and help them make a first choice. Create a turns list for Centers if necessary.

▶ **Center Time** (see pages 12–14)
Children spend time in Centers of their choice.

▶ **Story Time: 1st Reading**

Oonga Boonga

Author: Frieda Wishinsky

Summary: Family members try to soothe Baby Louise. Only her brother Daniel can make her stop crying by saying the words "Oonga boonga" and "Bunka wunka."

Theme Link: Family—Babies need a lot of care, and all family members try to help.

Purposes

Listens to stories read aloud. Demonstrates increasing levels of sustained and focused engagement. Increases the number of words in listening vocabulary. Develops understanding of main events.

Read the Story

As you read, vary the tone and pitch of your voice and the speed of your reading. Make comments that help children notice and track story details. Use voice, gestures, illustrations, or brief explanations to introduce new story words. Wait to discuss the story until after it has been read.

Suggested Vocabulary

Use these words often during Story Time and throughout the day.

brother a boy in a family with other children
faded went away little by little
family a mother, father, and their children; all of a person's relatives
gently softly and tenderly
harmonica a musical instrument
jig a lively dance
lullaby a song that quiets a baby
scampered ran away quickly
sobs cries with short quick breaths
tears water coming from the eyes; crying
unison together; at the same time
wails loud cries
whispered ke softly and low

> ### English Language Learners
> When reading aloud, support children in learning to say and understand new words. For example, point to pictures, use voice or gestures, and say words slowly and clearly a second time.

> ### Extending the Book
> For children who are ready for a challenge, have them help you read the title of the book. Use your finger to underline the title words, letter by letter, and sound them out to children.

Progress Monitoring

For information on Progress Monitoring, refer to page 47. Note which individual children focus on the story and reveal through facial expressions that they follow and understand story events. Observe whether children pay attention throughout the story, focus only after the story is well underway, or lose interest as soon as text reading ends. Listen to any comments and responses to discussion questions. These provide information about a child's understanding.

A MODEL FOR READING: *Use the following model to help you plan your book reading.*

Cover

Underline the title with your finger as you read it.

Frieda Wishinsky is the person who wrote this story. (Underline her name.) *She is the author. Carol Thompson drew the pictures. She is the illustrator.* Underline her name.

Oonga *and* Boonga *are funny words, aren't they? They are fun to say. I wonder why an author would use such funny words as the name of a book. Let's read the story and find out.*

pp. 2–3 (Read page 2.)

Define **tears**, pointing to the baby and then to the baby's tears splashing all over the page.

pp. 4–5 (Read page 5.)

Point to the **tears** and to the blue river in the illustration.

Oh, dear! Baby Louise didn't seem to like the little song her mother sang to her. That's too bad. She looks unhappy, doesn't she?

pp. 6–7 (Read page 7.)

As you read, define **gently** using the words *very softly and carefully.*

Baby Louise's cries, her **wails**, *were loud enough to shake the pictures off the walls. That's loud!*

pp. 8–9 (Read page 9.)

pp. 10–11 (Read page 11.)

Point to Grandpa's **harmonica**. Run your finger back and forth between Grandpa's two shoes to explain that a **jig** is a kind of dance.

Summarize the last two story events. *Nothing seems to work. Baby Louise didn't want the bottle of milk Grandma offered, and she didn't like Grandpa's* **harmonica** *music or his little dance.*

pp. 12–13 (Read page 12.)

Nothing seems to be working.

pp. 14–15 (Read page 14.)

Read with expression. Change your voice for each *oonga boonga* as if you were talking to a baby.

pp. 16–17 (Read page 16.)

*They all said "oonga boonga" at the same time. They all said it in **unison**, and it sure seemed to work, didn't it?*

Baby Louise looks happy now, doesn't she?

pp. 18–19 (Read page 18.)

Read with expression to convey concern and a sense of "Oh, no! Here we go again." After reading the word **faded**, provide the meaning, "went away, little by little." Point to pictures in sequence, and describe them.

Oh, no! Baby Louise is crying again.
I wonder why.

pp. 20–21 (Read page 20.)

That's strange. Oonga boonga *worked before. I wonder why it's not working now.*

This comment is intended to prompt children to think. Do not start a discussion just yet.

pp. 22–23 (Read page 22.)

pp. 24–25 (Read pages 24 and 25.)

When you come to the word **whispered**, lower your voice to suggest the word's meaning.

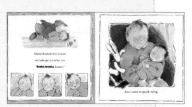

Story Discussion

That's the story of Oonga Boonga. Show cover and point to the title. *Where did the words in the title come from?*

Prompt discussion with questions like these: *Daniel could always get Baby Louise to stop crying, couldn't he? Baby Louise stopped crying when he was around. I wonder why. What do you think?*

We will read this story again on another day and we can talk more about why Baby Louise stopped crying when her brother talked to her.

▶ Outdoor Play

As you transition to Outdoor Play, say something like, *If your name starts with* D (hold up letter) *like* Daniel [L *like* Louise, G *like* Grandpa, N *like* neighbors, M *like* mother, F *like* father], *you may get up to go outside.* Provide others as needed for names in your classroom. See pages 10–11 for suggested conversation topics during this time.

▶ Songs, Word Play, Letters

Today children will be playing word games, singing songs, and reciting poems. Add your favorite game, song, or poem to this collection.

Songs

"If You're Happy"; "Eentsy, Weentsy Spider"; "Five Green and Speckled Frogs"

Poems

"Ten Little Fingers"; "Stand Up"

Literacy Skills

If Your Name Starts With [name a letter], Raise Your Hand

Purposes

Recognizes own name. Responds to own name and requests for action or information. Recites songs, rhymes, chants, and poems and engages in language and word play. Counts up to ten objects in a set using one-to-one correspondence.

Suggested Sequence for Today's Circle

1. "If You're Happy"
2. "Ten Little Fingers"
3. "Eentsy, Weentsy Spider"
4. If Your Name Starts With [name a letter], Raise Your Hand
5. "Stand Up"
6. "Five Green and Speckled Frogs"

Materials and Instructional Procedures

IF YOU'RE HAPPY

Materials: CD Track 1, Song Lyrics p. 159

Vocabulary: clap, hands, tap, knees

Procedure

- Sing one verse of the song slowly and do the motions (clapping hands) as you sing. Children can join in with both words and motions, but many will watch the first time, without participating fully.

- Tell children, *Let's do that again!* This comment acknowledges children's first efforts. Let them know that participation does not mean that they must know all the words and motions for a new song. This time, sing two verses, using clapping hands for the action in the first verse and tapping knees in the second.

TEN LITTLE FINGERS

Materials: Poetry Posters: Poem 1, CD Track 26

Vocabulary: fingers, shut, tight, open, wide, together, high, low, fold

Procedure

- Review the poem and write it on a small note card, if you need prompts. Read the poem aloud to children without showing the poster. Do all the motions as you recite and look directly at the children. Good eye contact signals children to join in as best they can. Pause briefly at the end of each

action to allow children to catch up with you, without pointing out individuals or demanding a specific level of participation.

- After reciting the poem, do it again, this time displaying the poster. You might say, *It's fun to use our hands.* Proceed as before. Show your own enthusiasm for the poem to help engage children.

EENTSY, WEENTSY SPIDER

Materials: CD Track 5, Song Lyrics p. 159

Vocabulary: up, spout, washed, out, dried

Procedure

- Proceed as you did with "If You're Happy." Go slowly and do the motions in a way that invites children to participate, if they wish. Sing the song just once today and tell children that you will do the song again another day.

IF YOUR NAME STARTS WITH [NAME A LETTER], RAISE YOUR HAND

Materials: uppercase alphabet cards, children's name cards

Vocabulary: letter, name, starts with, word

Procedure

- Say, *We're going to play a game with our names. I'm going to hold up a letter, like this.* (Hold up the letter that begins your own name.) *If your name starts with [name letter], raise your hand. My name starts with [name*

letter], *so I'm raising my hand.* [Child's name, if applicable]*'s name starts with* [name letter], *so he can raise his hand, too. I'll do a letter for everybody's name. Everyone will get a turn. Okay, let's start.*

- If a child whose name starts with the letter you are holding up does not respond, pull out that child's name card. Point to the first letter and say, *Your name starts with E, Eliot, so it's your turn to raise your hand.*

STAND UP

Materials: Poetry Posters: Poem 3, CD Track 28

Vocabulary: stand, turn around, clap, bow, stamp, wave, hand, bend, knees

Procedure

- Proceed as with "Ten Little Fingers." Recite the poem only once and tell children they will do the poem again on another day.

FIVE GREEN AND SPECKLED FROGS

Materials: CD Track 10, Song Lyrics p. 160, flannel board and flannel pieces

Preparation: Make these flannel board pieces: 5 green speckled frogs, 1 brown speckled log, 1 blue pool, several black bugs.

Vocabulary: green, speckled, log, delicious, pool, cool

Procedure

- Tell children that you will be singing a song about some frogs that jump off of a log, into a nice, cool pool. You might say, *Here's the log. Here are 1, 2, 3, 4, 5 frogs sitting on the log.* (Count the pieces as you place them.) *I'll put the cool pool right over here. Okay, here's how the song goes.*

- Sing the song, moving one frog each time. For verses 1, 2, and 3, quickly state the number of remaining frogs, while pointing to them, as a group. On the last three verses (two frogs, then one frog, then no frogs remain), pause briefly to allow children to notice the number of frogs remaining.

- Point to the bugs on the flannel board when you come to that point in the song. Model eating the bugs by saying *glub, glub.* Rub your tummy while singing *most delicious.*

- If you think children will enjoy singing the song another time, say, *Let's do that again. Let me get the frogs back over here on their log— 1, 2, 3, 4, 5 frogs.* (Count each frog as you move it to the log.) *Okay, we're ready. Let's sing it again!*

▶ Lunch/Quiet Time/Centers

This time is set aside for lunch, quiet time, and center activities. See pages 10–11 for suggested conversation topics during this time.

▶ Small Groups

For information on Small Groups, refer to pages 15–17.

▶ Let's Talk About It

Showing Empathy and Understanding

Purposes

Shows empathy and understanding to others. Expresses feelings through appropriate language.

Procedure

- Ask several children to tell you about a kindness that a child extended to them or that they extended to another child today. Children might need your assistance in telling about the event.

- Help children practice expressing empathy. For example, provide a short verbal description of a child in need. (A child is crying because he scraped his knee; a child just spilled paint on the floor.) You can ask children what they might do to make the crying child feel better or to help the child clean up the spill.

- Add to the children's ideas as appropriate. Practice with children what to say. You could use these examples: *Here's a tissue for your face.* Or, *I have some paper towels for cleaning up the spill.*

▲ Encourage children as they help one another. These children are helping each other clean up a paint spill.

▶ End-the-Day Centers

Children spend time in Centers of their choice. As children leave for home, say something that will help each child look forward to the next day. For example, tell children that they will read a new book, *Peter's Chair*, or that their name is on the turns list for a certain activity.

▶ **Start-the-Day Centers** (see pages 12–14)
Two or three Centers are available as you greet children and their families.

▶ **Morning Meeting** (see page 12)
Orient children to center activities and help them make a first choice.

▶ **Center Time** (see pages 12–14)
Children spend time in Centers of their choice.

▶ **Story Time: 1st Reading**

Peter's Chair
Author: Ezra Jack Keats

Summary: Peter's parents paint his old baby furniture for his new sister. Peter is angry about losing these items and not getting attention. He leaves home and takes his old chair. Peter then sees that he has outgrown his chair, so he helps his dad paint it.

Theme Link: Family—Children learn how to share the attention of adults with siblings and how to be a big brother or sister.

Purposes

Listens to stories read aloud. Demonstrates increasing levels of sustained and focused engagement. Increases the number of words in listening vocabulary. Develops understanding of main events.

Read the Story

Read *Peter's Chair* with expression to show Peter's strong feelings as he adjusts to being a big brother. Briefly explain that Peter fools his mother by leaving his shoes behind the curtain. To help children learn new story words, use voice and gestures, illustrations, or brief explanations. Wait to discuss the story until after you have read it.

Suggested Vocabulary

Use these words often during Story Time and throughout the day.

cradle a small bed for a baby, usually on rockers
crib a small bed with high sides to keep a baby from falling out
crocodile a large, scaly animal with a long body, four short legs, thick skin, a pointed snout, and a long tail
rascal a person who does playful tricks
signs clues
stretched reached out one's arms and legs
surprised feeling like something was unexpected

Extending the Book

For children who are ready for a challenge, ask them to help you read the title of the book. Underline the words and sound them out to children.

English Language Learners

Read s-t-r-e-t-c-h-e-d in a drawn-out way, *CRASH!* loudly, and *shhh!* softly to help demonstrate the word meanings. Also point to objects in pictures as you read about them.

Progress Monitoring

As you read, notice children's facial expressions and attentiveness. Who expresses curiosity at this new story? Who appears eager to see what will happen next? Which children point to pictures and answer *yes* and *no* to basic questions? Record your observations on copies of pages 155–156.

A MODEL FOR READING: *Use the following model to help you plan your book reading.*

Cover

The name or title of this book is Peter's Chair. *Underline the title with your finger as you read it.*

The author, or person who wrote this story, is Ezra Jack Keats. (Underline his name with your finger as you read it *is also the illustrator, the person who drew the pictures.*

This is Peter. What is he looking at? (Point to the chair.) Let's find out what happens in the story of Peter's Chair.

pp. 2–3 (Read page 2.)

Peter **s-t-r-e-t-ch-ed** *as high as he could. He had to stand on his tiptoes and reach as high as he could reach. He had to* **stretch** *to finish his building.*

pp. 4–5 (Read page 5.)

Use a quiet voice when you read Peter's mother's words.

Oh, Peter has a new brother or sister.

pp. 6–7 (Read page 7.)

A **cradle** *is a small bed for a newborn baby. Here's the long part of the* **cradle**, *and here's the top part.* Use your finger to trace the outline of the cradle.

pp. 8–9 (Read page 9.)

Read slowly and sadly to convey Peter's feelings when he whispers, "It's my high chair."

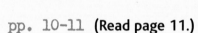

Oh, dear. First his cradle, and now his high chair. Peter looks quite unhappy. Point to Peter's face.

pp. 10–11 (Read page 11.)

Point to the **crib** and the chair as you read these words. When you read, "They didn't paint that yet!," say it with enthusiasm to convey Peter's joy.

Oh my, first his cradle, then his high chair, and now his crib. At least they didn't paint his little blue chair. I wonder what Peter is going to do next?

pp. 12–13 (Read page 12.)

Point to Peter as you read.

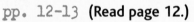

I wonder what he's going to do in his room.

pp. 14–15 (Read page 15.)

Point to Peter as you read.

Peter must be very upset about all of his baby things if he's thinking of running away from home. Well, let's see what happens.

pp. 16–17 (Read page 16.)

For now, at least, they aren't going to go far from home.

pp. 18–19 (Read page 18.)

Point to the chair and to Peter's bottom to emphasize that he is too big to fit.

Oh, Peter is too big for his chair. This must be a chair that he had when he was a lot younger, perhaps when he was a baby.

pp. 20–21 (Read page 20.)

Point to the window as you read the first sentence.

They didn't answer Peter's mother. They pretended they didn't hear her. Peter has an idea. Hmm, I wonder what it is.

pp. 22–23 (Read page 23.)

Point to the **crocodile**, to the bag, and to Peter's shoes as you read.

*A **rascal** is someone who likes to play tricks on people. Peter's mom called him a **rascal**.*

pp. 24–25 (Read pages 24 and 25.)

Point to Peter as you read page 25.

pp. 26–27 (Read page 26.)

Did you hear what Peter said to his father? I'm a little surprised by that. Are you? I thought he didn't want his sister, Susie, to have any of his baby furniture.

pp. 28–29 (Read page 29.)

What did Peter decide to do with his chair? (paint it for the baby)

That's the story of Peter's Chair.

Story Discussion

Prompt discussion with questions. For example:

What did Peter decide to do with his little blue chair? (paint it for the baby)

The ending was a little bit of a surprise for me because for a while, Peter was unhappy about his baby sister getting all of his furniture. Was the ending a surprise for you too?

We will read this story again another day, and we can talk about why Peter might have changed his mind.

▶ Outdoor Play

Dismiss children for Outdoor Play as you did yesterday, having children match first letters in their names to words in the story. Hold up the letters *P* for *Peter,* *B* for *bone,* *S* for *sidewalk,* and so on. See pages 10–11 for suggested conversation topics during this time.

▶ Songs, Word Play, Letters

Today children will be playing word games, singing songs, and reciting poems. Add your favorite game, song, or poem to this collection.

Songs

"If You're Happy"; "Eentsy, Weentsy Spider"; "Down by the Bay"

Poems

"Ten Little Fingers"; "Diddle, Diddle, Dumpling"

Literacy Skills

Chiming In With Rhyming Words; Those Words Begin With the Same Sound

Purposes

Finds words with the same beginning sound. Recites songs, rhymes, chants, and poems, and engages in language and word play. Says the words that complete rhymes, poems, or lines from stories either individually, or in a group. Uses new words in meaningful ways. Follows two-step directions and builds up to following multiple-step directions. Counts up to ten objects in a set using one-to-one correspondence.

Suggested Sequence for Today's Circle

1. "If You're Happy" (and Those Words Begin With the Same Sound)
2. "Ten Little Fingers" (and Chiming In With Rhyming Words)
3. "Eentsy, Weentsy Spider"
4. "Down by the Bay"
5. "Diddle, Diddle, Dumpling"

Materials and Instructional Procedures

If You're Happy (and Those Words Begin With the Same Sound)

Materials: CD Track 1, Song Lyrics p. 159

Vocabulary: clap, hands, stomp, feet, shout

Procedure

- Sing three verses, using clapping hands, stomping feet, and shouting "Hurray!" as motions.

- Proceed at a pace slow enough to allow children to complete motions with you.

- After singing "If You're Happy," say something like, *I noticed that some of the words in that song begin with the same sounds.* Happy and hands *begin with the same sound; they sound the same at the beginning:* /h/ happy and /h/ hand. *That's interesting, isn't it? Some words begin with the same sounds.*

Ten Little Fingers (and Chiming In With Rhyming Words)

Materials: Poetry Posters: Poem 1, CD Track 26

Vocabulary: fingers, shut, tight, open, wide, together, high, low, fold

Procedure

- Present the poem orally again on this day, without reference to the poster. Pause briefly at the end of each motion to give children a chance to catch up.

- You might say, *Let's do that again and this time you can say some of the words with me.* Display the poster. Pause briefly before the second word in each pair of rhyming words to let children chime in (*me/see*; *wide/hide*; *low/so*).

- Hold up both hands with fingers splayed, and ask children to do the same. You might say, *There's something else we can do with our fingers. We can count them.* Lead the counting. Fold down one finger at a time on one hand, and then on the other, until all have been counted.

- Some children will find it difficult to fold fingers down one at a time. Expect that some children will get involved watching their own fingers and will lose track of your model. Children will become more accustomed to this activity as you repeat it on subsequent days.

EENTSY, WEENTSY SPIDER

Materials: CD Track 5, Song Lyrics p. 159

Vocabulary: up, spout, washed, out, dried

Procedure

- Proceed as you did yesterday, performing the motions in a way that invites children to participate.

- You may want to add another verse from the book *The Itsy Bitsy Spider*. A source for this book is provided on this page.

DOWN BY THE BAY

Materials: CD Track 3, Song Lyrics p. 159, flannel board and flannel pieces

Preparation: Make these flannel board pieces: 3 watermelons, snake, cake, frog, dog, mouse, house, waves.

Vocabulary: bay, watermelons, snake, cake, frog, dog, mouse, house

Procedure

- Tell children, *We're going to sing a song about some silly animals*.

- Sing the song and place the appropriate animals on the flannel board as you sing. Remove the last piece before placing any new ones.

- Children may become silly; let the next verse of the song pull them back before they dissolve in laughter again.

- Remove flannel pieces and sing the song a second time, if you have time and think the children would enjoy it.

DIDDLE, DIDDLE, DUMPLING

Materials: Poetry Posters: Poem 2, CD Track 27; flannel board and flannel pieces

Preparation: Make these flannel board pieces: boy, bed, pair of socks (stockings), 2 shoes.

Vocabulary: son, stocking, on, off

Procedure

- Recite the poem slowly, pointing to the appropriate parts of the flannel board scene as you proceed. Do not present the illustration yet. Children should learn to attend to the words first. Some children will join you, but many will just watch during this first presentation.

- Tell children, *Let's do that again*. Repeat the poem as before, this time displaying the poem.

Progress Monitoring

Observe whether a child does the following: engages quickly, attempts verbal participation, attempts hand/finger/body motions, is attentive but not actively participating, or is withdrawn. Note which children anticipate and chime in quickly with rhyming words, which ones follow only after you have said the rhyming words, and any children who remain silent. Record your observations on copies of pages 155–156.

SUGGESTED RESOURCE

Book

Trapani, Iza. *The Itsy Bitsy Spider*. Watertown, MA: Charlesbridge Publishing, Inc. 1998.

▶ Lunch/Quiet Time/Centers

This time is set aside for lunch, quiet time, and center activities. See pages 10–11 for suggested conversation topics during this time.

▶ Small Groups

For information on Small Groups, refer to pages 15–17.

▶ Let's Find Out About It

Learning About the Care That Babies Need

Purposes

Uses own experiences to understand story events and expository text. Develops understanding that nonfiction texts are used to find information. Begins to recognize the needs and emotions of others.

Materials

book: *Oonga Boonga*; other information books about babies and baby care for young children (first books for toddlers showing daily activities of an infant or toddler); rattles and other baby toys (teething rings, cloth or chubby books)

Suggested Vocabulary

Introduce these words and use them in the discussion: baby, comfort, diapers; hungry, uncomfortable; burp, feed, rock

Procedure

- Remind children that babies must be cared for. Go through some pages in *Oonga Boonga* and show caring behavior (feeding, rocking, singing to) displayed by adults in the story.

- Select and show pictures from other books of babies being bathed, fed, put to bed, played with, and read to.

- Ask children in the group who have baby brothers or sisters to talk about them. Perhaps their siblings have special blankets or stuffed animals and sleep in a crib.

- Show baby playthings, if possible. Talk about why babies like these things and why they are safe (rounded corners of chubby books, non-breakable materials, nothing a baby can swallow).

> **Extending the Activity**
>
> Ask children who are ready for a challenge to tell you about a toy of theirs that would not be safe for a baby.

Center Time Connections

Baby play props can be added to the Dramatic Play area for use with baby dolls.

SUGGESTED RESOURCES

Books

Falwell, Cathryn. *We Have a Baby.* Boston: Houghton Mifflin, 1993.

Leuck, Laura (author) and Clara Vulliamy (illustrator). *My Baby Brother Has Ten Tiny Toes.* Chicago: Albert Whitman & Company, 1997.

Meyers, Susan (author) and Marla Frazee (illustrator). *Everywhere Babies.* Orlando, Florida: Harcourt, 2001.

> **English Language Learners**
>
> Name items or actions portrayed in books. Repeat the words, saying them clearly. Encourage children to say the words with you.

▶ End-the-Day Centers

Children spend time in Centers of their choice. As children leave for home, say something that will help each child look forward to the next day. For example, tell children that tomorrow they will learn a new song called "Open, Shut Them."

▶ **Start-the-Day Centers** (see pages 12–14)
Invite children to go to two or three open Centers.

▶ **Morning Meeting** (see page 12)
Discuss center activities and help children make a first choice.

▶ **Center Time** (see pages 12–14)
Children spend time in Centers of their choice.

▶ **Story Time: 2nd Reading**

Oonga Boonga
Author: Frieda Wishinsky

Purposes

Recalls some main events when asked, *What is happening in this story?* Links characters' basic emotions to their actions. Uses own experiences to understand characters' feelings and motivations. Expresses the main idea of a story or other text in a way that shows increasing understanding.

Read the Story Again

This time reconstruct the story with children. Help them recall events and characters' actions by asking, *What is happening here?* Use the following strategies as you read.

- Read the text first, then ask a question.
- Move the story along by reading the text without asking questions.
- Ask questions without reading, then confirm, clarify, or elaborate on children's answers and move on in the story.
- Ask questions, then read a sentence or two to confirm children's responses or clear up a misunderstanding.

- Continue to explain new words using explanations, tone of voice, facial expressions, and illustrations.

After reading, prompt discussion with the questions provided, or with similar ones.

Suggested Vocabulary

Use these vocabulary words as often as possible when discussing the story and during other activities in the school day.

brother a boy in a family with other children
faded went away little by little
family a mother, father, and their children; all of a person's relatives
gently softly and tenderly
harmonica a musical instrument
jig a lively dance
lullaby a song that quiets a baby
scampered ran away quickly
sobs cries with short quick breaths
tears water coming from the eyes; crying
unison together, at the same time
wails loud cries
whispered spoke softly and low

Extending the Activity

Invite children who are ready for a challenge to help read words tucked in illustrations (e.g., *meeow* on page 9, and *waaaah* on page 11). Use your finger to underline the words and sound them out to children after reading the main text.

English Language Learners

Find the page where the neighbors offer advice on how to get Baby Louise to stop crying. Point to your own body to explain *stomach* and *side* as you read the words on the page. Invite children to touch their own stomachs and their sides as they say the words with you.

Progress Monitoring

Note which children react positively, with recognition and delight, indifferently, or negatively. Note responses to these questions: *What is happening here? Who is this? What happened next?* Note individual answers about why Baby Louise stopped crying in response to Daniel. Record your observations on copies of pages 155–156.

A MODEL FOR READING: *Be sure to read all the text on each page. When you read it will vary, depending on the flow of conversations with children.*

Cover

You know this story, because we read it the other day. The name or title of this story is . . . (Pause.)

That's right. The name of the story is Oonga Boonga. *We are going to read the story again today, and talk about all the things that happen.*

pp. 2-3

What's happening here?

Yes, Baby Louise is crying and nobody can make her stop.

pp. 4-5

Who is trying here to get Baby Louise to stop crying? (her mother)

Yes, her mother. What did she do to try to get Baby Louise to stop crying? (held her close, sang a lullaby) *Who tries to make Baby Louise stop crying next? Do you remember?* (her father)

pp. 6-7

Yes, her father tried. He rocked her back and forth slowly—very **gently**—*and talked very softly to her, but it didn't work. Baby Louise kept crying—she was* **wailing** *so loudly that pictures fell off the walls!* **Wailing** *means she was crying loudly. So that didn't work. Who tried next?* (Grandma)

pp. 8-9

Yes, Grandma tried something next, and what did she try? Point to the bottle in Grandma's hands. (feeding the baby)

That didn't work. Baby Louise continued to **sob**, *or cry very sadly. This time, her* **sobs** *woke up some animals that lived in Louise's neighborhood.* Point to the dogs and cats in the illustrations to prompt recall, and ask, *What kinds of animals were they?*

So Grandma's idea didn't work. Do you remember who tries something next? (Grandpa)

pp. 10-11

Oh, my! Now Baby Louise has woken up the dogs and cats in the neighborhood—she's scared the birds and squirrels as well.

Grandpa thought music might help, but he didn't sing to Louise the way her mother did. He played a little musical instrument called a **harmonica** *and he did a little dance too. But music and the* **jig** *didn't seem to help.*

Okay, do you remember what happened next? (The neighbors tried to help.)

pp. 12-13

Nothing they tried worked, did it? Then something did work. Who came home from school? (Louise's **brother**, Daniel)

pp. 14–15

*Yes, Louise's **brother** Daniel came home, and what did he do?*

Point to the first picture. *When Daniel first said 'oonga boonga,' Louise looked up, but she was still crying. There still are **tears** streaming down her face.*

Point to the next picture. *Then he said 'oonga boonga' again, and she stopped **sobbing**, stopped crying. There's one little **tear**, right here, but that's all. No more **tears** are coming from her eyes.*

Point to the third picture. *Then Daniel said 'oonga boonga' a third time. What did Baby Louise do?* (She smiled.)

pp. 16–17

Read the first line on page 16. *What did Daniel tell his mother?* ("It's easy. You just say 'oonga boonga.'")

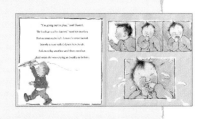

Read the second line. *So his mother, father, Grandma, and Grandpa all tried saying it.*
*Daniel pointed out that Louise liked it and then they all said "oonga boonga" in **unison**. In **unison** means at the same time.*

Baby Louise sure looks happy now, doesn't she? What happened next? (Daniel left.)

pp. 18–19

Then what did Baby Louise do? Point to each picture and describe with children how Baby Louise's emotions change. *When she realizes here that her big **brother** Daniel is gone, she starts to cry again.*

*Now what will the grown-ups in her **family** do to try to get her to stop?* (say *oonga boonga*) *And does that work?* (No.)

pp. 20–21

No, it doesn't work. Point to the grown-ups and say, *All the grown-ups are saying "oonga boonga," but Baby Louise is crying.*

Then what happens? Who comes back? (Daniel)

pp. 22–23

Confirm children's response by pointing to Daniel on this spread.

pp. 24–25

What's Daniel going to do this time? (Children respond.) *Yes, he says 'bunka wunka' this time, and she likes that.*

Story Discussion

Discuss with children whether it's what Daniel says that matters, or whether Baby Louise just likes to play with her big brother. You might ask, *What if Daniel had said 'lapta kapta'? Do you think Baby Louise would have stopped crying?* Then tell children that they can read this book again another day and talk more about it.

▶ Outdoor Play

Use color recognition to call children to Outdoor Play today. Point to items in the book. For example: *If you are wearing something blue like the letters in* Oonga Boonga, *you may get ready to go outside.* See pages 10–11 for suggested conversation topics during this time.

▶ Songs, Word Play, Letters

Today children will be playing word games, singing songs, and reciting poems. Add your favorite game, song, or poem to this collection.

Songs

"Open, Shut Them"; "Five Green and Speckled Frogs"; "Down by the Bay"

Predictable Book

Over in the Meadow

Literacy Skills

Chiming In With Rhyming Words; Let's Clap Our Names

Purposes

Separates words into syllables. Responds to own name and requests for action or information. Says words that complete rhymes, poems, or lines in a story individually, or in a group. Recites songs, rhymes, chants, and poems, and engages in language and word play. Identifies the position of objects in a line, pointing to each object and assigning the appropriate number to it. Counts up to ten objects in a set, using one-to-one correspondence.

Suggested Sequence for Today's Circle

1. "Open, Shut Them"
2. "Five Green and Speckled Frogs" (and Chiming In With Rhyming Words)
3. *Over in the Meadow*
4. "Down by the Bay" (and Chiming In With Rhyming Words)
5. Let's Clap Our Names

Materials and Instructional Procedures

OPEN, SHUT THEM

Materials: CD Track 9, Song Lyrics p. 160

Vocabulary: open, shut, clap, in, lap, chin

Procedure

- Sing the song while doing the motions. Go slowly enough so that children are able to follow along.

- Sing the song again, a little faster this time.

FIVE GREEN AND SPECKLED FROGS (AND CHIMING IN WITH RHYMING WORDS)

Materials: CD Track 10, Song Lyrics p. 160, flannel board and flannel pieces

Vocabulary: green, speckled, log, delicious, pool, cool

Procedure

- Tell children, *We're going to sing "Five Green and Speckled Frogs" again today, so I'm going to put the log on the flannel board, and then the five speckled frogs '1, 2, 3, 4, 5,' and then the cool blue pool.*

- Move frogs as usual and give children a chance to assess the 3, 2, and 1 frog(s) that remain in the last few verses. Use the same motions as before to accompany *glub, glub* and *most delicious.*

- Pause briefly when reaching the second word of a rhyming word pair (*frog/log; pool/cool*) so that children can chime in on these words.

- When finished say, *That was fun! Now I'm going to fold up the log, and my cool blue pool, and collect my five green and speckled frogs.*

Over in the Meadow

Materials: book: *Over in the Meadow*

Vocabulary: bask, crickets, dive, fireflies, lizard, muskrat, sand, shine, turtles

Procedure

- Read *Over in the Meadow*, keeping the natural rhythm of the verse. Point to pictures to identify objects named.

- Read the book just once on this day. Tell children, *We will read this book again on another day.*

Down by the Bay (and Chiming In With Rhyming Words)

Materials: CD Track 3, Song Lyrics p. 159, flannel board and flannel pieces

Vocabulary: bay, watermelons, snake, cake, frog, dog, mouse, house

Procedure

- Tell children, *Let's sing that song about those silly animals again.*

- Sing the song and place the appropriate animals on the flannel board as you sing. Remove the last piece before placing any new ones.

- Pause briefly before the second word in a rhyming word pair, so that children can chime in (*grow/go*; *snake/cake*; *frog/dog*; *mouse/house*).

- Remove flannel pieces and sing the song a second time, if time permits and children are having fun.

Let's Clap Our Names

Vocabulary: clap, name, parts

Procedure

- Tell children, *We are going to play a clapping game. First we say a name, and then we clap the parts we hear in the name. This is how we do it.*

- Model first, using several names that are not among the names of the children in the group (e.g., Priscilla, Anthony, Rosa, Ruth, Etta). First say the name slowly, emphasizing the syllables. Then say the name again, this time clapping with each syllable.

- Go around the circle, saying each child's name slowly, breaking it into syllables then saying the name again, clapping once for each syllable.

- All children should participate with you in clapping each child's name.

- Be sure to clap every child's name, going around the circle, so they know when their name will come up. This way they know they won't be left out.

▶ Lunch/Quiet Time/Centers

This time is set aside for lunch, quiet time, and center activities. See pages 10–11 for suggested conversation topics during this time.

▶ Small Groups

For information on Small Groups, refer to pages 15–17.

▶ Let's Talk About It

Learning to Regulate Behavior

Purposes

Follows rules and routines within the learning environment. Shows empathy and understanding to others. Expresses feelings through appropriate language.

Procedure

- Talk with children about rules for playing outdoors. Explain that the rules were made to keep everyone safe. Give examples of outdoor rules.

- Ask children to tell how they used the outdoor rules for playing safely outdoors today or yesterday.

- Children will probably tell of incidents in which they followed a rule, or when somebody else did not. If somebody else did not, you might say, *We'll ask* [child's name] *if she would like to talk about that in a minute. For your turn, we can talk about the rule you followed when you were being careful near the swings.*

- Go next to the child mentioned by the previous child and ask, [Child's name], *would you like to talk about how hard it was to follow a rule, or would you like to use your turn to tell us how you followed a rule?*

- Sum up after the discussion by telling children you appreciate their concern about the rules for playing outside because you don't want anyone to get hurt. For example, *I want everyone to have a good time playing outside.*

▶ End-the-Day Centers

Children spend time in Centers of their choice. As children leave for home, say something that will help each child look forward to the next day. For example, tell children that one activity tomorrow will be drawing pictures of families.

▶ **Start-the-Day Centers** (see pages 12–14)
Encourage children to explore two or three open Centers.

▶ **Morning Meeting** (see page 12)
Orient children to center activities and help them make a first choice.

▶ **Center Time** (see pages 12–14)
Children spend time in Centers of their choice.

▶ **Story Time: 2nd Reading**

Peter's Chair
Author: Ezra Jack Keats

Purposes

Recalls some main events when asked, *What is happening in this story?* Links characters' basic emotions to their actions. Uses own experiences to understand characters' feelings and motivations. Expresses the main idea of a story or other text in a way that shows increasing understanding.

Read the Story Again

Reconstruct the story. Help children recall events and characters' actions by asking, *What did (Peter, his mother, or his father) do next?*

Explain story events if necessary, including why Peter packed a bag with cookies and dog biscuits and why he didn't answer his mother when she spoke to him.

Provide more explanation of any new words in the story. For example, demonstrate **stretch** by raising your own arm up high.

After reading, prompt discussion with the questions provided or with similar questions.

Suggested Vocabulary

Use these words often during Story Time and throughout the day.

accident something that happens unexpectedly without being planned

change of heart a change in one's thinking and feelings

cradle a small bed for a baby, usually on rockers

crib a small bed with high sides to keep a baby from falling out

crocodile a large, scaly animal with a long body, four short legs, thick skin, a pointed snout, and a long tail

high chair a chair with a high seat and a tray, used for feeding babies

rascal a person who does playful tricks

signs clues

stretched reached out one's arms and legs

suggestion an idea to do something

surprise coming suddenly and without warning, a surprise ending

surprised feeling like something was unexpected

tiptoes walking on the tips of the toes

Extending the Book

For children who are ready for a challenge, point to *CRASH!* and let the children read the word with you. Say, *The big letters tell us to read that word loudly.*

English Language Learners

Raise your hand, like Peter's father, as you read *Hi, Peter*. Repeat the line. Children can raise their hands and say, *Hi, Peter* with you.

Progress Monitoring

Monitor facial expressions and attentiveness, such as who smiled or laughed when Peter tricked his mother. Note children's individual responses to the brief questions you pose while reading, the discussion questions at the end, and the question about whether children were surprised by Peter's decision. Record your observations on copies of pages 155–156.

A MODEL FOR READING: *Be sure to read all the text on each page. When you read it will vary, depending on the flow of conversations with children.*

Cover

We read this book a few days ago. This is the story of . . . (Pause.) *Right. The title of this book is Peter's Chair. We're going to read and talk about this story again today.*

pp. 2-3

Point to Peter and his block structure. Ask children, *What's happening here? Yes, Peter is putting his **crocodile** on the very top of his block building.* Now read page 2.

*The book said that he had to **stretch** as high as he could. He's on his **tiptoes**, **stretching** his arm as high as he can. What's going to happen to the block building? What will make it fall?*

pp. 4-5

Confirm the answer based on the picture. *Why do you think Willie ran into the block building?* Discuss how this was an **accident**, something he didn't mean to do.

Point to Peter's face and then in the direction of his gaze. *Does he hear something?* Guide children to recall that Peter's mother said "Shhhhh!" after she heard the crash.

Read the last three lines on page 5. Guide children's thinking toward how much a baby sleeps during the day.

pp. 6-7

Point to Peter and ask, *What's happening here?* Point to the cradle. *His mother is fussing around the **cradle**, the little bed for a new baby.*

Read the last two lines on page 6. *Is Peter happy that Susie has his **cradle**? No, he's not happy. He seems **surprised**, too.*

pp. 8-9

Point to Peter's father. *Who is this? What does he ask Peter?* (Children respond.)

*Yes, "Would you like to help paint sister's **high chair**?" That's a chair with long legs that babies sit in to eat. And Peter whispers to himself, "It's my **high chair**." Look at Peter's face. How do you think he's feeling right now?* Move on quickly. Talk just long enough to begin to establish some of Peter's possible feelings.

pp. 10-11

What does Peter find out here? Point to the pink crib in the picture first. *His **crib**, his baby bed, has also been painted pink. What else does he find out?* Point to the little blue chair.

Read the line, "'They didn't paint that yet!' Peter shouted." *It sounds like Peter is happy to find his old blue chair, doesn't it?*

pp. 12-13

Read page 12. *He picked it up and ran to his room.* Point to Peter. *And Willie followed him.*

pp. 14-15

Here are Peter and Willie in Peter's room. What does Peter suggest that they do? Yes, run away from home. Peter decided on a few things to take with him, and Willie got something, too . . .

Read page 15.

pp. 16-17

Turn the page and point to each item as you and the children name the items: *Peter's picture of himself as a baby, his toy* **crocodile**, *and his blue chair. What did Willie bring along? Point to the bone. Read page 16.*

pp. 18-19

What happened when Peter tried to sit down? He couldn't, could he? Why not? Right, he was too big. The chair is a little chair, maybe even one he had as a baby.

pp. 20-21

Point to Peter's mother in the window. Read the text on page 20. Then read the last two lines on page 20 again, and look out at the children. *What do you think is Peter's idea?*

pp. 22-23

Oh, on this page it says, "Soon Peter's mother saw **signs** *that Peter was home." That means she saw some clues. What were they?*

Point to the **crocodile**, the bag, and the shoes, and have children name them. *What did Peter's mother see behind the curtain? Yes, his mother saw his shoes. What did she think? Peter was playing tricks, being sort of a* **rascal**.

pp. 24-25

Peter's mother moves the curtain and discovers just his shoes. Peter's not there. He's behind her yelling, 'Here I am!'

pp. 26-27

Now where are Peter and his father? What are they doing? Yes, they are sitting down for lunch and Peter sat in a grown-up chair. What was the **suggestion** *Peter made for something that he and his father might do?*

Read page 26.

pp. 28-29

What is Peter doing here? Yes, he and his father are painting his little chair pink. He had a **change of heart**, *didn't he? He changed his mind about his chair.*

Story Discussion

Prompt discussion with questions. For example, *Why do you think Peter had a change of heart about giving his chair to his baby sister? Have you ever had a change of heart about something?*

That's all the time we have for Story Time today.

▶ Outdoor Play

Dismiss children for Outdoor Play as you did yesterday, using colors. Point to items in *Peter's Chair* as examples: *If you are wearing green like Peter's crocodile, you may get ready for Outdoor Play.* See pages 10–11 for suggested conversation topics during this time.

▶ Songs, Word Play, Letters

Today children will be playing word games, singing songs, and reciting poems. Add your favorite game, song, or poem to this collection.

Songs

"Old MacDonald Had a Farm"; "I'm a Little Teapot"; "If You're Happy"

Poems

"Ten Little Fingers"; "Stand Up"

Literacy Skills

Chiming In With Rhyming Words; If Your Name Starts With [name a letter], Raise Your Hand

Purposes

Recites songs, rhymes, chants, and poems, and engages in language and word play. Recognizes own name. Understands that pictures, print, and other symbols carry meaning. Listens with increasing attention. Identifies the position of objects in a line, pointing to each object and assigning the appropriate number to it. Counts up to ten objects in a set, using one-to-one correspondence.

Suggested Sequence for Today's Circle

1. "Old MacDonald Had a Farm"
2. "Ten Little Fingers" (and Chiming In With Rhyming Words)
3. "I'm a Little Teapot"
4. If Your Name Starts With [name a letter], Raise Your Hand
5. "Stand Up"
6. "If You're Happy"

Materials and Instructional Procedures

OLD MACDONALD HAD A FARM

Materials: CD Track 6, Song Lyrics pp. 159–160, flannel board and flannel pieces

Vocabulary: farm, chicks, ducks, cow, turkey

Preparation: Make flannel board pieces for animals named in the song: chicks, ducks, cows, turkeys.

Procedure

- Sing the song with children using the flannel board pieces for the animals you have chosen for the day. Leave pieces on the board, once you place them.

- Tell children that they will sing the song another day and that maybe there will be some different animals. Say, *For today, we'll put the chicks, ducks, cow, and turkey away.* Remove each animal from the flannel board as you name it.

TEN LITTLE FINGERS (AND CHIMING IN WITH RHYMING WORDS)

Materials: Poetry Posters: Poem 1, CD Track 26

Vocabulary: fingers, fold, high, low, open, shut, tight, together, wide

Procedure

- Present the poem orally to children once again. Do all the motions as you proceed at a normal pace, and look directly at the children. Pause briefly at the end of each motion to allow children to stay with you.

- Pause before the second word in a rhyming pair so that children can chime in (*me/see; wide/hide; low/so*).

- After reciting the poem, hold both hands up, fingers splayed, and count fingers, as you did before. Have children count their fingers, as you count yours, turning one finger down at a time, first on one hand, and then on the other.

I'M A LITTLE TEAPOT

Materials: CD Track 8, Song Lyrics p. 160

Vocabulary: teapot, short, stout, handle, spout, tip, pour

Procedure

- Ask children to stand up.

- Model how children should position themselves, with one arm up for a teapot spout and the other hand on a hip for a handle.

- Sing the song slowly, using appropriate motions to accompany the song.

- Sing it a second time, then ask children to sit down.

If Your Name Starts With [name a letter], Raise Your Hand

Materials: uppercase alphabet cards, name cards

Vocabulary: first, letter, name, raise, starts with

Procedure

- Play this game just as you did on Monday of this week.

- Continue to be supportive of children who do not quickly respond when the letter at the beginning of their name is shown. Use name cards, and point to the first letter to help children learn the meanings of *first* and *starts with*, as well as the letter.

Stand Up

Materials: Poetry Posters: Poem 3, CD Track 28

Vocabulary: bend, bow, clap, hand, knee, stamp, stand, turn around, wave

Procedure

- Present the poem orally again, without displaying the poster.

- Pause briefly after each action is named, to make sure children keep up.

If You're Happy

Materials: CD Track 1, Song Lyrics p. 159

Vocabulary: clap, hands, feet, stomp, shout

Procedure

- Sing three verses of the song, using clapping hands and stomping feet, as motions.

- Do one verse of "If You Are Sad and You Know It," and rub your eyes crying, *waa waa*, as the motion. Comment that this might be a good song for Baby Louise in *Oonga Boonga*.

Progress Monitoring

Note children's responses to the first letter in the name activity. Observe which children need prompting. For example, when prompt is given, does the child respond with some recognition ("Oh, yes!"), or does the response indicate that the name and the letter are unfamiliar? Record your observations on copies of pages 155–156.

▶ **Lunch/Quiet Time/Centers**

This time is set aside for lunch, quiet time, and center activities. See pages 10–11 for suggested conversation topics during this time.

▶ Small Groups

For information on Small Groups, refer to pages 15–17.

▶ Let's Find Out About It

The Harmonica and Other Musical Instruments

Purposes

Develops understanding that nonfiction texts are used to find information. Uses and explores objects.

Materials

book: *Oonga Boonga*; a real harmonica or a toy harmonica; books on musical instruments (see the suggestion on this page); bleach solution

Suggested Vocabulary

Introduce these words and phrases and use them in the discussion: harmonica, musical instruments, musical notes, musician, names of musical instruments in resource books

Procedure

- Find the page in *Oonga Boonga* where Grandpa plays his harmonica and point out the instrument.

- Show a real harmonica or a toy replica. Demonstrate, or have a guest musician demonstrate, how the harmonica is played.

- Give children turns blowing into the harmonica, if this is possible. To clean the harmonica between turns, dip it in a bleach solution ($\frac{1}{4}$ cup of bleach to 1 gallon of water), then rinse with clean water and wipe dry.

- Show books that have pictures of musical instruments and information about them. Read about the harmonica and a few other instruments. Place books in the book area for children to look at independently later.

> **English Language Learners**
>
> Point to each picture of a musical instrument and say its name slowly and clearly. Have children say the name after you.

Songs, Word Play, Letters Connections

Invite musicians to the classroom who can play other instruments. If possible, play songs that feature the instruments during Songs, Word Play, Letters. For example, a harmonica is one instrument used in "Riding in an Airplane," "Down on Grandpa's Farm," and "Bumping Up and Down" by Raffi.

SUGGESTED RESOURCES

Books

Cox, Judy (author) and Elbrite Brown (illustrator). *My Family Plays Music*. New York: Holiday House, 2003.

CDs

Raffi. "Bumping Up and Down." Raffi. *Singable Songs for the Very Young*. Rounder Records compact sound disc. 1996.

Raffi. "Down on Grandpa's Farm" and "Riding in an Airplane." Raffi. *One Light*, *One Sun*. Shoreline Records compact sound disc. 1996.

> **Extending the Activity**
>
> Have children listen to a song where instruments stand out clearly. Show pictures of the instruments they will hear and help children name them.

Progress Monitoring

Observe which children attend closely to explanations and to information you share from a book about musical instruments. Note which children recognize the harmonica and can name it right away, and which children begin using the word as the discussion proceeds. Record your observations on copies of pages 155–156.

▶ End-the-Day Centers

Children spend time in Centers of their choice. As children leave for home, say something that will help each child look forward to the next day. For example, tell children, *Tomorrow you will learn how to make your very own bottle shakers. You can use your shakers during Songs, Word Play, Letters time, to play along with the songs we sing.*

▶ **Start-the-Day Centers** (see pages 12–14)
Make available two or three Centers as children and their families arrive.

▶ **Morning Meeting** (see page 12)
Gather children to talk about center activities. Help children make a first choice.

▶ **Center Time** (see pages 12–14)
Children spend time in Centers of their choice.

▶ **Story Time: 3rd Reading**

Oonga Boonga
Author: Frieda Wishinsky

Read the Story Again

Slow down as you begin to read some words to invite children to chime in with short parts of the story. This gives children the opportunity to say many of the new words. Saying the first sound of a word will prompt children's recall. If children do not chime in quickly, supply the word or phrase and keep reading.

Story Discussion

After reading, thank children for helping to read the story and tell them they did a wonderful job. Use these or other questions to discuss Baby Louise's actions and the possible reasons for her behavior:

- *Everybody tried to get Baby Louise to stop crying. Why didn't they just let her cry? Why did they try to get her to stop?*

- *Is there any other reason why people might try to get a baby to stop crying?* (You might need to ask questions about why a baby cries—hunger, pain, fear, boredom, missing someone.)

- *Why do you think Baby Louise was crying?* (Return to the story to confirm children's ideas.)

If there is time to read a second book, use *Into My Mother's Arms* (see page 7), which follows a young girl through her day.

Words and Phrases for Chiming In

(Vocabulary words appear in **dark** type.)

crying – pp. 2, 5, 7, 9, 11, 12, 18, 20, 25
mother – pp. 5, 16, 18, 20
lullaby – p. 5
tears ran like rivers to the sea – p. 5
father tried – p. 7
gently in his arms – p. 7
whispered softly in her ear – p. 7
wails shook the pictures on the walls – p. 7
bottle – p. 9
eat, eat – p. 9
dogs and cats – p. 9
sobs – p. 9
harmonica – p. 11
jig – p. 11

> **Extending the Book**
>
> For children who are ready for a challenge, underline letters in the title with your finger and let children read it by themselves. Welcome a child's chiming in with you for more of the text.

> **English Language Learners**
>
> Read the book one more time before asking children to help you read it. Slow down in a few spots to signal children to chime in, and repeat the key words and phrases you select. Some children will chime in with you the second time, not the first. Add comments in places, to use key words again. (*Yes, Baby Louise's smile faded. It faded away.*)

▶ **Outdoor Play**

As you transition to Outdoor Play, hold up letters and ask children to match them to the beginning letters in their names. Use story words from *Oonga Boonga*. For example: *If your name starts with* T *like* tears [H *like* harmonica, B *like* bottle, S *like* sobs, W *like* wails, P *like* pictures], *you may go outside.* See pages 10–11 for suggested conversation topics during this time.

▶ Songs, Word Play, Letters

Today children will be playing word games, singing songs, and reciting poems. Add your favorite game, song, or poem to this collection.

Songs

"Five Green and Speckled Frogs"; "Head and Shoulders, Knees and Toes"

Predictable Book

Over in the Meadow

Literacy Skills

Chiming In With Rhyming Words; If Your Name Starts With [name a sound], Raise Your Hand

Purposes

Segments the beginning sounds in words. Shows a steady increase in the number of words in their listening vocabulary. Says the words that complete rhymes, poems, or lines from stories, either individually or in a group. Follows two-step directions and builds up to following multiple-step directions. Identifies the position of objects in a line, pointing to each object and assigning the appropriate number to it. Counts up to ten objects in a set, using one-to-one correspondence.

Suggested Sequence for Today's Circle

1. "Five Green and Speckled Frogs" (and Chiming In With Rhyming Words)

2. *Over in the Meadow* (and Chiming In With Rhyming Words)

3. "Head and Shoulders, Knees and Toes"

4. If Your Name Starts With [name a sound], Raise Your Hand

Materials and Instructional Procedures

FIVE GREEN AND SPECKLED FROGS (AND CHIMING IN WITH RHYMING WORDS)

Materials: CD Track 10, Song Lyrics p. 160, flannel board and flannel pieces for the song

Vocabulary: green, speckled, log, delicious, pool, cool

Procedure

- Tell children, *We're going to sing "Five Green and Speckled Frogs" again today, so I'm going to put the log on the flannel board, and then the five green speckled frogs 1, 2, 3, 4, 5. (Count frogs as you place them.) I won't forget the cool blue pool.*

- Manipulate frogs and other pieces as usual, and give children a chance to assess the 3, 2, and 1 frog(s) that remain in the last few verses.

- As you remove the frogs from the flannel board, count them again.

OVER IN THE MEADOW (AND CHIMING IN WITH RHYMING WORDS)

Materials: book: *Over in the Meadow*

Vocabulary: bask, crickets, dive, fireflies, lizard, muskrat, sand, turtles, shine

Procedure

- Read *Over in the Meadow*, keeping the natural rhythm of the verse. Point to pictures to identify objects named.

- After the first reading, say to the children, *I'm going to read this book again and, this time, you can help me with some of the words.* Pause when you come to the second word in a rhyming word pair (e.g., *sun/one*), to signal children to chime in with you. Say the first sound in the word to prompt children's recall.

HEAD AND SHOULDERS, KNEES AND TOES

Materials: CD Track 4, Song Lyrics p. 159

Vocabulary: head, shoulders, knees, toes, eyes, ears, mouth, nose

Procedure

- Stand up and ask the children to stand up too. Sing "Head and Shoulders, Knees and Toes" for the first time and model the motions for children, touching the different parts of the body when singing about them. Go slowly enough for children to keep up.

- Sing the song slowly again.

IF YOUR NAME STARTS WITH [NAME A SOUND], RAISE YOUR HAND

Vocabulary: hand, name, raise, sound, starts with

Procedure

- Model for children by using a first sound not used in the children's names. Say, *I'm going to say a sound, /t/, /t/. Let's pretend that someone named Tanika is in our class. If I said /t/ and then said, 'If your name starts with /t/, raise your hand,' then Tanika would raise her hand.*

- *I'm going to say some sounds that I know are at the beginning of your names. When I say a sound, think about your own name. If it begins with the sound I say, then raise your hand. I'll help you, if you need it. I will say enough sounds so that everyone will have a turn to raise his or her hand.*

- Proceed with the game, using initial sounds found in names of children in the group. If a child whose name starts with the sound called does not respond, say, *Terrel, your name starts with /t/. Terrel /t/, so you can raise your hand.* Children may not yet be familiar with thinking of their names as having a sound at the beginning. Be sure to say the target sound (/t/, /t/), and not the letter name *t*. Hang on to the sound long enough to give children time to compare it to the beginning sound in their name.

▶ Lunch/Quiet Time/Centers

This time is set aside for lunch, quiet time, and center activities. See pages 10–11 for suggested conversation topics during this time.

For information on Small Groups, see pages 15–17.

▶ Let's Find Out About It

Making Bottle Shakers

Purposes

Understands that print carries meaning. Develops understanding that nonfiction texts are used to find information. Attends to directions.

Materials

books: *Oonga Boonga* and *Let's Make Music*; tag board, sample bottle shaker you have made

Preparation

- On tag board write the three-step directions from page 5 of *Let's Make Music*. Add illustrations to match (paper clips, beads, caps).
- Make a sample bottle shaker following the directions in *Let's Make Music* (pages 4–7).

Suggested Vocabulary

Introduce these and use them in the discussion: beads, bottle pipes, directions, drum, musical instruments, paper clips, pebbles, shakers; first, second, third (steps)

Procedure

- Find the pages in *Oonga Boonga* where Grandpa is playing a harmonica.
- Remind children that they've seen some other musical instruments (yesterday in Let's Find Out About It), and that in this book (hold up *Let's Make Music*) there are directions for making some musical instruments.
- Show the cover of *Let's Make Music* and talk with children about what they see.

> **English Language Learners**
>
> Hold up some of the materials children will use to make their bottle shakers, such as beads, pebbles, and paper clips. Say the name of each item and have children say it after you.

- Turn briefly to the contents page and say, *The contents page tells us what information is in a book.* Read the headings of the instruments the book tells how to make.
- Flip through the book, telling children, *This is where it tells us how to make ____.* Then read the pages about bottle shakers. Show your sample, describing the items you put inside. Tell children that they will make bottle shakers in Center Time next week.
- Show children the directions chart you have made and read it, running your finger under the lines of print, saying, *The first thing we do is ____. The second thing we do is ____.*

Center Time Connections

Children will make their own bottle shakers during Center Time, where it is scheduled at the art table.

Songs, Word Play, Letters Connections

Children can use their shakers to keep the beat to songs sung during this circle.

> **Extending the Activity**
>
> Invite children to look further at *Let's Make Music* and tell you about the steps in another activity.

Connect With Families

In a note to parents, suggest they ask children about playground safety rules, what toys are safe for babies, how a harmonica is played, or about someone they played with this week.

▶ End-the-Day Centers

Children spend time in Centers of their choice. As children leave for home, say something that will make each child look forward to the next week. On the calendar, show them today (Friday), the weekend days, and Monday, when they'll return to school.

notes to Teachers

Here are some tips and suggestions for organizing and managing Center Time and Small Groups.

Center Time

Managing the Centers

The Centers are designed to be flexible for both teachers and children. You can set up as many Centers as you would like at the start of the week, and add or reduce the number as the week progresses. Refer to pages 12–14 to select the Center Time activities that you would like children to experience on a particular day. Modify or substitute these activities as needed.

Once the Centers are set up, introduce the activities that require a demonstration. Have children sign up for the Center in which they want to participate. If space in one Center fills up, help children sign up on a turns list so that they can have a later opportunity to explore that Center. Then move from Center to Center and observe the children as they explore the activities independently. Provide assistance as necessary.

Moving From One Center to Another

When children appear to be ready to move to another Center, help them look around to see where they might go next. Some Centers will be full because there might be limited space. You may want to use a turns list so children can later participate in the Center of their choice. Point out other Centers where space is currently available.

Small Groups

Organizing and Managing Small Group Activities

Organize children into three small groups of five or six children. It is recommended that you keep the same groups for the entire unit and evaluate how the Small Groups work together at the end of the unit. If necessary, adjust group membership for the next unit.

Note that some Small Groups will continue into the following week, and some Small Groups will continue into the following unit.

Progress Monitoring

You may wish to make copies of pages 155–156 and use them to record your observations about children's behavior, learning, and attention to the activities throughout this unit. Continue to update information about each child so you can refer to your notes later while doing a more formal assessment.

Greeting and Parting

On the first day or two of school, post a note to each parent on a parent bulletin board or by some other method. Welcome parents and remind them to bring an extra set of clothing for the child's cubby drawer.

Make suggestions about how parents can tell you about any issues of immediate concern. Point out that only brief conversations can take place as parents come and go each day.

Weekly Planner

	Day 1	Day 2	Day 3
Start-the-Day Centers 30 Minutes	Greet children and open selected Centers.		
Morning Meeting 15 Minutes	Introduce Center Time activities.		
Center Time 60 Minutes pp. 50–52	**Sand and Water:** Exploring Air and Water; **Book Area:** Exploring Books; **Art Area/Table:** Making Paper Collages; Making Musical Instruments; **Art Area/Easel:** Painting With Primary Colors; Paint Mixing; **Blocks:** Playing With Family Figures; **Puzzles and Manipulatives:** Exploring Letters and Paint Chips; **Dramatic Play:** Painting Furniture; **Writing Center:** Using Name Cards		
Toileting/Snack 15 Minutes			
Story Time 20 Minutes	**1st Reading** – *Noisy Nora* pp. 57–60	**4th Reading** – Reread *Oonga Boonga* or another book of your choice. p. 64	**2nd Reading** – *Noisy Nora* pp. 68–71
Outdoor Play 35 Minutes	**Conversations:** Observe turn-taking with wheel toys. Help children wait by telling them when their turn will come.	**Conversations:** Observe children's use of toys and comment when children work together.	**Conversations:** Observe for displays of anger. Help the child understand the problem and identify other responses.
Songs, Word Play, Letters 20 Minutes	**Songs:** "Bingo"; "Down by the Bay" **Predictable Book:** *Time for Bed* **Literacy Skills:** If Your Name Starts With [name a letter], Raise Your Hand; Those Words Rhyme! pp. 61–62	**Songs:** "Five Green and Speckled Frogs"; "Head and Shoulders, Knees and Toes" **Poems:** "Diddle, Diddle, Dumpling"; "Hands" **Literacy Skills:** Those Words Begin With the Same Sound; Can You Think of Words That Begin With the Same Sound as ____? pp. 65–66	**Songs:** "Bingo"; "Old MacDonald Had a Farm" **Poems:** "Stand Up"; "Hands" **Predictable Book:** *Time for Bed* **Literacy Skills:** Chiming In With Rhyming Words pp. 72–73
Handwashing/Toileting 10 Minutes			
Lunch/Quiet Time/ Center Time 90 Minutes	**Conversations:** *This weekend did you do something special with a family member?* Be sensitive to children who do not live with parents.	**Conversations:** *Have there been times you wanted more attention?* Link to characters in books.	**Conversations:** *Did anyone make a good instrument?* Help child tell about how he or she made the instrument and related emotions.
Small Groups 25 Minutes pp. 53–55	**Mathematics:** Watch Me Count **Writing:** Draw and Label Pictures of Family **Book Browsing:** Exploring Books	**Science:** Paper Fans and Airplanes **Language and Print Manipulatives:** Alphabet Puzzles, Alphabet Letter Matching, and Name Matching; Paint Chip Matching **Book Browsing:** Exploring Books	**Science:** Paper Fans and Airplanes **Language and Print Manipulatives:** Alphabet Puzzles, Alphabet Letter Matching, and Name Matching; Paint Chip Matching **Book Browsing:** Exploring Books
Let's Find Out About It/ Let's Talk About It 20 Minutes	**Paper Airplanes and Other Folded Paper Objects** p. 63	**Paint Mixing and Paint Chips** p. 67	**Developing Self-Control: Waiting** p. 74
End-the-Day Centers 20 Minutes	Open selected Centers and prepare children to go home.		

Day 4	Day 5
3rd Reading – *Peter's Chair* p. 75	**4th Reading** – Reread *Peter's Chair* or another book of your choice. p. 79
Conversations: Observe and talk with children about taking turns in the playhouse to prevent crowding.	**Conversations:** Observe one or two children who are slow to join in play. Support them in trying a new activity.
Songs: "Eentsy, Weentsy Spider"; "Five Little Ducks"; "Five Green and Speckled Frogs" **Predictable Book:** *Over in the Meadow* **Literacy Skills:** Those Words Rhyme!; I'm Thinking of ____ Clue Game pp. 76–77	**Songs:** "Down by the Bay"; "Open, Shut Them"; "If You're Happy"; "I'm a Little Teapot" **Poems:** "Ten Little Fingers"; "Diddle, Diddle, Dumpling" **Literacy Skills:** Interesting-Sounding Words pp. 80–81
Conversations: *Is there something you like to do with a brother or a sister?* Guide recall and learn siblings' names.	**Conversations:** *Do babies eat the same things we eat?* Help children realize the ways food is the same as well as different.
Science: Paper Fans and Airplanes **Language and Print Manipulatives:** Alphabet Puzzles, Alphabet Letter Matching, and Name Matching; Paint Chip Matching **Book Browsing:** Exploring Books	**Mathematics:** Which Bear Is First in Line? **Science:** Exploring Sound Cans **Book Browsing:** Exploring Books
Social Skills Development: Sharing p. 78	**Cookbooks and Recipes** p. 82

Half-Day Program Schedule

2 hours 45 minutes
A half-day program includes two literacy circles.

10 min.	**Start-the-Day Centers** Writing Center, Book Area, Puzzles and Manipulatives
10 min.	**Morning Meeting**
60 min.	**Center Time** Include mathematics, science, and writing activities from Small Groups. Paint and paint chips are introduced in Let's Find Out About It, Day 2.
20 min.	**Story Time** Use discussion questions from Let's Talk About It to address social-emotional issues. Use discussion questions from Let's Find Out About It to address concept development.
35 min.	**Outdoor Play**
20 min.	**Songs, Word Play, Letters**
10 min.	**End-the-Day Centers** Writing Center, Book Area, Puzzles and Manipulatives

Connect With Families

- Suggest to families that they read poetry or rhyming books to their children for about ten minutes each day. Encourage them to stop before a rhyming word and ask their child to chime in with the word. Provide several book titles listed in Suggested Resources for Songs, Word Play, Letters for families to find in their local libraries.

- Encourage families to tell stories through pictures and words. Suggest they ask children to draw a picture of whatever they like, then tell about their pictures. Parents can write labels for pictures that their children draw.

Start-the-Day Centers

- Open two to three Centers for children to visit independently upon their arrival.

Morning Meeting

- Introduce children to Centers by showing some selected objects from each Center and briefly demonstrating activities to help them make a first choice.

- For example, on **Monday:** At the water table, hold an empty bottle under water to show how to fill it and demonstrate how to use pumps to move water from one container to another. Show a finished bottle shaker and explain and model the steps needed to make one by demonstrating use of the materials from the art table. **Tuesday:** At the easel, demonstrate mixing two colors of paint with a paintbrush to create new colors. Show how to spell children's names using alphabet letter cards and name cards at the Writing Center. On all mornings, show the paint chips that have been added to Puzzles and Manipulatives for playing matching games and to Dramatic Play for pretending to paint furniture. Also, show family figures that have been added to the Blocks area.

- You might want to modify or substitute an activity to meet your children's needs. For more information on adapting these Center Time activities to your classroom, see the Notes to Teachers on page 83.

- Use the suggested vocabulary words and phrases in a manner so that their meanings are clear.

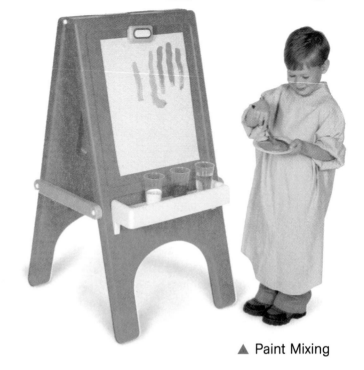

▲ Paint Mixing

SAND AND WATER

Exploring Air and Water

Purposes: Asks and answers questions. Uses simple tools and equipment for investigation. Observes and explores materials, objects, or events in the environment.

SCIENCE

Materials: empty plastic containers with pumps (e.g. lotion or liquid soap bottles), containers for filling and pouring, tubs of water

Suggested Vocabulary: Add these words to those introduced in Week 1 (p. 12): bubbles, container, lotion, pump, soap, water; inside, empty; fill, prime (a pump), push, refill

- Encourage experimentation as children play freely with materials. You might provide a prompt like, *When you hold an empty container under water, first it makes bubbles, then it fills up with water.*

- Engage children in conversation about their actions. You might say, *It takes a long time to fill the bottle that way, doesn't it?*

- Provide information as needed. For example, *If you take the top off and look inside you will see a tube. When you push (prime) the pump, first the air in the tube comes out and makes bubbles, then the water squirts out.*

BOOK AREA

Exploring Books

Purposes: Chooses independently to read or pretend to read books in the book area.

Materials: Add *Noisy Nora, Peter's Chair,* and *Over in the Meadow* to the book collection later in the week (after they have been in Small Groups).

- Encourage children to explore books together or independently.

- Join children for brief periods. Read parts of books aloud and/or ask children about them. You might ask, *What happened in the story* Peter's Chair? *What's your favorite part of the story?*

Making Paper Collages

- Continue the activity from Week 1 (p. 13).

Making Musical Instruments

Purposes: Uses simple tools and equipment to increase understanding. Learns conservation by using materials for multiple purposes. Builds finger dexterity.

Materials: small plastic drink bottles with screw caps, paper clips, small beads or pebbles, small flat dishes, stickers, white glue (for teacher), directions chart, sheet of address labels, markers

Preparation: Give each child an empty bottle. Arrange paper clips, beads, and/or pebbles on separate dishes within easy reach of children. Give each child a few stickers on a sheet and an address label they can use to put their names on their instruments.

Suggested Vocabulary: beads, bottle, cap (bottle), label, musical instrument, paper clips, pebbles, percussion, sheet, sounds, stickers; inside, outside; remove, close, decorate, shake, stick, fill

- Observe children as they make instruments by filling their bottles with objects and decorating them with stickers. Make a connection to the bottle shakers they read about in the book *Let's Make Music*.

- Help children apply glue inside bottle caps and screw them on the bottles.

- Encourage children to write their names on address labels. You might say, *Write your name on the label with a marker and stick it on the bottom of your shaker. That way we'll know which one is yours.* Provide help if needed.

- If children want to use their bottle shakers in Songs, Word Play, Letters, invite them to sing "Bingo." You might say, *Let's sing "Bingo" and instead of clapping our hands for each missing letter, we can shake our bottle shakers!*

Painting With Primary Colors

Purposes: Creates original artwork to express ideas. Explores and experiments with paint. Uses and cares for art materials.

Materials: easel, paper, 3 cups for paint, 3 primary-color paints (red, yellow, blue), cup for water, paintbrushes, smocks

Preparation: Place 3 cups of paint, each containing a different primary color, plus a sheet of paper on the easel. Have children wear painting smocks. Keep a cup of water nearby for rinsing brushes.

Suggested Vocabulary: brush, chair, colors, crib, cup, easel, high chair, paint, painting, paper, walls; extra, favorite, blue, green, red, yellow; dip, drip

- As children paint freely at the easel, show those who need help how to dip a brush in paint and apply it to the paper. Describe your actions as you demonstrate. For example, *Dip your paintbrush in the paint like this. Try to wipe off the extra paint so it doesn't drip too much.*

- Encourage children to talk about their paintings. You might comment, *I see you are using lots of red paint. Tell me about your painting.*

Paint Mixing

Purposes: Explores and experiments with paint. Uses art materials safely and appropriately. Explores and experiments with color. Uses a variety of tools to strengthen hand grasp, flexibility, and coordination.

Materials: tempera paint, paint cups, cups for water, easel brushes ($\frac{1}{3}$" size), small plastic palettes, newsprint easel paper

Preparation: Provide two cups of paint on each side of the easel. Colors paired over the week should include: red and yellow; red and white; black and white; red and blue; blue and yellow. Put no more than a 1" depth of paint in each cup. Provide one brush for each side of the easel, one cup of rinsing water, and one small palette.

Suggested Vocabulary: bristles, color names (red, blue, yellow, orange, green, purple, pink, lavender, white, black, gray), handle, paintbrush; dark, light, pastel; mix, rinse, shade, spread

- Encourage children to create new colors as they paint freely at the easel.

- Remind children to rinse their brush in water between dips of paint.

- Engage children in a conversation about their paintings. For example, you might say, *What a pretty color you made. How did you do that?*

- Have children write their names on their paintings. Provide help if needed. Display paintings on a bulletin board, grouped and labeled by colors, if possible.

BLOCKS

Playing With Family Figures

SOCIAL STUDIES

Purposes: Engages in conversation and uses language to enter into play. Begins to understand family needs, roles, and relationships. Uses classroom materials purposefully and respectfully. Builds awareness of directionality and position in space.

Materials: unit blocks, family figures

Suggested Vocabulary: Add these words to those introduced in Week 1 (p. 13): apartment, aunt, boy, brother, building, cousin, family, father, friend, girl, grandfather, grandmother, house, mother, neighbor, people, sister, uncle; visit

- Observe children and ask them to describe the scenes they create with blocks and family figures. For example, *Tell me about your building. Oh, so a baby lives there. Is there a big brother or sister in that family or just a baby?*

- Relate scenes to books when possible. For example, *Oh, that's an apartment building? That's the kind of building where Peter lived.*

PUZZLES AND MANIPULATIVES

Exploring Letters and Paint Chips

Purposes: Makes comparisons among objects. Understands the concepts of letter and word. Builds finger dexterity. Demonstrates self-direction in use of materials.

Materials: Add the following to the materials from Week 1 (pp. 16–17): alphabet letters, paint chips, small dishes for sorting, laminated background boards with tiles from Small Groups.

Suggested Vocabulary: Add these words to those introduced in Week 1 (pp. 16–17): alphabet, colors, letter names, letters, paint chips; bigger, smaller; match

- Review directions for playing Alphabet Letter Matching and Paint Chip Matching from Small Groups, if needed.

- Encourage children to play these games and puzzles independently or with a friend.

- Observe children and engage them in conversation. You might ask, *Where is the other dark blue paint chip to match this one? Both of these are blue, but are they the same shade of blue?*

DRAMATIC PLAY

Painting Furniture

SOCIAL STUDIES

Purposes: Uses language while participating in dramatic play. Initiates interaction with other children. Engages in socio-dramatic play. Uses play to explore social roles and emotional states.

Materials: Add to existing materials: empty paint cans, large paintbrushes, chair, crib, paint chip brochures (from hardware stores), teacher-made cookbooks.

Suggested Vocabulary: Add these words to those introduced in Week 1 (p. 14): baby, boys, brother, chair, color, crib, furniture, girls, paint, paintbrush, pink, sister

- Support children's play with comments and questions. For example, *Oh, dear, the baby is upset. Do you think holding her or patting her back would help?* Or, *What color are you pretending the chair will be when you're done? That's a pretty big paintbrush, but you're doing a great job with it.*

- Help children make connections to painting scenes in *Peter's Chair*. You might say, *I see you're painting the baby's crib, just like Peter's dad did in the story. What color will the crib be when you're done?*

WRITING CENTER

Using Name Cards

Purposes: Recognizes his or her name. Experiments with making words by stringing letters together. Shows interest and curiosity in trying new experiences. Seeks adult help when encountering a problem.

Materials: name cards from Week 1, alphabet letter cards (uppercase and lowercase)

Preparation: Print 3–4 complete sets of alphabet letters in upper and lowercase pairs, as seen in typical alphabet charts, each set on a sheet of paper. Cut paper so that half of the alphabet can be pasted onto one side of a piece of tag board and the other half on the other side. Laminate if possible, then place the alphabet charts at the writing table for children to use as a reference.

Suggested Vocabulary: Add these new words to those introduced in Week 1 (p. 14): alphabet, card, finger, name, row; first, last, next; find, matches, spell

- Help children write their names, using the name cards and alphabet cards for reference. Comment as you provide support. For example, *The second letter in your name is t, which looks like this.* Point to alphabet card. *Let's see if we can draw one that looks like it.*

- Accept approximations. Model letter formation on paper if children ask for help.

- Observe children's experimentation in making lines and designs.

Small Groups Overview

- Each day there are three different Small Groups activities. The same three activities are made available for three days. Groups of five or six children should spend one day in each activity, then rotate to a new activity on the following day. Small Groups work best when children are at tables.

- On Day 1, complete the rotation of children through the three groups from days 4 and 5 of Week 1.

- On Days 2, 3, and 4, children make paper fans and airplanes, match paint chips, browse information books, and continue the alphabet and letter activities from the previous week.

- On Day 5, children count bears, explore sound with cans and boxes, and continue to browse information books. These Small Groups will continue on Days 1 and 2 of Week 3.

- Use the suggested vocabulary words and phrases in a manner so that their meanings are clear.

▲ Exploring Sound Cans

MATHEMATICS

Watch Me Count: Day 1 — High support

- Continue the activity from Week 1 (p. 17). You might say, *Last week you might have seen other children playing a counting game. Now it's your turn.*

WRITING

Draw and Label Pictures of Family: Day 1 — Medium support

- Proceed with the activity from Week 1 (p. 17). You might say, *Last week other children drew a picture of their family. Today it's your turn.*

- *ELL* Help children verbally label their drawings.

BOOK BROWSING

Exploring Books: Day 1; Days 2, 3, 4; Day 5 — Low support

Purposes: Chooses independently to read or pretend to read books. Holds a book upright and turns its pages from front to back while reading or pretending to read.

Materials: Add *Oonga Boonga, Peter's Chair,* and *Over in the Meadow* to the book collection.

- Encourage children to look at books together or independently.

- Observe and ask questions about the books they are reading. For example, *What is the baby doing in that book? What's happening in this picture? Show me the cover of the book you're reading.*

SCIENCE

Paper Fans and Airplanes: Days 2, 3, 4 — High support

Purposes: Uses simple tools and equipment for investigation. Follows two-step directions and builds up to following multiple-step directions.

Materials: paper, crayons (optional), book: *Paperfolding*

Preparation: Illustrate the five steps to making a paper fan and airplane on chart paper, using the book *Paperfolding* or other books on paper crafts. Display the chart at the table.

Suggested Vocabulary: airplane, crease, fan, steps; cool, lengthwise, straight; folding

Procedure

- Tell children they will make paper fans and airplanes. Remind children that in *Oonga Boonga*, Daniel played with a paper airplane. Also remind children about the paper folding activity from Let's Find Out About It. You might say, *Today you can make a fan to cool yourself or an airplane to fly, by just folding a piece of paper.*

- Demonstrate and explain steps to make a simple paper fan. Show children a finished fan and point to illustrated steps as you demonstrate.

Continued on next page

1. Place a sheet of paper (lengthwise) on the table in front of you.
2. Fold the bottom of the sheet up about 1 inch and crease it all the way across.
3. Flip the paper over and make another 1-inch fold and crease it all the way across.
4. Repeat steps until entire sheet is folded into a narrow strip.
5. Gather the bottom in your hand and fan yourself!

- *EXTRA SUPPORT* Check with children after each step and assist those who need it. Have children work with partners if appropriate.

- *EXTENDING THE ACTIVITY* Demonstrate steps to make a simple airplane. Show children a finished plane and point to illustrated steps.

1. Take a sheet of paper and fold it in half lengthwise.
2. Fold down the front two corners, toward the inside of the airplane, making the edge of the paper meet the fold.
3. Fold down the sides again, making the edges of the fold meet each other in the center.
4. Fold the sides in again.
5. Hold the center and open the wings out. Now, throw! **Note of Caution:** Tell children to be careful when throwing the airplanes. Airplanes are pointy and could cause injury if they hit someone, especially in the eye.

- *SOCIAL-EMOTIONAL SUPPORT* Collect items when done. Remind children that the best place to play with their fans and airplanes is outside, where there is plenty of room.

LANGUAGE AND PRINT MANIPULATIVES

Alphabet Puzzles, Alphabet Letter Matching, and Name Matching: Days 2, 3, 4
Medium support

- Proceed with the activity from Week 1 (p. 15). You might say, *Last week we played with three different games where we matched letters and our names. You may play with any of those again or you can try a new game where you match colors.*

Paint Chip Matching: Days 2, 3, 4

Purposes: Makes comparisons among objects. Arranges sets of objects in one-to-one correspondence.

Materials: paint chips (from hardware store), tag board or poster board, double-sided tape; matching color tiles made of tag board, laminating machine (optional)

Preparation: Mount 5–6 paint chips in left column of tag or poster board. Laminate if possible. Make paint chip tiles of matching colors. Add double-sided tape on back of tiles and on poster board in the right column, opposite paint chips. Make 3–4 different posters that pairs of children can share.

Suggested Vocabulary: color names, hardware store, paint chips; match, stick (as in "stick to" something)

Procedure

- Tell children they are going to match colors using chips of paint from the hardware store. Help children understand what paint chips are by making a connection to a story. For example, *Paint chips like these are used to help people like Peter's dad decide what color to paint something. You can find them at hardware stores where they sell paint. Today you will match colors on the paint chips.*

- Show children the color tiles. Find one that matches the first paint chip on the poster and stick it in the right column next to it. Engage children in conversation about the activity. For example, *Do you think these two paint chips match? Why?*

- *ELL* Have children match paint chips and name the colors they see. Review color names if needed by naming the colors on the matching set a child is using, and then help the child to name them.

- *SOCIAL-EMOTIONAL SUPPORT* Have children work with a partner. Encourage them to work together and take turns.

MATHEMATICS

Which Bear Is First in Line?: Day 5
High support

Purposes: Learns to use ordinal number names to identify the position of objects in a line, pointing to each object, and assigning the appropriate ordinal number to it.

Materials: Activity Aids 4, 5

Preparation: Photocopy and cut the sections containing bears along the dotted lines. Set aside 5 bears for each child, making each bear in the set a different color (1 blue, 1 green, 1 purple, 1 red, and 1 yellow). Make enough copies of Activity Aid 5 for each child to have his or her own path and blackberry bush. Also make a set of these materials for you to use in your demonstration.

Suggested Vocabulary: first, second, third, fourth, fifth, blue, green, purple, red, yellow

Procedure

- Introduce the activity to the children by lining up your set of bears on the path. You might say, *We are going to play a game with a bear family that wants to follow this path to the blackberry bush. They need to get in line.*

- Point to each of your bears and give each an ordinal number (first through fifth). The bear nearest the bush should be first. Provide prompts like, *This bear is first in line. This bear is second in line.*

- Tell children to line up their bear family on their path and ask them to identify each bear's position in line. For example, *Point to the bear that is first in line. Now point to the bear that is second in line.* Continue until children have pointed correctly to each bear.

- Next, have children remove their bears from the path and line them up this way: You might say, *Put the red bear first in line, put the green bear second in line* until the five bears are in the designated order.

- Use ordinal numbers when asking children about the bears. You might say, *Point to the first bear in line. Now, point to the third bear in line.* Be sure to skip around so you can tell if children know the meanings of the ordinal number words.

- *EXTRA SUPPORT* If a child makes an error, or if a child is imitating another child's pointing, use your materials to point to each bear and name its ordinal position (first, second, etc.). Then let the child try some part of the activity again.

- *EXTENDING THE ACTIVITY* If time permits, extend the activity upward for any children who conducted the entire activity correctly. You might point to the second bear on the child's path and say, *Where in the line is this bear?*, so that children will have to produce ordinal number words.

Use copies of pages 155–156 to record your observations. Note any ordinal number words or color names the child did not learn. List children who were ready to extend the activity.

SCIENCE

Exploring Sound Cans: Day 5

High support

Purposes: Uses simple tools and equipment for investigation. Uses strength and control to perform simple tasks. Follows multiple-step directions.

Materials: small metal, 1-lb coffee cans or smaller cans with snap-on lids (e.g., baking soda cans), small boxes with lids (e.g., jewelry boxes), small plastic bottles with screw caps, variety of small objects (e.g., beads, pebbles, popcorn kernels, paper clips), polystyrene foam pieces or cotton balls, dishes to hold small objects, printed labels for dishes

Preparation: Place small objects in labeled dishes within easy reach of children. Give each child first a box, then a metal can.

Suggested Vocabulary: beads, cardboard, cotton balls, metal, noise, paper clips, pebbles, plastic, popcorn kernels, sound; loud, noisy, soft; bang, clang, collide, knock, muffle, rattle, shake

Procedure

- Tell children they will explore objects to learn how to create and muffle sounds. Make connection to the noises Nora makes in *Noisy Nora*. For example, *Why was Nora called "Noisy Nora"?* (Because she made a lot of noise.) *Today you will learn about ways to make loud and soft noises.*

- Take a box and fill it with a type of small object that will make a loud sounds. Secure the lid to the box and shake it. Ask children to listen to the sounds it makes. You might say, *That makes a loud sound, doesn't it?* Add cotton balls or pieces of polystyrene foam to box and ask children if they think the sound will change. You might ask, *Will the sound become softer when I add these to the box?*

- Give children boxes and invite them to make their own. Suggest a method. For example, *You can use beads, paper clips, popcorn kernels, or pebbles to make your noisy boxes.* Or, *I think you must have pebbles in your box because I hear a loud noise.*

- *EXTENDING THE ACTIVITY* Collect boxes and show children how to do the same activity with a metal can. Encourage experimentation with a variety of objects. Discuss how the sounds are different inside cans than in cardboard boxes.

- *SOCIAL-EMOTIONAL SUPPORT* Remove basic materials, and return sound boxes to children. Allow each child to demonstrate his or her sound maker. Ask others to describe the sounds they hear. Collect boxes/cans first if children have difficulty keeping theirs still while others demonstrate.

- *EXTENDING THE ACTIVITY* If time permits, follow same procedure to explore making sounds with plastic bottles.

SUGGESTED RESOURCES

Books

Ehlert, Lois. *Eating the Alphabet: Fruits & Vegetables from A to Z.* San Diego: Harcourt Brace, 1989.

Mayo, Margaret (author) and Alex Ayliffe (illustrator). *Dig Dig Digging.* New York: Henry Holt, 2001.

Mitton, Tony and Art Parker. *Dazzling Diggers.* London: Kingfisher, 2000.

Developing Children's Language Through Conversation

It is important to engage children in good conversations about things that interest them. This teacher's guide suggests topics you might want to talk about, but only you can decide what is most interesting for children at any given moment. Try to have conversations that encourage children to talk about their *memories* of things from the past, their *plans* for the future, and their *ideas* about why things happen or why people do things. Also help children talk about *feelings* and *problems* that need to be solved. Respond honestly and with interest. Try to avoid automatic answers that are not genuine or specific to the conversation (e.g., *Wow! Good girl! Fantastic! That's great. Isn't that nice.*). Instead, make a comment that responds to the child such as, *It must have been fun to sleep over at your grandma's house.*

Empathy and Helping Others

Watch for times when children show that they are aware of the feelings of other children and notice things they do to help others. Notice times when children invite others to play or when they help or comfort someone. Soon after you see the event, have a conversation with the children. Help them describe what they did and why they did it, as well as their feelings. Later, during Let's Talk About It, you can tell the group about the event.

Center Time: Talk About Empathy

Watch for opportunities during Center Time to talk about children's feelings. For example, two girls and a boy are playing with the burp cloths and other baby props in the dramatic play area. Georgina is watching and looking sad. One girl, Carmen, stops suddenly and offers Georgina a baby doll. A few minutes later, talk with the children about what happened. Be sure to make clear the steps in the event: 1) Carmen noticed that Georgina was watching and looking interested in her play; 2) Carmen offered her a toy doll; and 3) Georgina joined and played happily as a group member. Summarize by saying that other children like it when they are included in play.

A Model for Conversation

Conversation About Empathy

Carmen: Here, you want to take care of Baby? She's crying.

Georgina: [eagerly accepts] Yes! I can make her stop crying.

Carmen: Okay, good. I gotta make dinner now. [pretends to cook]

A couple of minutes later they break, and the teacher gently pulls Carmen and Georgina aside:

Teacher: *I was watching a few minutes ago when Georgina was watching you play. Georgina, did you want to join them?*

Georgina: Yes.

Teacher: *And then Carmen gave you the baby to hold, while she cooked.*

Carmen: I wanted to cook something and somebody needed to hold the baby or she'd cry.

Teacher: *That worked out for both of you then, didn't it? You both got to play. It feels good to be included in a game, doesn't it?*

Good Conversations

Continue to engage children in conversations about families. Help them see connections between their lives and characters or events from *Oonga Boonga* or *Peter's Chair*. Encourage children to use precise names for relationships (e.g. father, grandma, sister, uncle). Often families have special names for relatives ("nana" for grandmother). Accept these names and tell children other commonly used names for the relationship (grandmother, grandma).

▶ **Start-the-Day Centers** (see pages 50–52)
Make available two to three Centers as children arrive.

▶ **Morning Meeting** (see page 50)
Gather children and review plans for the day. Then orient children to center activities. Create a turns list for Centers if necessary.

▶ **Center Time** (see pages 50–52)
Children spend time in Centers of their choice.

▶ ## Story Time: 1st Reading

Noisy Nora

Author: Rosemary Wells

Summary: Nora's parents are busy with her sister and baby brother. Nora tries lots of naughty, noisy ways to distract them. Finally, she pretends to run away from home. In the end, she bursts out of a closet to surprise her family—noisily, of course.

Theme Link: Family—Every child wants loving attention from parents, but when there are several children, attention must be shared.

Purposes

Listens to stories read aloud. Demonstrates increasing levels of sustained and focused engagement. Shows a steady increase in the number of words in listening vocabulary. Develops understanding of main events.

Read the Story

As you read *Noisy Nora*, draw children in by reading with expression. When Father says, "Quiet!" put an edge of irritation in your voice. Likewise, sound exasperated when reading sister Kate's standard line.

Help children notice and track story events by summarizing the action in short asides.

Suggested Vocabulary

Use these vocabulary words when discussing the story and during other activities.

banged used a hand or hit two objects together to make a sudden loud noise
burping patting a baby's back so that air comes up from the baby's tummy
cellar a basement or room under a building
family father, mother, and children
felled caused to fall; struck down
filthy very dirty
kite a toy made of material on a frame attached to a string and flown in the air
marbles small glass balls, used in games
moaned made a long low sound of suffering
monumental very, very big
shrub a bushy plant
slammed shut fast and hard, causing noise

Extending the Book

For children who are ready for a challenge, have them help you read the title of the book, *Noisy Nora*. Underline the words with your finger letter by letter and sound them out to children. Comment that *Noisy* and *Nora* both begin with *N*.

English Language Learners

When reading aloud, point to pictures (*marbles*), vary your tone of voice (*moaned*), gesture (pat on shoulder for *burping*), and say words slowly and clearly a second time (*Jack was filthy. Filthy.*).

Progress Monitoring

Do children come to this new story with enthusiasm? Do individual children attend throughout the reading? Notice which children call out answers and attempt to participate in the discussions. Record your observations on copies of pages 155–156.

A MODEL FOR READING: *Use the following model to help you plan your book reading.*

Cover

The title of this book is Noisy Nora. *Underline the title with your finger as you read it.*

The name of the person who wrote this story is Rosemary Wells. (Underline her name with your finger as you read it.) She's the author, and she is also the illustrator, the person who drew the pictures.

The title of this book is a girl's name—Noisy Nora. Do you think this might be Nora here, this little girl mouse? (Point to Nora.) Oh, it looks like the green chair is about to fall over. (Point to the chair and then to the pot and lid.) And the red pot and lid are going to fall on the floor too. Hmm, I wonder if Noisy Nora had anything to do with the chair and the pot and lid falling? Let's read the story and see what we can find out about Noisy Nora.

pp. 2-3 (Read pages 2 and 3.)

Point to Jack (in high chair) and Kate (playing chess) as you read their names.

pp. 4-5 (Read pages 4 and 5.)

Point to Jack as you read page 4.

Hmm . . . Nora's Mom and Dad are busy with the other children. They can't play with Nora or talk to her. She has to wait. Hmm . . . she might not like that.

Now read page 5. Use tone of voice and hand gestures when you say the word **banged** to demonstrate the meaning of the word. Then say, *I wonder why she's **banging** the window.*

pp. 6-7 (Read page 6.)

Stress the words *then* and **slammed.** Use a hand gesture to convey the meaning of the word **slammed** and point to the door on the page.

Oh, my! (Raise your eyebrows in surprise.) I wonder why Nora is doing these things.

Now read page 7. Point to a few of the marbles as you read. *Oh, I bet that made a lot of noise. They weren't even Nora's marbles. They belonged to her sister, Kate.*

pp. 8-9 (Read pages 8 and 9.)

*Nora's mother and father are scolding her. They don't like the noise. And her sister Kate called her a bad name, which is something we shouldn't do. Maybe she's mad about the **marbles.** I wonder— how do you think Nora is feeling now that she knows everyone in her family is kind of upset with her?* Children respond. Accept children's comments about Nora's feelings, but return quickly to reading the story.

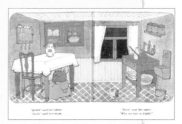

pp. 10–12 (Read pages 10 to 12.)

Define *filthy* as very dirty. Point to Jack in the tub and Kate cooking.

When you read page 12, slow your pace on the last four words to convey a sense of waiting. *Nora has to wait a lot, doesn't she? Do you think she likes waiting?* (Children comment.)

p. 13 (Read page 13.)

Stress the words *first* and *then*. Point to the lamp and chairs and explain the meaning of **felled**. *She used a cord to make the chairs fall over.*

pp. 14–15 (Read pages 14 and 15.)

Point to the **kite** and stress the word *then*.

Nora is doing a lot of things that she shouldn't do, I think. Do you think she's still angry because she has to wait? (Yes.) *I think so, too.*

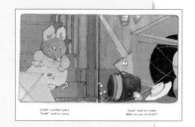

pp. 16–17 (Read pages 16 and 17.)

Seems like everybody in Nora's family is still upset with her, doesn't it?

pp. 18–19 (Read pages 18 and 19.)

Point to Jack when reading page 18 and to Kate when reading page 19.

Hmmm. Looks to me like Nora is poking her sister Kate with a stick in her back. I think Nora is mad at Kate, but it's not nice to poke somebody, is it? Do you think maybe Nora thinks Kate gets too much attention from her parents? (Children comment.)

pp. 20–21 (Read pages 20 and 21.)

Point to Jack while reading and exaggerate, "Nora had to wait," by reading slowly.

As you read page 21, raise your eyebrows and look a bit astonished.

pp. 22–24 (Read page 22.)

Hmm . . . It's very quiet in the house. Nora isn't there making noise right now. I wonder what will happen next.

Read page 23. Point to the father and then to the mother as you read. Then turn the page, and read page 24 to complete the rhyming verse. Look at the children with concern. *Do you think Nora's parents and her sister know that she is gone?*

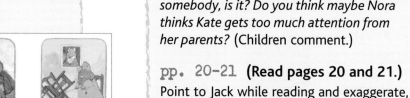

Continued on next page

p. 25 (Read page 25.)

Read with a tone of concern and even alarm.

pp. 26–27 (Read pages 26 and 27.)

Point to mailbox and **shrub** as you read page 26. Express concern and alarm with your tone of voice. *Nora's mommy and daddy can't find her. I wonder what will happen.*

Read page 27 with emotion, as if Nora's mother is *very* worried. Show worry in your facial expression.

Nora's mommy and daddy can't find her. Do you think they might be scared or worried about where she is? (Children respond.)

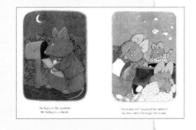

pp. 28–29 (Read pages 28 and 29.)

Draw out *mon-u-men-tal* and say it rather loudly.

Well, that was a surprise ending, wasn't it? I think Nora's parents are feeling better now that they know Nora is there. They are smiling now. (Point to parents' faces.) *And Kate is smiling too! Everyone is glad to see Nora.*

Story Discussion

Prompt discussion with questions. For example:

That's the story of Noisy Nora. Did you like the story? (Children comment.) If there is time, ask each child which part he or she liked the best.

▶ Outdoor Play

Have children leave for Outdoor Play when they match the beginning letters in their names to story words. For example: *If your name starts with N* (hold up letter) *like Nora . . . K like Kate . . . J like Jack . . . F like father,* and so on. Be aware of which children had to wait a long time on other days and call their letters early on. See pages 48–49 for suggested conversation topics during this time.

▶ Songs, Word Play, Letters

Today children will be playing word games, singing songs, and reciting poems. Add your favorite game, song, or poem to this collection.

Songs

"Bingo"; "Down by the Bay"

Predictable Book

Time for Bed

Literacy Skills

If Your Name Starts With [name a letter], Raise Your Hand; Those Words Rhyme!

Purposes

Recites songs, rhymes, chants, and poems, and engages in language and word play. Discriminates between sounds that are the same and sounds that are different. Uses pictures to understand a book. Notices first letter in own name. Listens to predictable texts read aloud.

Suggested Sequence for Today's Circle

1. "Bingo"
2. If Your Name Starts With [name a letter], Raise Your Hand
3. *Time for Bed* (and Those Words Rhyme!)
4. "Down by the Bay"

Materials and Instructional Procedures

BINGO

Materials: CD Track 12, Song Lyrics p. 159, flannel board and pieces for the song

Preparation: Make flannel board pieces for farmer, dog, and the letters *B*, *I*, *N*, *G*, and *O*.

Vocabulary: farmer, dog, name, clap

Procedure

- Place the flannel pieces on the board. You might say, *This is the farmer and this is the farmer's dog. The dog's name is* Bingo *and these are the letters we use to write* Bingo: *B-I-N-G-O.*

- Sing the verse through once with clapping to accompany naming of letters in *Bingo*, as you point to each one. Some children will join in.

- Turn the *B* over, and sing the song a second time, clapping for *B* instead of saying the letter's name. Continue turning one letter over, per verse, until the entire name is clapped. Sing the song slowly enough so children can follow along.

IF YOUR NAME STARTS WITH [NAME A LETTER], RAISE YOUR HAND

Materials: children's name cards (written conventionally, with first letter only capitalized), uppercase alphabet cards (all first letters and first letter combinations such as *Ch, Sh,* and *Th* found in children's names)

Vocabulary: starts with, hand, head, letter, name, pat, raise

Procedure

- Ask children if they remember the name game. Hold up a letter. Say, *If your name starts with* [name letter], *you raise your hand* (model). *Everyone will get a turn.*

- Play one round of the game as usual. If a child whose name starts with the letter does not respond, quickly find that child's name card, point to the first letter, and say, *Keisha, your name begins with* K, *so you may raise your hand.*

- For the second round, tell children that you will have them use a different motion to tell you that they know a letter is the first one in their name. You might say, *When I hold up the letter that begins your name, pat your head. Instead of raising your hand, like this* (model), *pat your head, like this* (model).

TIME FOR BED (AND THOSE WORDS RHYME!)

Materials: book: *Time for Bed*

Vocabulary: bee, bird, cat, calf, deer, fish, foal, goose, house, laugh, loose, mouse, pup, sheep, snake, wish, word

Procedure

- To start, show children the cover of *Time for Bed*, read the title, and underline it with your finger.

- As you read each page, point to the picture of the baby animal named and follow the rhythm of the verse on each page. When you are finished reading, you might say, *That book was about animal mommies trying to get their babies to go to sleep. I noticed that some words in the book rhyme, or have the same sound at the end.* (Turn back to appropriate pages.) *Mouse and house rhyme, pup and up rhyme, and so do deer and here! That's interesting that words can have the same sound at the end like that.*

- Tell children that you will read this book again another day.

DOWN BY THE BAY

Materials: CD Track 3, Song Lyrics p. 159, flannel board and flannel pieces for the song

Vocabulary: bay, watermelon, dare, snake, cake, frog, dog, mouse, house

Procedure

- Sing the song, placing the appropriate flannel pieces on the board one verse at a time. Remove the pieces for each verse before putting on the new ones.

- Sing the song a second time if children respond enthusiastically the first time.

▶ Lunch/Quiet Time/Centers

This time is set aside for lunch, quiet time, and center activities. See pages 48–49 for suggested conversation topics during this time.

▶ Small Groups

For information on Small Groups, refer to pages 53–55.

▶ Let's Find Out About It

Paper Airplanes and Other Folded Paper Objects

Purposes

Shows a steady increase in the number of words in listening vocabulary. Develops understanding that nonfiction texts are used to find information. Listens to explanations involving multiple-step directions.

Materials

books: *Oonga Boonga* and *Paperfolding*; other books on origami and paper crafts, sample airplane, newspaper

Preparation

Make a sample paper airplane from newspaper.

Suggested Vocabulary

Use these words in a manner that makes their meanings clear: directions, fan, origami, paper; first, second; crease, fold

Procedure

- Find the pages in *Oonga Boonga* where Daniel is holding a paper airplane. Point it out and ask children what it is. Confirm that it is an airplane, and explain that Daniel made his airplane by folding paper.

- Show children the paper airplane you have already made. Ask them what kind of paper you used. If they don't know, tell them it is newspaper. Show them a newspaper and how parts can be separated. Show children how you folded the newspaper to make the airplane. Do this slowly so they can see each step. Talk about the steps in the process. For example, *The first thing we do is . . .; the second thing, . . .*. Also demonstrate making a simple newspaper fan.

English Language Learners

Say and demonstrate words associated with making a paper airplane, such as *fold*, *wing*, and *crease*. Invite children to repeat after you.

- Look through craft books, such as *Paperfolding*, with children. Read some of the directions and show pictures of how to make paper airplanes and fans.

- Tell children they will get to make their own paper airplanes and fans in Small Groups.

Extending the Activity

Show origami objects to children, if possible. Discuss what they are and how they were made.

Extensions

Have a guest visit the classroom and demonstrate origami.

Small Groups Connections

Children make paper airplanes and fans. They will be given step-by-step instructions again as they work.

Outdoor Play Connections

After making paper airplanes in Small Groups, children can fly them.

SUGGESTED RESOURCE

Book

Stevens, Clive. *Paperfolding*. Chicago: Heinemann Library, 2001.

▶ End-the-Day Centers

Children spend time in Centers of their choice. As children leave for home, say something that will help each child look forward to the next day. For example, tell children who enjoy songs that tomorrow they will sing "Five Green and Speckled Frogs" again.

▶ **Start-the-Day Centers** (see pages 50–52)

Make available two to three Centers as children arrive.

▶ **Morning Meeting** (see page 50)

Orient children to center activities and help them make a first choice.

▶ **Center Time** (see pages 50–52)

Children spend time in Centers of their choice.

▶ **Story Time: 4th Reading**

Oonga Boonga

Author: Frieda Wishinsky

Read *Oonga Boonga* Again

Assign children the part of Daniel, while you read the other characters' parts. Participating in this way draws children's attention directly to the characters and their relationships. All children have the same part so that everyone can say the words together.

Taking On the Roles of Story Characters

Daniel: Oonga Boonga. – p. 14
It's easy. You just say Oonga Boonga. – p. 16
See, she likes it. – p. 16
I'm going out to play. – p. 18
What's wrong? – p. 22
Bunka wunka, Louise. – p. 24

Story Discussion

Here is a question you might use to prompt discussion:

If you had been Baby Louise's big brother or big sister, what would you have tried to get her to stop crying? Can you think of something new to try? Invite children to express their ideas.

Other Book Suggestions

If you think that children will not be interested in a fourth reading of *Oonga Boonga*, substitute a reading of *New Moon* (see page 7) or another theme-related book of your choice. *New Moon* is the story of another big brother and little sister. In this book, the big brother teaches his sister to say *moon,* and to look for it in the sky.

Making Connections: Help children connect the book to their own experience by asking questions like these: *If you have a baby brother and sister, are there things that you try to teach them? New words? How to play with a toy? If you have big brothers or sisters, are there things they help you learn?*

▶ **Outdoor Play**

Use clothing items to dismiss children today. Point to the pictures in *Oonga Boonga*. For example, *If you are wearing long sleeves like Louise, you may get ready to go outside now. If you're wearing short sleeves like this neighbor . . . something with a pocket like Grandpa,* and so on. See pages 48–49 for suggested conversation topics during this time.

▶ Songs, Word Play, Letters

Today children will be playing word games, singing songs, and reciting poems. Add your favorite game, song, or poem to this collection.

Songs

"Five Green and Speckled Frogs"; "Head and Shoulders, Knees and Toes"

Poems

"Diddle, Diddle, Dumpling"; "Hands"

Literacy Skills

Those Words Begin With the Same Sound; Can You Think of Words That Begin With the Same Sound as ____?

Purposes

Finds words with the same beginning sounds. Counts objects in a set using one-to-one correspondence. Uses sets of concrete objects to represent and decompose small numbers. Moves body with balance and control. Sings and listens to songs with repetitive phrases and rhythmic patterns.

Suggested Sequence for Today's Circle

1. "Five Green and Speckled Frogs"

2. "Diddle, Diddle, Dumpling" (and Those Words Begin With the Same Sound)

3. Can You Think of Words That Begin With the Same Sound as ____? (and *Oonga Boonga*)

4. "Hands"

5. "Head and Shoulders, Knees and Toes"

Materials and Instructional Procedures

FIVE GREEN AND SPECKLED FROGS

Materials: CD Track 10, Song Lyrics p. 160, flannel board and flannel pieces

Vocabulary: green, speckled, log, delicious, jumped, pool, cool

Procedure

- Say something like, *We're going to sing* "*Five Green and Speckled Frogs*" *again today. Here is the log* (put the piece on the flannel board), *and here are the frogs. Help me count them.* Count the frogs as you place them on the log. *And here is the cool blue pool.*

- Sing the song, moving one frog each time. Rub your tummy for *most delicious.* Children will enjoy chiming in with *yum yum, glub glub,* and with other parts, as well. Sing slowly enough to help children keep up.

- Ask children to count the frogs with you as you remove them.

DIDDLE, DIDDLE, DUMPLING (AND THOSE WORDS BEGIN WITH THE SAME SOUND)

Materials: Poetry Posters: Poem 2, CD Track 27

Vocabulary: off, on, son, stockings

Procedure

- Read the poem slowly, but with rhythm and expression. (Do not point to words or underline the lines of text. Read expressively, as if reciting from memory.)

- When you finish, you might say, Diddle *and* dumpling *begin with the same sound, /d/, /d/, /d/. Diddle. . . /d/ dumpling* (emphasize /d/ at beginning of each word). Tell children that both words begin with /d/, and that you think this is interesting.

- Point to the illustration and comment about how it shows what happened in the poem. Underline the print with your finger, read a line at a time, and point out in the illustration where that part is depicted.

- Recite the poem again. Invite children to chime in.

CAN YOU THINK OF WORDS THAT BEGIN WITH THE SAME SOUND AS ____? (AND OONGA BOONGA)

Materials: book: *Oonga Boonga*, Picture Card: tears

Vocabulary: silly, sink, soap, sobs

Procedure

- Show the book to children and remind them they read it in Story Time. Tell children that you are going to play a game using some of the words from this book.

- Tell children that this is a thinking game. To play, you are going to say a word, and they are to try to think of other words that begin with the same sound. Say, *Let's start with* tears. Show the Picture Card. *Baby Louise cried a lot of tears.* Tears *starts with* /t/, *and so do* toe *and* top.

- Tell children that you will go around the circle to see if anybody has an idea for another word that begins with /t/ like *tears*.

- Go around the circle, asking each child if they have an idea. If a child does not answer quickly, move on, saying, *Okay, you keep thinking. We'll see if* [child's name] *has an idea.* Few, if any, children may think of words on this first time of playing.

- After giving each child a chance to offer a word, suggest a word yourself (*table, tongue*), and say, for example, *I think* table *starts like* tears. . . *with* /t/. Offer one more idea, if children do not offer any, then tell children that they will play this game again another day.

HANDS

Materials: Poetry Posters: Poem 4, CD Track 29

Vocabulary: chin, fingers, hands, nose, toes

Procedure

- Recite the poem slowly once. Do all the motions, pausing briefly between lines to allow children to follow along if they feel ready.

- Tell them that they did great and that you will do the same poem tomorrow. Then ask children to stand up to get ready for the song about parts of the body.

HEAD AND SHOULDERS, KNEES AND TOES

Materials: CD Track 4, Song Lyrics p. 159

Vocabulary: head, shoulders, knees, toes, eyes, ears, mouth, nose

Procedure

- Tell children they are going to sing "Head and Shoulders, Knees and Toes," which they sang last week. Sing slowly and model the motions. Children follow your lead with words and motions.

- Sing the song a second time, a little faster. Model the motions again, as you sing.

Progress Monitoring

Note whether a child focuses on an activity quickly, participates in the singing, attempts hand/finger/body motions, is attentive but not actively participating, or is unfocused or withdrawn. Note which children chime in on the poetry reading and which indicate with facial expressions, nods, or words that they recognize similar beginning sounds. Record your observations on copies of pages 155–156.

▶ **Lunch/Quiet Time/Centers**

This time is set aside for lunch, quiet time, and center activities. See pages 48–49 for suggested conversation topics during this time.

▶ **Small Groups**

For information on Small Groups, refer to pages 53–55.

▶ **Let's Find Out About It**

Paint Mixing and Paint Chips

Purposes

Understands that print carries meaning. Shows a steady increase in the number of words in listening vocabulary. Uses language to discuss observations. Performs fine-motor tasks.

Materials

book: *Peter's Chair*; paint can, paint chip booklets, white paint, red paint

Suggested Vocabulary

Use and discuss meanings of these vocabulary words with children: color names, booklet, palette; mix, tint

Procedure

- Find the page in *Peter's Chair* that shows Peter's father painting. Ask children to offer ideas about where Peter's father might have bought the paint. Expand children's likely answer of "the store" to explain that a hardware store or paint store is where people often buy paint.

- Show a paint can to children and point out the name of the paint color printed on the can or label. Explain that a paint store has many colors from which to choose. Tell them that people look at the samples, called paint chips, that come on cards or in booklets, and that they always name the color shown.

- Show paint sample booklets and explain that customers pick the colors they want from there. Then the store clerk mixes the paints to make the color a customer chooses.

- To show children how paint is mixed to make a specific color, fill a bowl with white paint and add drops of red paint to it to make pink. Invite children's predictions and observations. Point out that the store

probably had to mix paint like this to make pink paint for Peter's father.

- Read any information on the paint booklets that is appropriate. If available, show pages from the book *Color* where circles of color overlap and create a new color, or use pages from the book *Mouse Paint* to do the same.

Small Groups Connections

Cut apart paint chip booklets to make color-matching manipulatives. Make 6–8 matching colors for each set to use in Small Groups.

Center Time Connections

Add paint chip booklets, empty paint cans, and brushes to the Dramatic Play area for props. Put paint chip manipulatives at the Puzzles and Manipulatives table after children use them in Small Groups.

SUGGESTED RESOURCES

Books

Heller, Ruth. *Color*. New York: Grosset & Dunlap, 1995.

Walsh, Ellen Stoll. *Mouse Paint*. New York: Harcourt, 1995.

> **English Language Learners**
>
> As you show the paint chips, repeat color names and invite children to say them along with you.

> **Extending the Activity**
>
> Ask children what color they think would result if you mixed ____ and ____ [name two colors].

Progress Monitoring

Notice which children add color names to their speaking vocabulary. You may wish to record who indicates an understanding that the print on cans and brochures is meaningful, and who shows interest in the color changes. Record your observations on copies of pages 155–156.

▶ **End-the-Day Centers**

Children spend time in Centers of their choice. As children leave for home, tell them that tomorrow they will read *Noisy Nora*. This will help them look forward to returning to school.

▶ **Start-the-Day Centers** (see pages 50–52)
Make available two to three open Centers as children arrive.

▶ **Morning Meeting** (see page 50)
Help children make a first Centers choice after you demonstrate activities.

▶ **Center Time** (see pages 50–52)
Children spend time in Centers of their choice.

▶ **Story Time: 2nd Reading**

Noisy Nora

Author: Rosemary Wells

Purposes

Recalls some main events when asked, *What is happening in this story?* Links characters' basic emotions to their actions. Uses own experiences to understand characters' feelings and motivations. Expresses the main idea of a story or other text in a way that shows increasing understanding.

Read the Story Again

This time reconstruct the story. Help children recall events and characters' actions by asking, *What is happening on this page? What did Nora do next?* Help children connect Nora's actions to her feelings of impatience and anger. Specific guidance is provided for each page of the book. Adapt, as necessary, for your children.

Suggested Vocabulary

Use these vocabulary words as often as possible when discussing the story and during other activities in the school day.

banged used a hand or hit two objects together to make a sudden loud noise
burping patting a baby's back so that air comes up from the baby's tummy
cellar a basement or room under a building
family father, mother, and children
felled caused to fall; struck down
filthy very dirty
kite a toy made of material on a frame attached to a string and flown in the air
marbles small glass balls, used in games
moaned made a long low sound of suffering
monumental very, very big
shrub a bushy plant
slammed shut fast and hard, causing noise

Extending the Book

Invite children who are ready for a challenge to read the word *tralala* on page 22 of *Noisy Nora*. Use your finger to underline the word letter by letter, and sound it out to children. Then ask the children to sing *tralala* along with you to demonstrate the word's meaning.

English Language Learners

After you read *Hush!* on page 8, explain that people sometimes put a forefinger in front of their lips when they want others to be quiet. Invite children to make the gesture themselves while repeating the word *hush*.

Progress Monitoring

Be aware of cues to individual children's understanding. Notice which children respond to events in the story with smiles, frowns, giggles, and shaking heads. Notice any quizzical looks as well. Observe who understands why Nora was naughty. Record your observations on copies of pages 155–156.

A MODEL FOR READING: *Be sure to read all the text on each page. When you read it will vary, depending on the flow of conversations with children.*

Cover

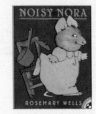

We read this story the other day, and you know that the title of this book is . . . (pause) Noisy Nora.

Tell children that you are going to read the story again today and talk about it.

pp. 2-3, 4-5

Read page 2 and point to the print.

Oh, Jack had dinner early. (Point to the highchair.) *This baby mouse right here, in the highchair, is Jack. Mother mouse is feeding him.*

Point to Nora and ask who is down there. Flip back to the book cover and match her orange dress there to the one here, if needed, to help children identify her.

Yes, this is Nora, and what is she doing? (waiting, looking at Mother, or pulling on Mom's dress) Agree that Nora has to wait because her Mom is busy feeding her baby brother, Jack.

Read pages 3 and 4.

Point to characters as you read their names. *What is Nora doing?* (She is tossing chess pieces, putting a bowl on her head.) Summarize that she's waiting and trying to find something to do.

Link **burping** to feeding of Jack, and explain the need to **burp**. *Burp means to pat a baby's back to help air come up from the tummy, which makes a "burp!" sound. Nora's mom is **burping** Jack right here.* Point to the picture.

Read page 5.

Emphasize **banged** and explain how Nora is making that loud noise, pointing to the picture.

pp. 6-7

Read page 6, emphasizing **slammed**. *Slamming a door would make a loud noise, wouldn't it?* You might suggest that Nora is getting pretty angry now.

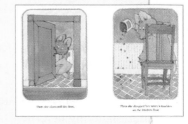

Do you remember what Nora is doing here? Point to the picture on page 7.

What does she have in her hand? What are these little round things falling to the floor? (Point to the **marbles**.) *Yes, she's dumping **marbles** that belonged to her sister, Kate, out of a can, and they are falling on the kitchen floor.* Remind children that they talked before about the loud noise marbles make when they hit the floor.

Read page 7.

pp. 8-9

Read pages 8 and 9.

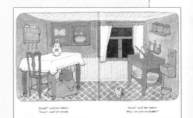

Do Nora's father and mother and sister like all the noise she's making? (No.) *They tell Nora to be quiet—and to hush—and her sister calls her a bad name—dumb, which means that Kate thinks Nora is not very smart, or doesn't have good ideas for things to do.*

Where is Nora now? (Point to her under the table. Establish that Nora looks sad and left out.) *Poor Nora. Her mother and father don't have time for her, and now they might be mad about all the noise. Do you remember what happens next?*

pp. 10-11, 12-13

Read pages 10 to 12. Identify characters and what each is doing. Emphasize *filthy* as you read it. Explain again that it means "very, very dirty," and link it to why Jack needs a bath on page 10.

Identify objects and what Nora is doing with them. Draw out that she's not getting any attention, that she wants something to do, and she is probably angry at her Mom and Dad for ignoring her. Then, read page 13.

Explain *felled*. *Nora didn't just knock chairs over with her hand. She used something to make them fall over; she* ***felled*** *them.*

pp. 14-15

Identify objects and what Nora has done with them. Read pages 14 and 15.

pp. 16-17

Read pages 16 and 17. *Everyone is mad at Nora again, and Kate calls her that bad name. That's mean. She shouldn't do that, even if she is mad at Nora.*

Does anyone remember what happens next?

pp. 18-19, 20-21

Read pages 18 to 20 to prompt recall.

Help children identify characters and what they are doing. Summarize the action and emphasize again that Nora is having to wait. *Does anyone remember what happens next? Let's see.*

Read page 21.

Discuss the picture. Point out the features outside the door—grass and trees, moon in the sky. Comment that it's nighttime. *Nora seems to be leaving the house—going outside—at night.*

We know that she didn't really go outside, don't we? Where did she actually go to hide from her family? (into the closet)

pp. 22-23, 24-25

Does everybody realize Nora is gone?
(Children respond.) *Looks like it. So they
are going to hunt for her, try to find her,
aren't they?* Read pages 22 to 24.

Where are they now? **Cellar** *is another
name for basement.* Comment that maybe
some children have a cellar in their house or
apartment building. Comment on the old
tub in Nora's cellar. Explain that sometimes
people put things they aren't using anymore
down in their **cellar** or their basement.
Read page 25.

pp. 26-27

Read page 26. Explain **shrub**—a bushy
plant—and point it out.

Sound worried. *They can't find Nora,
can they?*

Now read page 27.

*Sounds like Nora's mother is very upset
because Nora is missing. She's crying.*
Demonstrate how her mother might act
and sound.

What happens next? (Children respond.)

pp. 28-29

Read pages 28 and 29.

*That was a very big crash. Do you think
Nora's parents are glad that she's back?*
Call attention to their faces.

Story Discussion

Prompt discussion with questions. For example:

*Nora reminded me a little of Peter, with that surprise ending. She was sort of a
rascal like Peter. Do you know why I think so?*

Ask children who wish to, to tell one thing they liked best about this story. Do
not insist that each child answer or that each one have a unique comment.
Other children might offer something they didn't like.

*Okay, that's all the time we have today for Story Time. We'll read this book again
another day.*

▶ Outdoor Play

Point to pictures in *Noisy Nora* and use colors to call children to
Outdoor Play: *If you are wearing something red like this pan . . . orange like
Nora's dress . . . green like the chair . . . blue like the cover's background,
and so on.* See pages 48–49 for suggested conversation topics during
this time.

▶ Songs, Word Play, Letters

Today children will be playing word games, singing songs, and reciting poems. Add your favorite game, song, or poem to this collection.

Songs

"Bingo"; "Old MacDonald Had a Farm"

Poems

"Stand Up"; "Hands"

Predictable Book

Time for Bed

Literacy Skills

Chiming In With Rhyming Words

Purposes

Recites songs, rhymes, chants, and poems, and engages in language and word play. Listens with increasing attention. Says the words that complete rhymes, poems, or lines from stories, either individually or in a group. Sings and listens to songs with repetitive phrases and rhythmic patterns. Moves body with balance and control. Names many uppercase letters.

Suggested Sequence for Today's Circle

1. "Bingo"
2. "Old MacDonald Had a Farm"
3. *Time for Bed* (and Chiming In With Rhyming Words)
4. "Stand Up"
5. "Hands"

Materials and Instructional Procedures

BINGO

Materials: CD Track 2, Song Lyrics p. 159, flannel board and flannel pieces

Vocabulary: farmer, dog, name, clap

Procedure

- Name *farmer* and *dog*, as you put these pieces on the flannel board. As you place the first flannel letter on the board, ask, *What is the name of this farmer's dog?* (Bingo)

- Sing the first verse, and point to letters in *B-I-N-G-O*, when singing that part. Continue singing more verses, clapping for letters as they are turned over, one at a time. When finished, remove the dog and letters, but leave the farmer.

OLD MACDONALD HAD A FARM

Materials: CD Track 6, Song Lyrics pp. 159–160, flannel board and chick, duck, cow, turkey pieces, plus a new animal piece (e.g., pig)

Vocabulary: farm, chick, duck

Procedure

- Tell children that you are now going to sing a song about another farmer, one that doesn't have a dog named Bingo, as far as you know. Explain that he does have lots of other animals. Place the chick, duck, cow, and turkey on the board.

- Sing slowly enough for children to follow along. Do the sounds for each animal. If you have time and the children are interested, add the new animal.

- Remove the animals one at a time, naming each one as you pick it up.

TIME FOR BED (AND CHIMING IN WITH RHYMING WORDS)

Materials: book: *Time for Bed*

Vocabulary: bee, bird, calf, cat, deer, fish, foal, goose, house, loose, laugh, mouse, pup, sheep, snake, wish, word

Procedure

- Read the title on the cover, underlining words with your finger. Remind children that this is a book about baby animals that need to go to sleep. Tell them that you are going to read it again today. Read the book through once, pointing to the picture of the baby animal named on each page.

- Tell children that maybe they have trouble going to sleep sometimes, just like the baby animals. Or, suggest that maybe they don't want to stop playing and go to bed.

- Tell children that you are going to read the book again, and that they can say some of the words this time. Tell them that some words in this book have the same sound at the end—they rhyme. *Mouse* and *house* rhyme, and so do a lot of other words.

- As you read the book a second time, pause before the last word on each page to let children chime in with the word. It always rhymes with an earlier word. Prompt recall by holding onto the first sound of the word longer than you would normally.

STAND UP

Materials: Poetry Posters: Poem 3, CD Track 28

Vocabulary: bend, bow, clap, hand, knees, stamp, stand, turn, wave

Procedure

- Recite the poem slowly enough for the children to follow you as you go through the motions.

- Show children the poem and talk about the illustrations, referring to lines of the text, as appropriate. Then, recite the poem with its motions a second time. Do not point to the text. Model motions again. Tell children that they did a great job and that now you are going to do another poem.

HANDS

Materials: Poetry Posters: Poem 4, CD Track 29

Vocabulary: chin, fingers, hands, nose, toes

Procedure

- Recite the poem the first time without referring to the poster. Do all the motions, pausing briefly between lines, to allow children to follow along if they feel ready.

- Show the poem to children and talk about the illustrations, reading selected lines of text that match. Then, recite the poem again. Do not underline text on the poster. Focus on leading the children through the motions and on observing whether individual children are learning the words.

▶ Lunch/Quiet Time/Centers

This time is set aside for lunch, quiet time, and center activities. See pages 48–49 for suggested conversation topics during this time.

▶ Small Groups

For information on Small Groups, refer to pages 53–55.

▶ Let's Talk About It

Developing Self-Control: Waiting

Purposes

Follows rules and routines within the learning environment. Uses speech to communicate wants, needs, or thoughts.

Procedure

- Introduce the topic. For example, you might say, *Sometimes at school you need to wait for a turn, maybe when you're playing in the block area or playing at the water table. We have a turns list in our school so that things are fair. Can someone tell me what "being fair" means at school?* (Children may answer that being fair means everyone has a turn.)

- Ask individual children to tell about a time today when they wanted to play in an area that was busy and they had to wait for a turn. Support children who want to cite an example by asking questions to help them clarify their ideas.

- Point out that today, several children's names were written on the turns lists. For example, explain that Jamie's name is on the list for the water table, and that this means that he will have a turn tomorrow. Explain that Lily's name is on the turns list for blocks. Add that at Morning Meeting tomorrow, you will call on her to play in blocks.

- Sum up with, *We make sure that everyone has turns in school so that our classroom is a place that is fair.*

▶ End-the-Day Centers

Children spend time in Centers of their choice. As children leave for home, say something that will help each child look forward to the next day. For example, tell children that tomorrow they will sing "Five Green and Speckled Frogs" again.

▶ **Start-the-Day Centers** (see pages 50–52)
Make available two to three Centers as children arrive.

▶ **Morning Meeting** (see page 50)
Orient children to center activities by showing some of the items. Help children make a first choice.

▶ **Center Time** (see pages 50–52)
Children spend time in Centers of their choice.

> **Extending the Book**
>
> For children who are ready for a challenge, point again to "And they did" on the last page. Hold the book out for children to see the words and read them along with you.

▶ **Story Time: 3rd Reading**

Peter's Chair

Author: Ezra Jack Keats

Read the Story Again

In the third reading of *Peter's Chair*, pause as you read so children can chime in with the story and say many of the new words.

Move the reading along quickly. Prompt children's recall by saying the first sounds in words or first words in phrases, and by pointing to pictures of nouns like *cradle*.

Story Discussion

After reading, use these or other questions to discuss Peter's actions:

- *Why was Peter upset in the beginning?*

- *Why do you think Peter changed how he felt about his baby furniture?* Focus on Peter's realization that he was too big for his chair.

Reread *Oonga Boonga* today if there is time, or substitute a book of your choice.

Words and Phrases for Chiming In

stretched – p. 2
mother – p. 5
new baby – p. 5
cradle – p. 6
pink – p. 6
high chair – p. 9
crib – p. 11
"My **crib**. It's painted pink too". – p. 11
shouted – p. 11
ran to his room – p. 12
bag – p. 15
". . . blue chair, my toy **crocodile**, and the picture of me when I was a baby." – p. 15
bone – p. 15
in the chair – p. 18
for lunch – p. 20
idea – p. 20
signs – p. 23
rascal – p. 23
"Here I am". – p. 25
chair – p. 26
". . . paint the little chair pink for Susie". – p. 26
they did – p. 29

> **English Language Learners**
>
> Repeat some key words and phrases. Some children will chime in the second time, not the first. Add comments in places to provide an opportunity to use key words again. For example, *Yes. They painted the cradle pink!*

▶ **Outdoor Play**

Point out clothing items in *Peter's Chair*, directing children to leave for Outdoor Play if their clothes match: *If you are wearing long sleeves like Peter . . . short sleeves like Peter's father . . . sneakers with laces . . . a turtleneck like Peter,* and so on. See pages 48–49 for suggested conversation topics during this time.

▶ Songs, Word Play, Letters

Today children will be playing word games, singing songs, and reciting poems. Add your favorite game, song, or poem to this collection.

Songs

"Eentsy, Weentsy Spider"; "Five Little Ducks"; "Five Green and Speckled Frogs"

Predictable Book

Over in the Meadow

Literacy Skills

Those Words Rhyme!; I'm Thinking of _____ Clue Game

Purposes

Discriminates between sounds that are the same and sounds that are different. Understands that pictures, print, and other symbols carry meaning. Shows a steady increase in understanding new words. Communicates using verbal and nonverbal cues. Sustains attention to activity appropriate for age. Sings and listens to songs with repetitive phrases and rhythmic patterns.

Suggested Sequence for Today's Circle

1. "Eentsy, Weentsy Spider"

2. "Five Little Ducks"

3. *Over in the Meadow* (and Those Words Rhyme!)

4. I'm Thinking of _____ Clue Game (and *Oonga Boonga* and *Peter's Chair*)

5. "Five Green and Speckled Frogs"

Materials and Instructional Procedures

EENTSY, WEENTSY SPIDER

Materials: CD Track 5, Song Lyrics p. 159

Vocabulary: up, spout, washed, out, dried

Procedure

- Place your fingers in position to start the song, and ask children if they remember what song starts like this.

- Sing the song, leading the children in the motions. If they enjoy it, sing the song a second time, going a little faster. Then try a new song called "Five Little Ducks."

FIVE LITTLE DUCKS

Materials: CD Track 11, Song Lyrics p. 160

Vocabulary: out, over, back, far away

Procedure

- Tell children they are going to try a new song called "Five Little Ducks." Sing the song slowly, using hand motions to show the hills and the quacking. After the first verse or two, encourage children to join in on the hand motions and *Quack, quack, quack.*

- Say something like, *We'll sing that song again another day.*

OVER IN THE MEADOW (AND THOSE WORDS RHYME!)

Materials: book: *Over in the Meadow*

Vocabulary: bask, crickets, dive, fireflies, lizard, muskrat, sand, shine, turtles

Procedure

- Read *Over in the Meadow*, keeping the natural rhythm of the verse. Point to the pictures to show the children the animals and other objects as they're named in the text.

- Tell children you are going to go back and read some pages again, so that you can talk about some words that rhyme. Read the first page. Say, Sun *and* one *rhyme—they have the same sound at the end.* Flip to the page with the fish, and read it. Say, Blue *and* two *rhyme, don't they?*

- Tell children that this is all for now, but you will read this book another day.

I'm Thinking of ____ Clue Game (and *Oonga Boonga* and *Peter's Chair*)

Materials: books: *Oonga Boonga*, *Peter's Chair*; Picture Cards: cradle, harmonica, high chair

Vocabulary: cradle, harmonica, high chair

Procedure

- Show children the two books and read the titles. Explain that you will play a game with them using some words from these stories. Set the books aside.

- Tell children that you are going to go back and read some pages again. You will give clues to guess what word you are thinking of that is in one of these books. They should listen to the clues, and when they have an idea, raise their hand.

- For *harmonica*, use these clues: *I'm thinking of a word that is the name of a musical instrument. Baby Louise's grandpa blew into this instrument to play music for her. This instrument's name starts with /h/. When children guess the word, show the picture to confirm.*

- For *cradle*, use these clues: *This is a bed a tiny baby sleeps in. When Peter was a baby, his parents rocked him in one of these. The name of this kind of baby bed starts with /k/. If children need another clue say, The name of this bed for a tiny baby rhymes with* ladle.

- For *high chair*, use these clues: *A baby sits in one of these when she eats dinner. The name of this piece of baby furniture starts with /h/, and rhymes with* fair.

- After the children guess each word, show the Picture Card and explain the word again: *This is the cradle, the kind of bed for a very young baby. It has rockers so parents can rock the baby to sleep.*

Five Green and Speckled Frogs

Materials: CD Track 10, Song Lyrics p. 160, flannel board and flannel pieces

Vocabulary: green, speckled, log, delicious, pool, cool

Procedure

- Ask the children to count the frogs with you, as they are placed on the flannel board.

- Sing the song slowly enough for children to keep up. Count frogs as you remove them from the flannel board after singing.

Progress Monitoring

Notice which children sing along or attempt hand motions as you sing and which ones say numbers clearly and confidently. Note which children remain engaged during the word guessing game, which ones understand the object of the game, and which attempt to call out answers. Record your observations on copies of pages 155–156.

▶ Lunch/Quiet Time/Centers

This time is set aside for lunch, quiet time, and center activities. See pages 48–49 for suggested conversation topics during this time.

▶ Small Groups

For information on Small Groups, refer to pages 53–55.

▶ Let's Talk About It

Social Skills Development: Sharing

Purposes

Develops a beginning understanding of interacting appropriately with other children—cooperating, helping, sharing, and expressing interest. Uses speech to communicate needs, wants, or thoughts.

Procedure

- Talk about sharing. For example, *Let's talk about sharing. At school, the toys and materials are for all of the children to use. Sometimes children must share materials with each other, so that everyone can have a good time at school.*

- Give an example of how two or more children shared today.

- Explain to children that sometimes sharing means that they must divide the materials, such as the blocks or markers, with other children as they play. Add that it sometimes means they must take turns.

- Have children help role-play a situation in which sharing might be necessary. Choose two children to be the helpers. Put four or six blocks between them. Ask, *Can you think of a fair way to divide the blocks, to share them?* (Children probably decide to divide the blocks evenly.)

- Then gather the blocks and select two other children to help. Add one more block to the collection, making an odd number, and ask children to be fair in dividing them. Discuss with all the children that "fair" may not mean "same number."

- Sum up the discussion. For example, *It's important that we share at school so everyone can have a good time. Sometimes we must divide materials, and sometimes we must wait for a turn, or give a turn.*

▶ End-the-Day Centers

Children spend time in Centers of their choice. As children leave for home, tell them that you were so happy to have shared your day with each one of them, and that you are looking forward to seeing them tomorrow.

▶ **Start-the-Day Centers** (see pages 50–52)
Make available two to three Centers as children arrive.

▶ **Morning Meeting** (see page 50)
Help children make a first choice in Centers after you orient them to the activities.

▶ **Center Time** (see pages 50–52)
Children spend time in Centers of their choice.

▶ **Story Time: 4th Reading**

Peter's Chair

Author: Ezra Jack Keats

Read *Peter's Chair* Again

Ask all the children to say the words Peter speaks. This draws children's attention to the characters and their relationships. Encourage children to shout or whisper as Peter does.

Taking On the Roles of Story Characters

Peter: That's my **cradle**, and they painted it pink! – p. 6; It's my **high chair**. – p. 9; My **crib**. It's painted pink too. – p. 11; They didn't paint that yet! – p. 11; Let's run away, Willie. – p. 15; We'll take my blue chair, my toy **crocodile**, and the picture of me when I was a baby. – p. 15; This is a good place. – p. 16; Here I am! – p. 25; Daddy, let's paint the little chair pink for Susie. – p. 26

Story Discussion

After reading, guide discussion toward the understanding that Peter felt neglected because his parents spent so much time with the new baby. Reread the mother's dialogue on page 20 and discuss it. You might say, *I wonder if what his mother said helped Peter have a **change of heart** about the baby furniture. What do you think?*

Other Book Suggestions

If you think children will not enjoy listening to a fourth reading of *Peter's Chair,* you can substitute *A Baby Sister for Frances* (see page 7) or another theme-related book of your choice. In *A Baby Sister for Frances* the older sister, Frances, doesn't get much attention because of the new baby, and she "runs away" by sitting under the table. Her parents encourage her to "return home," and she does.

Making Connections: You might point out that Peter's mother invited him to a nice lunch. Suggest that this helped Peter to realize that he was loved. In *A Baby Sister for Frances*, point out that Frances's parents talked about her when she was "away" under the table, so that she would realize what a good big sister she was and "return" home.

▶ **Outdoor Play**

Hold up letters one by one and call children to Outdoor Play like this: *If your name starts with B like baby and bag . . . C like crib and crocodile . . . H like high chair . . . P like paint and Peter . . . W like Willie, and so on.* See pages 48–49 for suggested conversation topics during this time.

▶ Songs, Word Play, Letters

Today children will be playing word games, singing songs, and reciting poems. Add your favorite game, song, or poem to this collection.

Songs

"Down by the Bay"; "Open, Shut Them"; "If You're Happy"; "I'm a Little Teapot"

Poems

"Ten Little Fingers"; "Diddle, Diddle, Dumpling"

Literacy Skills

Interesting-Sounding Words

Purposes

Sings and listens to songs with repetitive phrases and rhythmic patterns. Responds to their names and requests for action or information. Participates successfully as a member of a group. Recognizes and describes or represents emotions such as happiness, surprise, anger, fear, and sadness. Discriminates between sounds that are the same and sounds that are different.

Suggested Sequence for Today's Circle

1. "Down by the Bay"
2. "Open, Shut Them"
3. Interesting-Sounding Words (and *Oonga Boonga* and *Peter's Chair*)
4. "If You're Happy"
5. "Ten Little Fingers"
6. "Diddle, Diddle, Dumpling"
7. "I'm a Little Teapot"

Materials and Instructional Procedures

DOWN BY THE BAY

Materials: CD Track 3, Song Lyrics p. 159, flannel board and flannel pieces

Vocabulary: bay, watermelons, pig, cow, hen

Procedure

- Sing the song, placing the appropriate flannel pieces on the board. Remove the pieces for each verse before putting on the new ones.

OPEN, SHUT THEM

Materials: CD Track 9, Song Lyrics p. 160

Vocabulary: open, shut, clap, lap, creep, chin

Procedure

- Tell children that now they're going to sing a song that they sang once before. Tell them it has a funny little surprise at the end.

- Make the open-shut hand motion once to signal how to start.

- Sing the song slowly with the children, modeling the hand motions. Say, *That was fun! We'll sing that song again another day.*

INTERESTING-SOUNDING WORDS (AND *OONGA BOONGA* AND *PETER'S CHAIR*)

Materials: books: *Oonga Boonga, Peter's Chair;* chart paper, easel, marker

Vocabulary: crash, fussing, muttered

Procedure

- Show children the covers of the books and read the titles aloud. Say, for example, *These books have some interesting-sounding words in them.*

- Flip through *Oonga Boonga* and read these words and phrases out loud: *oonga boonga; meeow; woof; grr; wah, wah, wah; bunka wunka.* Comment on the words as you read them. You might say, *These dog sounds are fun to say: Woof! Grr!*

- Do the same with *Peter's Chair*, using the words *muttered, fussing, crash,* and *shhhh.* Compare the loud word *crash* with the quiet word *shhhh.*

- Write the words *shhhh* and *crash* on the easel. As you write, name the letters you are using to make the sounds. Point out that *shhhh* starts with /sh/, while *crash* ends with /sh/, and that this sound is written with the letters *s* and *h*.

If You're Happy

Materials: CD Track 1, Song Lyrics p. 159

Vocabulary: clap, hands, stomp, feet

Procedure

- Tell children that you are going to sing, "If You're Happy." Tell them that they know this song pretty well by now.

- Sing the first two verses ("clap your hands," "stomp your feet") as usual. Start out slowly to give the children a chance to remember the song from last week.

- If you like, add verses using interesting sounding words from *Oonga Boonga* and *Peter's Chair*. Examples:

   If you're sad and you know it,
   cry wah, wah, wah!

   If you're silly and you know it,
   yell oonga boonga!

   If someone's noisy and you know it,
   whisper shhhh!

Ten Little Fingers

Materials: Poetry Posters: Poem 1, CD Track 26

Vocabulary: fingers, fold, high, low, open, shut, tight, together, wide

Procedure

- Show children the poster, underline the title of the poem, and present it by modeling the motions, while looking at them. Do the motions slowly enough for children to follow along.

- If you have time, have children hold up their hands again and lead them in counting their ten fingers.

Diddle, Diddle, Dumpling

Materials: *Poetry Posters*: Poem 2, CD Track 27

Vocabulary: off, on, son, stockings

Procedure

- Recite the poem with children, without referring to the book.

- Show the poster to children and talk with them about the illustration, referring to the text, and then back to the illustration.

- Recite the poem again with children.

I'm a Little Teapot

Materials: CD Track 8, Song Lyrics p. 160

Vocabulary: teapot, short, stout, handle, spout, tip, pour

Procedure

- Ask children to stand up. Tell them that they are going to sing "I'm a Little Teapot."

- Remind children how to make a handle and a spout by modeling the arm positions.

- Sing the song, doing the motions with children.

▶ Lunch/Quiet Time/Centers

This time is set aside for lunch, quiet time, and center activities. See pages 48–49 for suggested conversation topics during this time.

▶ Small Groups

For information on Small Groups, refer to pages 53–55.

▶ Let's Find Out About It

Cookbooks and Recipes

Purposes

Develops understanding of different kinds of texts. Understands that print carries meaning. Develops beginning understanding of standard units of measurement and terminology. Counts up to ten objects in a set using one-to-one correspondence.

Materials

book: *Noisy Nora*; measuring utensils, boxes or containers of ingredients, muffin pan, children's cookbook

Preparation

On a large piece of craft paper, write out a simple recipe.

Suggested Vocabulary

Model use and discuss meanings of these vocabulary words: cookbook, directions, ingredients, pans, recipe; bake

Procedure

- Find the page in *Noisy Nora* where Kate cooks with her mother. Point out that there is no cookbook or recipe shown in the picture, but people often use recipes when they cook. Explain that recipes give directions on how to make food.

- Point out the pan Nora is playing with in the picture. Ask children if they can guess what type of pan it is (a muffin pan). If possible, show a muffin pan and have children help you count the muffin mold spaces.

- Show children the recipe you wrote. Point out that ingredients and cooking tools are listed, and that directions are given for mixing and for cooking.

English Language Learners

Hold up various cooking tools and say their names. Ask children to say the names with you.

- Explain that a cookbook is a book with many recipes. Show a children's cookbook and point out the organization and pictures. Invite comments from children about recipes or cookbooks in their homes.

- Show and explain the uses of cooking utensils, such as measuring spoons and cups and cooking pans. Also show children boxes or containers of common ingredients, such as sugar, butter, and flour.

Small Groups Connections

At snack time, provide a simple recipe, ingredients, and tools (popsicle sticks for spreading) for making jelly sandwiches with crackers, or use a recipe for mixing cream cheese and pineapple to create a topping for crackers. **Be sure you know whether any children have food allergies!**

Extending the Activity

Write the names of cooking tools, such as *pan*, *cup*, *spoon*, and *pot*, on large sticky notes. Sound out the words with children. Then put the notes on the objects they match.

Center Time Connections

Make recipe cards for children to use for play with modeling clay or dough. Add pots, pans, empty ingredients boxes, and cookbooks to the house area for play.

Connect With Families

Tell parents that children have been learning about beginning letters in their names. Suggest that parents help their child write his or her name.

SUGGESTED RESOURCE

Book

Watt, Fiona. *The Usborne Farmyard Tales: Children's Cookbook.* Tulsa: EDC, 2003.

▶ End-the-Day Centers

Children spend time in Centers of their choice. As children leave for home, say something about the following week that will help the children look forward to Monday.

Notes to Teachers

Adapting Activities to Your Program

It is important to observe and sustain children's interest in activities. Throughout *Opening the World of Learning,* in Notes to Teachers, suggestions are made for ways that you might adjust activities in response to children's interests.

Center Time

Blocks: Add Paper for Sign-making

Place half sheets of white paper, a few markers, and a roll of masking tape in a shoebox lid or plastic tub and place it in the Blocks area. When appropriate, make suggestions. For example, *I could help you write* pirate ship *if you'd like a sign for your boat.* Accept any form of writing children may use as they make signs, even if it is scribble writing.

Blocks: Playing With Family Figures

If materials are limited to one set, suggest that each child take the role of one family figure (e.g., mother, father, baby), so children can play together. If social skills can't accommodate interactive play, work out a turns system for using the set.

Dramatic Play: Writing Phone Messages and a Telephone Book

Place small pieces of paper in a card box and a marker next to a play phone to encourage message writing. Make a small telephone book for the area. Include phone numbers for a pizza shop, the doll babies' pediatrician's office, poison control, the library, a baby sitter, and so on. Draw simple pictures to indicate the places included in the phone book. Place a second phone in the Blocks area that is fairly close to the house area to encourage incoming and outgoing calls.

Art Area/Table: Making Paper Collages

Include narrow strips (4"–5" long) of construction paper and scissors with the collage supplies. As children create some of their own collage pieces, they will also develop skills in cutting.

	Day 1	Day 2	Day 3
Start-the-Day Centers 30 Minutes **Morning Meeting** 15 Minutes **Center Time** 60 Minutes pp. 86–88	Greet children and open selected Centers. Introduce Center Time activities. **Sand and Water:** Marble Box Play; **Book Area:** Exploring Books; **Art Area/Table:** Clay Dough With Baking Props and Recipe Cards; **Art Area/Easel:** Painting With Marbles; **Blocks:** Playing With Family Figures; **Puzzles and Manipulatives:** Exploring Alphabet Puzzles and Fabric Swatches; **Dramatic Play:** Reading Aloud to Dolls; **Writing Center:** Story-Related Word Cards		
Toileting and Snack 15 Minutes			
Story Time 20 Minutes	**1st Reading –** *Whistle for Willie* pp. 93–95	**3rd Reading –** *Noisy Nora* p. 99	**2nd Reading –** *Whistle for Willie* pp. 103–106
Outdoor Play 35 Minutes	**Conversations:** When accidents occur, help children understand that others did not try to hurt them.	**Conversations:** Observe and comment when children solve problems by taking turns going down the slide, or by dividing sand toys fairly.	**Conversations:** Talk with a child about what you are doing when you clean a scrape or hold an ice pack on a bump.
Songs, Word Play, Letters 20 Minutes	**Songs:** "Bingo"; "The Wheels on the Bus" **Poems:** "Ten Little Fingers"; "Stand Up" **Literacy Skills:** I'm Thinking of ____ Clue Game; Those Words Rhyme! pp. 96–97	**Songs:** "Five Green and Speckled Frogs"; "Clap Your Hands"; "I'm a Little Teapot" **Predictable Book:** *Time for Bed* **Literacy Skills:** If Your Name Starts With [name a letter], Raise Your Hand; Those Words Rhyme! pp. 100–101	**Songs:** "Five Little Ducks"; "Down by the Bay"; "The Wheels on the Bus" **Poem:** "Ten Little Fingers" **Predictable Book:** *Brown Bear, Brown Bear, What Do You See?* **Literacy Skills:** Those Words Rhyme!; I'm Thinking of ____ Clue Game pp. 107–108
Handwashing/Toileting 10 Minutes			
Lunch/Quiet Time/ Center Time 90 Minutes	**Conversations:** *How many pieces of ____ do we have today?* Count food provided; match to children.	**Conversations:** *Does anyone have a dog?* Talk about dogs; be open to expressions of fear as well as pleasure.	**Conversations:** *When you played with marbles, what did you notice?* Help children describe and explain.
Small Groups 25 Minutes pp. 89–91	**Mathematics:** Which Bear Is First in Line? **Science:** Exploring Sound Cans **Book Browsing:** Exploring Books	**Mathematics:** Which Bear Is First in Line? **Science:** Exploring Sound Cans **Book Browsing:** Exploring Books	**Science:** Marble Play **Games:** Alphabet Bingo **Book Browsing:** Exploring Books
Let's Find Out About It/ Let's Talk About It 20 Minutes	**Chess and Other Games** p. 98	**Developing Self-Control: Turns List** p. 102	**Birth Announcements and Birth Weight** p. 109
End-the-Day Centers 20 Minutes	Open selected Centers and prepare children to go home.		

Day 4	Day 5
4th Reading – *Noisy Nora* p.110	**1st Reading –** *Corduroy* pp. 114–117
Conversations: If a child has trouble stopping an activity, prepare the child to go inside by alerting him or her before it is time to go in.	**Conversations:** Observe and talk with children when a group of children is excluding a child or being unkind in another way.
Songs: "If You're Happy"; "Head and Shoulders, Knees and Toes"; "I'm a Little Teapot" **Literacy Skills:** If Your Name Starts With [name a sound], Raise Your Hand; Chiming In With Rhyming Words pp. 111–112	**Songs:** "Bingo"; "Clap Your Hands" **Predictable Book:** *Over in the Meadow* **Literacy Skills:** We Can Change It and Rearrange It; Chiming In With Rhyming Words; Can You Think of Words That Rhyme With ____? pp. 118–119
Conversations: *Do pets need the same kind of food as people?* Guide thinking about how food helps animals.	**Conversations:** *Who has a special stuffed animal?* Support telling about who gave it to them, and so on.
Science: Marble Play **Games:** Alphabet Bingo **Book Browsing:** Exploring Books	**Science:** Marble Play **Games:** Alphabet Bingo **Book Browsing:** Exploring Books
Birth Announcements and Birth Length p. 113	**Social Skills Development: Compliments** p. 120

Half-Day Program Schedule

2 hours 45 minutes

A half-day program includes two literacy circles.

10 min.	**Start-the-Day Centers** Writing Center, Book Area, Puzzles and Manipulatives
10 min.	**Morning Meeting**
60 min.	**Center Time** Includes small group work in writing, mathematics, and science.
20 min.	**Story Time** Include topics from Let's Talk About It and Let's Find Out About It as discussion questions. Read a second book on some days.
35 min.	**Outdoor Play**
20 min.	**Songs, Word Play, Letters**
10 min.	**End-the-Day Centers** Writing Center, Book Area, Puzzles and Manipulatives

Connect With Families

- Families can help children learn new words. Encourage parents to name objects around the house, for example, in the kitchen, in the baby's room, in the living room. They can talk with children about how to use some of the things they name.

- Involve parents in children's literacy learning. If you have set up a lending library with additional copies of storybooks, have each child check out a book and take it home to read with a family member.

- Invite family members who play musical instruments to visit your class. Have them play several tunes, including if possible the songs children are singing this week. Then ask if they will show children how the instruments work.

Start-the-Day Centers

- Open two to three Centers for children to visit independently upon their arrival.

Morning Meeting

- Introduce children to Centers by showing some selected objects from each Center and briefly demonstrating activities to help them make a first choice.

- For example, on **Monday:** Demonstrate use of a marble box. Show the recipe card and demonstrate materials and steps needed to make clay dough cookies. **Tuesday:** Demonstrate how to paint with marbles. **Wednesday:** Show the fabric swatches and discuss their connection to *Corduroy*. Show and talk about story word cards from the Writing Center and encourage children to use them to practice writing words. On all mornings, point out that *Whistle for Willie* has been added to the Book Area and encourage children to read aloud stories to the dolls in Dramatic Play.

- You might want to modify or substitute an activity to meet your children's needs. For more information about Center Time, see the Notes to Teachers on page 121.

- Model the suggested vocabulary words and phrases in a manner that makes their meanings clear.

▲ Marble Box Play

SAND AND WATER

Marble Box Play

SCIENCE

Purposes: Observes and explores materials. Explores simple machines. Shows interest and curiosity in trying new activities. Participates successfully as a member of the group.

Materials: 25–30 glass marbles, 2 medium-size cardboard boxes, 8–10 long cardboard tubes, scissors, duct tape, small plastic dishes

Preparation: Cut holes in sides of box and box lid to fit long tubes. Use duct tape to attach tubes to box. Some tubes should run diagonally through the inside of box so that the marbles do not always empty directly across from the hole into which they are dropped. Other tubes can be attached to the outside of the box by taping them against the sides. Vary the incline of the tubes inside and outside the box to vary the speed at which the marbles will run through them. Place one box at each end of the table. Place two children near each box.

Suggested Vocabulary: box, marble, side, sound, tube, tunnel; hard, noisy, round; clang, click, disappear, drop, exit, reappear, roll

- Observe as children send marbles through the tubes and catch them as they exit. Remind them that the child closest to the exit hole retrieves the marble, but the marble should always be returned to the child who sent it.

- Provide a prompt for a conversation about the movement of the marbles. For example, *Look! When I put the marble in the tube on this side of the box, it comes out on this side. If I put the marble in this tube, where will it come out?*

- Provide information. For example, you might say, *Sometimes the marble comes out on the same side of the box where it went in, but sometimes it comes out on the other side.*

- Engage children in conversation about the sounds the marbles make when they roll and collide with each other. For example, *When the marbles roll through the tubes or bump into each other, what sounds do you hear? I hear sounds like "clang" and "click." Do you? It's a pretty noisy game!*

BOOK AREA

Exploring Books

Purposes: Retells familiar stories. Requests that favorite stories be read aloud. Sustains attention to a task appropriate for age.

Materials: Add *Whistle for Willie* to the book collection late in the week.

- Encourage children to explore books together or independently.

- Join children for brief periods. Read parts of books aloud and talk with children about them, making connections to the family theme. For example, *What does Peter wear to make him feel grown-up? That's right, his father's big hat. How do Peter and his parents feel when he learns to whistle? They feel proud and happy.*

ART AREA: TABLE

Clay Dough With Baking Props and Recipe Cards

Purposes: Observes and explores materials. Describes properties of materials. Uses simple tools and machines. Understands that print carries meaning.

Materials: recipe card with simple, clearly written/illustrated recipe, homemade clay dough (see recipe below), rolling pins, cookie cutters, cookie sheet, small cardboard box, hot pads, spatula, kitchen timer

Preparation: Make clay dough ahead of time. (Recipe: 1 c flour, 1 c water, $\frac{1}{2}$ c salt, 2 tbs oil, drop of food coloring; mix and heat over medium burner, stirring constantly; turn out to knead.) Wrap heavy foil around stiff cardboard to make small cookie sheets. Cut one side panel on cardboard box on three sides to create a door. Draw temperature dial

above oven door opening. Place plastic placemats or clay boards at each place at the table. Prepare recipe cards on tag board. Write the following steps and illustrate them with ideas provided.

Cookie Dough

1. Put lump of dough on placemat. (Draw lump of dough on a board.)
2. Use rolling pin to flatten out the dough. (Draw rolling pin on top of dough.)
3. Push cookie cutters into dough to form cookies. (Draw cookie cutter in dough.)
4. Lift cookie shapes off and place on cookie sheet. (Draw dough with cookie shape holes and cookie sheet with cookies.)
5. Put cookie sheet in oven and cook for 10 minutes. (Draw oven with door open.)
6. Remove cookies and let cool. (Draw cookie sheet held by a hand with hot pad.)
7. Enjoy! (Draw smiley face.)

Suggested Vocabulary: cookie cutters, cookie sheet, cookies, directions, hot pad, oven, recipe, recipe card, rolling pin, spatula, steps; sticky; bake, follow, pretend, roll

- Observe children as they work together to follow recipe steps. Provide help where needed. Describe as you demonstrate. For example, you might say, *Don't forget step number two. It's much easier to use the cookie cutters when the dough is flat. Watch how I use the rolling pin.* Or, *Is the cookie sheet hot? Here is a hot pad to help you hold it.*

- Remind children of the scene in *Noisy Nora* where Nora's mother is cooking with her sister Kate, and of the cookbooks and recipes they explored in Let's Find Out About It and Small Groups.

ART AREA: EASEL

Painting With Marbles

Purposes: Explores and experiments with paint. Describes the physical properties of objects. Coordinates body movements to complete simple tasks. Shows interest and curiosity in trying new activities.

Materials: marbles, liquid paint (2 different colors), small plastic bowls, plastic spoons, box lids ($8\frac{1}{2}$" × 11"), bucket of water, paper towel (wet and dry), pre-cut paper to fit inside box lids, markers

Preparation: Give children a box lid and arrange them in pairs within easy reach of bowls of paint, spoons, pre-cut paper, and markers. A bucket of water should be placed on floor out of children's way.

Suggested Vocabulary: box lid, coat (of paint), color names, game, level, line, paper, side, sound, spoon, tracks, water; across, upside down; bump, clang, clean, collide, dip, mix, rinse, rolls, tilt

- Suggest that children use markers to write their name on the back of the piece of paper that goes inside their box lid.

- As children paint with marbles, make a connection to Nora's sister Kate playing with marbles in *Noisy Nora.* You might say, *Maybe this is something Kate would do with her marbles, too.*

- Point out to children that a marble can be re-coated with paint by dipping it again with their spoon.

- Engage children in a conversation about the activity, making comments or asking questions. For example, *What happens when you tilt the box? See it go from side to side and up and down? It makes a line, or track, of paint. What happens when one color mixes with another?*

Continued on next page

- Prompt children to clean up when they are done. You might say, *Put your marbles and spoons in the water to clean off the paint when you're done. Put your picture on the shelf to dry. Now your space is ready for someone else who wants to paint with the marbles.*

- Display dry paintings in the center for all to enjoy.

BLOCKS

Playing With Family Figures

- Continue the same activity from Week 2 (p. 51).

PUZZLES AND MANIPULATIVES

Exploring Alphabet Puzzles and Fabric Swatches

Purposes: Develops personal preferences. Sustains attention appropriate for age. Performs fine-motor tasks. Asks questions about, and describes, materials. Names letters.

Materials: Add to materials from Week 2 (p. 52): alphabet puzzles and fabric swatches.

Suggested Vocabulary: Add these words to those introduced in Weeks 1–2 (pp. 14, 52): corduroy, corners, edges, fabric, overalls, patterns, puzzles, ridges, shoulder strap, swatch; bumpy; feel, touch.

- Help children examine and describe the objects as they play with them by asking questions. For example, *What are you playing with?* Or, *An alphabet letter is missing from the puzzle. Can you find it?* Or, *Touch the fabric. What does it feel like?*

- Make a connection between the fabric swatches, buttons, and *Corduroy.* You might ask, *What kind of fabric are Corduroy's overalls made from? What does corduroy feel like? It has rows of ridges. Is there a button that you could use to fix the shoulder strap on Corduroy's overalls?*

DRAMATIC PLAY

Reading Aloud to Dolls

Purposes: Engages in socio-dramatic play. Initiates interaction with other children. Uses play to explore and practice social roles. Retells stories. Handles books appropriately.

Materials: Add to materials from Weeks 1–2 (pp. 14, 52): board books including *Peter's Chair* and *Whistle for Willie.*

Suggested Vocabulary: Add these words to those introduced in Weeks 1–2 (pp. 14, 52): page, pictures, story, story time; hear, listen, read aloud

- Help children arrange dolls in a circle for story time, as they do when you read to them. Explain that babies love it when mommies and daddies read to them.

- Show them how to hold the book upright so the dolls can see the book. Remind children that they can use the pictures to help them remember the story. Provide prompts when needed. You might say, *Chris, will you help Maria hold the book up so all the dolls can see? In this picture, Peter looks happy. What do you think happened here?*

WRITING CENTER

Story-Related Word Cards

Purposes: Understands that print carries meaning. Shows interest in trying to write familiar words from storybooks. Explores writing tools and experiments with making marks.

Materials: Add to materials from Weeks 1–2 (pp. 14, 52): tag board strips, computer print-outs of key words from unit stories, line drawings of word meanings, paste, laminating machine (optional), hole puncher, metal rings

Preparation: Make computer print-outs (32-point font) of these key words and simple line drawings of each word to fit on tag-board strips: *Peter's Chair:* blue, bone, chair, pink; *Oonga Boonga:* baby, bottle, cat, tears; *Noisy Nora:* kite, lamp, marbles, tub; *Whistle for Willie:* chalk, dog, hat, rope; *Corduroy:* button, flashlight, lamp, overalls. Attach to tag-board strips. Laminate if possible, and then punch hole in one end. Secure 3–4 cards with a metal ring and give each pair of children a set.

- Encourage children to practice writing story words using word cards as a reference. Accept rudimentary marks.

- Show children a sample of a word card, pointing to the picture and the word. Encourage them to look at the other word cards on a ring and think and talk about what they say. For example, you might say, *What is this a picture of? It looks like a pair of pants, but it's a special kind of pants that Corduroy wore. Do you remember what they are called? Overalls, that's right.*

Small Groups Overview

- Each day there are three different Small Groups activities. The same three activities are made available for three days, and each group of five or six children spends one of the three days in each activity. Small Groups work best when children are at tables.

- On Days 1 and 2, children continue the mathematics, science, and book-browsing activities they started the previous week.

- On Days 3, 4, and 5, children investigate sound with marbles, play alphabet games, and browse books.

- For more information about managing Small Groups, refer to Notes to Teachers on page 121.

- Model the suggested vocabulary words and phrases in a manner that makes their meanings clear.

▲ Marble Play

MATHEMATICS

Which Bear Is First in Line?: Days 1, 2  High support

- Continue the activity from Day 5 of Week 2 (p. 55). You might say, *You may have noticed that some children were playing a game with bears last week. Today it is your turn to play.*

SCIENCE

Exploring Sound Cans: Days 1, 2 High support

- Continue the activity from Day 5 of Week 2 (p. 55). You might say, *You might have noticed that some children were exploring sounds with cans last week. Today it is your turn.*

BOOK BROWSING

Exploring Books: Days 1, 2; Days 3, 4, 5 Low support

Purposes: Chooses independently to read or pretends to read books. Uses and shares books in play. Holds a book upright and turns its pages from front to back while reading or pretending to read.

Materials: Add *Noisy Nora* and *Time for Bed* to the book collection. Also add some nonfiction books that might be of interest.

Procedure

- Encourage children to look at books together or independently.

- Observe children and ask questions about the books they are reading. For example, *Which book did you pick today? Can you tell me what it's called?* Or, *You know how to hold your book and turn the pages carefully. That's great. Can you show me a picture you like? Why do you like it?*

- If interest in books wanes, pair children to look at the Picture Cards and find the same or similar pictures in the book illustrations. Some children may want to play the Picture Card Word Clue Game. One child looks at the card and gives meaning and sound clues. The other child guesses the picture.

SCIENCE

Marble Play: Days 3, 4, 5 High support

Purposes: Uses simple tools and equipment for investigation. Learns properties of objects, and makes comparisons among objects.

Materials: 18–20 glass marbles (with colors streaked through, if possible), long cardboard tubes, hand-held magnifying glasses (one per child), three large boxes and box lids to hold small dishes of hard and soft materials, such as salt, cotton balls, small rocks, polystyrene foam peanuts, paper clips

Continued on next page 89

Preparation: Put three to five small containers of hard and soft materials inside three large box lids and place within reach of all children.

Suggested Vocabulary: names of materials in small containers (e.g. rocks, paper clips), glass, lens, magnifying glass, toy, tube; colorful, smooth; borrow, clang, collide, plop, roll, thud, tilt, trade

Procedure

- Tell children they are going to play with marbles. Make a connection to *Noisy Nora,* For example, *Nora dumped marbles on the floor. Her sister Kate didn't like that, did she? We're going to play with marbles today, and find out why Kate might have liked to play with marbles.*

- Give each child a marble. Explain that they are going to look at the marble using a magnifying glass, which is a special kind of glass that makes things look bigger than they really are. Ask children to describe the marble. You might ask, *What does it feel like in your hand?* (hard, smooth, round) *What do you see through the magnifying glass? I see colored lines, or streaks, in mine. What colors can you see? I see orange and red.*

- Collect marbles and magnifying glass and explain that you are moving on to the next step in the activity. You might say, *Now that we've learned what marbles feel like and look like, let's find out what they sound like.*

- Explain that because marbles are round, they roll and can easily fall off the table, it's a good idea to keep them in a container, like a box. Distribute boxes and three marbles per child, one at a time, placing them in each child's box as you count out loud, *1, 2, 3.*

- Show children how to tilt their box to make their marbles roll around and invite them to experiment. Provide prompts like, *Listen to the sounds the marbles make when they bang into the side of the box or into each other. Which sound is louder? That's right, it's louder when the marbles bang into each other.*

- Collect all but one marble per child. Take a soft material, like cotton balls, and give each child some to place in the corner of their box. Have children tilt their boxes so the marble rolls into the cotton balls and point out that almost no sound is created. Then have children tilt their boxes in the other direction so the marble hits the side of the box. Compare the two sounds. Comment about the activity. For example, *The cotton balls, which are soft, don't make sound, do they?*

- *EXTENDING THE ACTIVITY* Collect boxes. Let children touch and identify each of the materials in the dishes on the table, saying whether it is hard or soft. Take a cardboard tube and place one end inside one of the dishes containing a hard material, such as rocks. Drop a marble in the top of the tube and ask children to listen for the sound it makes when it falls into the material. Guide children in noticing that the sound is louder when the marble lands on a hard material than on a soft material.

- *EXTENDING THE ACTIVITY* Have children take turns dropping marbles through tubes into various materials. Ask children to predict whether the sound will be loud or soft, and talk about the results. For example, *Your marble made a loud sound when it landed in the dish of paper clips. Who can make a soft sound with their marble?*

- *EXTRA SUPPORT* Encourage children to swap marbles with each other so they can examine different kinds under the magnifying glass. Or, have children work in pairs as a way to promote sharing.

GAMES

Alphabet Bingo: Days 3, 4, 5

High support

Purposes: Associates the name of a letter with its shape. Names many uppercase letters.

Materials: teacher-made or commercial alphabet bingo game (uppercase only), containing individual playing boards, chips, and cards

Procedure

- Distribute playing boards and chips to each child. Explain that you are going to hold up a card with a letter printed on it. If they find that letter on their card, they should cover it with a chip. Demonstrate an example. For instance, *This card has an A on it. I found an A on my card, so I put a chip over it, like this. This card has a C on it. I don't have a C on my card, so I can't put a chip on my card.*

- Explain that there are three ways to cover a row—horizontally, vertically, and diagonally. You might say, *There are three kinds of rows you can make with your chips.* Point to your card and show the three kinds of rows. Explain that when they fill a row with chips, they should shout "Bingo!" to let everyone know. Ask children to repeat "Bingo!" after you.

- *SOCIAL-EMOTIONAL SUPPORT* Explain that you will continue playing until each child has one whole row covered with chips. As you explain this, show three ways to cover a row. Have children repeat "Bingo!" after you. Then watch the other children continue to play, until everyone has "Bingo!" You can encourage children who don't have a row covered yet by saying, *Soon you'll have a whole row covered.*

SUGGESTED RESOURCES

Books

Mitton, Tony and Ant Parker. *Terrific Trains*. London: Kingfisher, 1998.

Stickland, Paul and Henrietta Stickland. *Dinosaur Roar!* New York: Puffin, 1994.

Developing Children's Language Through Conversation

Teachers sometimes feel that there is little time to have conversations with children, but there are many opportunities during the day for talking. Use transitions, such as when waiting with children to go outdoors, when helping children with toileting or hand washing, and when the first few children have arrived for the day. Talk with children when they are outdoors and during meals and snacks. Meals are wonderful times for conversations. When children are eating, their minds are not occupied fully, which presents a natural time to talk about things that are related to the curriculum and class activities.

Regulating Behavior

Watch for times when children show that they are striving to behave in appropriate ways. For example, you might observe this when a child tells others what the rules are. Soon after you see a child exercising self-control, have a conversation with the children involved. Help them talk about what happened, how they felt, what they decided to do, and the consequences of their behavior for themselves and others. Later you can tell the full group about the event during Let's Talk About It. Encourage the children involved to help tell about the event.

Mealtime: Talk About Regulating Behavior Using Rules

Sit at a table with several children as they eat snacks or lunch. Listen to what they are talking about and join by asking them to say more or to make clearer the ideas they are trying to communicate. By this time in the unit, children will be familiar with three books: *Noisy Nora, Oonga Boonga,* and *Peter's Chair.* Try to help children understand the stories and their own experiences by making connections between the books and classroom life.

Good Conversations

Do not correct the child's grammar. Do repeat and expand what the child has said. For example, if a child says, "I runned home." You can simply say, "Oh, you ran home yesterday." Model the correct usage and add a bit of extra information.

A Model for Conversation

Mealtime: Conversation About Rules and Regulating Behavior

Teacher: *Today over in Blocks it sounded a little like Noisy Nora or like when Peter's dog knocked over his tower! Did you hear the crash?*

Juan: Yeah, it was pretty loud!

Jamie: It hurt my ears!

Teacher: *Yes, it was a monumental crash! I'm glad no one got hurt. It kind of scared me. How about you?*

Juan: Me, too. I jumped. Wow, that was loud!

Teacher: *Does anyone remember the rule we have that makes it so we don't have such big accidents?*

Jamie: Umm, don't build so big?

Teacher: *Yes. Can anyone remember how high we can build?*

Juan: Up to here (points to his chest).

Teacher: *That's right, Juan. We don't build any higher than our chest unless a teacher is right there to help. Do you know why we have the rule?*

Jamie: So we don't get knocked on the head and hurt.

Teacher: *Right!*

Good Conversations

Use varied vocabulary and speak naturally to children. Most children benefit from hearing language that is somewhat more complex than the language they can use on their own.

▶ **Start-the-Day Centers** (see pages 86–88)
Make available two or three Centers as you greet children and their families.

▶ **Morning Meeting** (see page 86)
Gather children and review plans for the day. Orient children to center activities and help them make a first choice. Create a turns list for Centers if necessary.

▶ **Center Time** (see pages 86–88)
Children spend time in Centers of their choice.

Extending the Book

Help children who are ready for a challenge notice that this book was written by the same author who wrote *Peter's Chair*.

▶ **Story Time: 1st Reading**

Whistle for Willie

Author: Ezra Jack Keats

Summary: Peter wants to learn to whistle. He tries and gives up several times, until he finally learns this new skill.

Theme Link: Family—As they grow up, through practice children learn new skills, in which the whole family can take pride.

Purposes

Listens to stories read aloud. Demonstrates increasing levels of sustained and focused engagement during read-aloud times. Shows a steady increase in the number of words in listening vocabulary. Develops understanding of main events.

Read the Story

In *Whistle for Willie*, Peter moves from yearning and disappointment to the thrill of learning a new skill. Use a lot of expression as you read, to convey these emotions. *"Ooooh, how Peter WISHED he could . . ." "He tried and tr-i-i-i-ed . . ."* Raise your eyebrows and open your mouth to reflect Peter's surprised delight when he finally manages to whistle.

Throughout the story, use brief comments and explanations to help children notice and keep track of what Peter is doing.

Suggested Vocabulary

Use these words during Story Time and throughout the day.

balance the ability to keep your body steady

dizzy likely to fall; unsteady

errand a trip to accomplish a task

practice do something again and again to learn to do it well

proud feeling good about an accomplishment

quick as a wink very fast

raced ran fast

reflection a likeness in a mirror

scrambled moved quickly on hands and knees

shadow the shade made by blocking a beam of light

whistle make a shrill sound by blowing air past one's lips

wink a blink of an eye

wished desired; wanted

English Language Learners

Whenever possible, demonstrate word meanings. Read, "He blew and blew and blew," then pucker your lips and blow air through them.

Progress Monitoring

Note which children attend closely to the story and show, with facial expressions or answers, that they understand story events. Notice if words like *dizzy*, *shadow*, or *reflection* are already in individual children's oral vocabulary or are new and unfamiliar. Make a note if children are unable to sustain their focus through the whole story. Record your observations on copies of pages 155–156.

A MODEL FOR READING: *Use the following to help you plan your book reading.*

Cover

The title of this book is Whistle for Willie. *The author, or the person who wrote the story, is Ezra Jack Keats.*

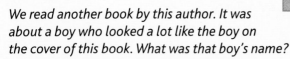

We read another book by this author. It was about a boy who looked a lot like the boy on the cover of this book. What was that boy's name?

Yes, the boy's name was Peter, and the story was Peter's Chair. *In the story we are going to read today, Peter doesn't have a baby sister yet, although he does have his dog. What was his name? Yes, Willie.*

I wonder what will happen in this story? Let's read and find out.

pp. 2–3 (Read page 3.)

Read with emotion that conveys longing. *Peter really wanted to* **whistle**. *He* **wished** *he could, but he wasn't able to. Peter looks a bit sad here, doesn't he?*

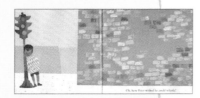

pp. 4–5 (Read page 4.)

Read with expression to convey Peter's wonder at this boy's skill. Show an expression that says, "That's quite amazing!" *I wonder if Peter would like to be able to do that with Willie.*

Now read page 5. Read the first line with a tinge of fatigue and frustration in your voice.

He kept spinning around and around—he whirled. Oh, look here. (Point to Peter's mouth.) *It doesn't look as if Peter is trying to* **whistle** *right now. I guess he decided to stop for a while and do something else.*

pp. 6–7 (Read pages 6 and 7.)

Point to the traffic lights and to Peter in the pictures as you read.

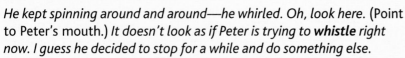

It looks like Peter's about to lose his **balance** and fall over. What do we call the feeling people get when they go around and around? Yes, **dizzy**.

pp. 8–9 (Read pages 8 and 9.)

Vary tone of voice to help convey meaning. Read page 8 briskly, and point to the box to explain **carton**. Then read page 9. *Oh, Peter must be disappointed. He keeps trying to* **whistle**, *but it doesn't seem to be working.*

pp. 10–11 (Read pages 10 and 11.)

When Peter got out of the **carton**, *where did he go?* Point to the carton.

Yes, he went home.

pp. 12–13 (Read page 13.)

Use your voice to express fatigue and frustration about the lack of success despite such effort. Slow your pace as you read the last two lines, sadly.

pp. 14–15 (Read page 15.)

Read the last sentence with expression that conveys Peter's disappointment.

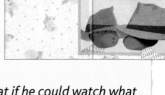

We can see two pictures of Peter here. One is the actual Peter and the other a **reflection** *of Peter in the mirror.* (Point first to Peter and then to his reflection.) *Maybe Peter thought that if he could watch what he was doing, by looking at his* **reflection** *in the mirror, he might be able to figure out how to* **whistle**. *I wonder also if Peter thought that if he looked more grown-up—wearing his father's hat—that he might be able to* **whistle**.

pp. 16–17 (Read pages 16 and 17.)

Read in a lower tone when Peter is pretending to be his father.

pp. 18–19 (Read page 19.)

Point to Peter's **shadow**. Remind children of a time when they may have seen their **shadows**.

pp. 20–21 (Read pages 20 and 21.)

Point to Peter jumping and to his **shadow**. Read page 21 with anxious surprise.

Oh, here's Peter looking around the corner. There's Willie. (Point to Willie.) Willie's head is turned away from Peter. I don't think Willie sees Peter.

pp. 22–23 (Read pages 22 and 23.)

Define **scrambled** by explaining that Peter crawled quickly under the box.

Read with surprise, enthusiasm, and delight as Peter manages to **whistle**.

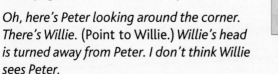

pp. 24–25 (Read page 25.)

*Willie ran very fast over to Peter. He **raced** to him. Look at the smile on Willie's face!*

pp. 26–27 (Read page 27.)

pp. 28–29 (Read pages 28 and 29.)

*It looks as if Peter and Willie are going home after doing an **errand**. I think they got something at the grocery store. See? They are both carrying something, and look! Peter is **whistling**! I wonder if he'll **practice**—keep **whistling** so he gets better at it—now that he's learned how. What do you think?*

Story Discussion

Guide a short discussion. For example:

What a good story about how Peter learned to whistle. He sure was happy at the end of the story when he finally could whistle, wasn't he? Peter's parents, his mom and dad, seemed very happy and proud of him too. I am sure there are things you have learned to do that make you feel proud or happy that you can do them now. Listen to responses and guide a short discussion.

We need to stop for the day, but we'll read Whistle for Willie *again.*

▶ Outdoor Play

Point to clothing items in *Whistle for Willie* and tell children they can go to their cubbies and Outdoor Play if they are wearing long pants like the boy, a long sleeved shirt like Peter, a dress like the girls jumping rope, and so on. Refer to page 121 for information on adapting Outdoor Play activities to your classroom. Also, see pages 84–85 for suggested conversation topics during this time.

▶ Songs, Word Play, Letters

Today children will be playing word games, singing songs, and reciting poems. Add your favorite game, song, or poem to this collection.

Songs

"Bingo"; "The Wheels on the Bus"

Poems

"Ten Little Fingers"; "Stand Up"

Literacy Skills

I'm Thinking of _____ Clue Game; Those Words Rhyme!

Purposes

Recites songs, rhymes, chants, and poems, and engages in language and word play. Understands that pictures, print, and other symbols carry meaning. Communicates using verbal and nonverbal cues. Sings and listens to a variety of songs. Responds to a variety of rhythms with body movements. Identifies the position of objects in a line, pointing to each object and assigning the appropriate number to it.

Suggested Sequence for Today's Circle

1. "Bingo"
2. "The Wheels on the Bus"
3. I'm Thinking of _____ Clue Game (and *Noisy Nora* and *Peter's Chair*)
4. "Ten Little Fingers" (and Those Words Rhyme!)
5. "Stand Up"

Materials and Instructional Procedures

BINGO

Materials: CD Track 2, Song Lyrics p. 159, flannel board and flannel pieces

Vocabulary: farmer, dog, name, clap

Procedure

- Say the names of the letters as you place them on the flannel board to spell B-I-N-G-O. *First, we need* B, *and second, we need* I. *Next, we need* N; *then* G. *Lastly, we need* O.

- Sing the verse through, pointing to each letter as its name is sung. Say, *I'm going to turn the* B *over. Now, let's sing it again and clap instead of saying* B.

- Tell children that you are going to turn over the *I*, and everyone will clap two times this time, once for the *B* that's turned over, and once for the *I*. Repeat with remaining letters, replacing each with a clap.

- Accept singing or clapping throughout song as children will not master it right away.

THE WHEELS ON THE BUS

Materials: CD Track 7, Song Lyrics p. 160

Vocabulary: wheels, bus, round, town, people, up, down, horn, wiper

Procedure

- Sing several verses, performing an appropriate motion for the item on the bus that is making a sound or moving. Go slowly enough that children can keep up with the motions.

I'M THINKING OF _____ CLUE GAME (AND *NOISY NORA* AND *PETER'S CHAIR*)

Materials: books: *Peter's Chair*, *Noisy Nora*; Picture Cards: crocodile, marbles, kite, shrub, crib, high chair

Vocabulary: crocodile, kite, marbles

Procedure

- Show children *Peter's Chair* and *Noisy Nora* and tell them you will be playing a game with words from those stories.

- Tell children you are going to give them clues to guess what word you're thinking of and they are to try to guess which word it is. Say, *Be sure to listen to everything I say before you raise your hand to let me know you have an idea.* Model raising your hand.

- For *crocodile*, use these clues: *This is a long animal with scaly skin and a big mouth with sharp teeth. These animals live in water in swamps. In* Peter's Chair, *Peter played with a stuffed animal like this.*

- For *marbles,* use these clues: *These are little glass balls that children like to play with. In* Noisy Nora, *Nora's sister Kate had some of these and Nora dumped them on the floor. They made a lot of noise.*

- For *kite,* use these clues: *This is a toy that flies through the air as you hold onto it with a string. Nora flew her brother's down the stairs. Its name rhymes with* bite.

Ten Little Fingers (and Those Words Rhyme!)

Materials: Poetry Posters: Poem 1, CD Track 26

Vocabulary: fingers, fold, high, low, open, shut, tight, together, wide

Procedure

- Display the poetry poster, read the title as you underline it with your finger, and then recite the poem naturally, as you look at children and lead them in performing the motions.

- When you finish, tell children there are some words in that poem that rhyme, or that have the same sound at the end. Read the first four lines of the poem again. You might say, me *and* see *rhyme. They have the same sound at the end.*

- Read the next four lines and say something like, Wide *and* hide *rhyme too!* Tight *and* together *begin with the same sound—* /t/, tight, together—*but they don't rhyme, do they?* Me *and* see *rhyme, and so do* wide *and* hide. *It's fun to find words that rhyme, isn't it?*

Stand Up

Materials: Poetry Posters: Poem 3, CD Track 28

Vocabulary: bend, bow, clap, hand, knees, stamp, stand, turn, wave

Procedure

- Display the poster and read the title of the poem as you underline it with your finger. Tell children that you need to look at the words sometimes to help you remember the poem.

- Recite the poem while looking at the children and modeling the motions.

- If time permits, try another poem called "Good Morning, Mrs. Hen." See Poetry Posters: Poem 20 or use the CD.

▶ Lunch/Quiet Time/Centers

This time is set aside for lunch, quiet time, and center activities. See pages 84–85 for suggested conversation topics during this time.

▶ **Small Groups**

For information on Small Groups, refer to pages 89–91.

▶ **Let's Find Out About It**

Chess and Other Games

Purposes

Understands that pictures and print carry meaning. Understands that print is used for different purposes. Listens with increasing attention. Shows interest and curiosity in learning new concepts.

Materials

book: *Noisy Nora*; checkers and chess boards and pieces, age-appropriate games with directions

Suggested Vocabulary

Model use and discuss meanings of these vocabulary words with children: checkers, chess board, chess pieces, directions, rules

Procedure

● Find the page in *Noisy Nora* where Nora's sister Kate is playing chess with her father. Explain that they are playing a game called *chess*. Point out the chessboard and pieces. Remind children that Nora's sister Kate is a little older than Nora and explain that chess is a game for children who are a little older than they are.

● Show children a checkerboard and pieces. Explain that checkers is a board game, like chess. Ask if some children have begun to learn checkers and talk about the rules of the game.

● Bring out the directions for checkers, if you have them. If not, show another game with directions. Explain that directions tell how to do something and read a bit of them to children.

● Tell children that they will be playing Alphabet Bingo soon and then a bit later, and that everyone will get a chance to play.

● Invite children to talk about other games they play at home. You also might ask if they have ever seen someone reading directions to learn how to do something. Consider having a personal experience prepared to share.

Small Groups Connections

Children play Alphabet Bingo this week.

> **Extending the Activity**
>
> Invite children to give examples of their favorite games and say why they like them.

> **English Language Learners**
>
> As you read the game directions, point to the parts of the game and say their names slowly and clearly.

▶ **End-the-Day Centers**

Children spend time in Centers of their choice. As children leave for home, say something that will help each child look forward to the next day. For example, if a child enjoys stories, predict that tomorrow will be fun because you will be reading *Noisy Nora* again.

▶ **Start-the-Day Centers** (see pages 86–88)

Make available for children two or three Centers.

▶ **Morning Meeting** (see page 86)

Help children make a first choice in Centers after you orient them to the activities.

▶ **Center Time** (see pages 86–88)

Children spend time in Centers of their choice.

Extending the Book

Invite children who are ready for a challenge to read two words with you—*banged* and *slammed*.

▶ **Story Time: 3rd Reading**

Noisy Nora

Author: Rosemary Wells

Read the Story Again

As you read *Noisy Nora*, pause to let children chime in with the story. This gives them the opportunity to say many of the new words. Children may especially enjoy shouting out the sound words such as *crash* and *hush*.

Story Discussion

After reading, thank children for helping to read the story. Use these or other questions to help children relate to the characters' actions and feelings, and the reasons for them:

● *Are there times when you have to wait—times when you wish you could get more of a grown-up's attention? How do you feel when you have to wait?*

● *Why do you think Nora changed her mind about leaving home and going outside?*

If there is time for a second book, try *Where the Wild Things Are* (see page 7) about a naughty boy who goes on an imaginary adventure.

Words and Phrases for Chiming In

(Vocabulary words appear in **dark** type.)

Kate – pp. 3, 19
burping – p. 4
banged the window – p. 5
slammed the door – p. 6
marbles on the kitchen floor – p. 7
Hush! – pp. 8, 16
filthy – p. 10
lamp down – p. 12
felled some chairs – p. 13
brother's **kite** – p. 14
father – p. 16
sleepy – p. 18
had to wait – p. 20
I'm never coming back! – p. 21
Mercy! – p. 24
tralala from Jack – p. 22
song – p. 23
wrong – p. 24
cellar – p. 25
shrub – p. 26
moaned – p. 27
monumental crash – p. 28

English Language Learners

Always provide sound prompts for key words when you wish children to chime in. If children do not chime in quickly, say the whole word or phrase yourself, slowly and clearly. Then repeat, lingering on the first sound, to invite children to chime in.

▶ **Outdoor Play**

Hold up letter cards and tell children they can leave for Outdoor Play when the first letters of their names match the first letter in a word. Use words from the story: B *like* burp, W *like* window, D *like* door, L *like* lamp, M *like* marbles, and so on. See pages 84–85 for suggested conversation topics during this time.

▶ Songs, Word Play, Letters

Today children will be playing word games, singing songs, and reciting poems. Add your favorite game, song, or poem to this collection.

Songs

"Five Green and Speckled Frogs"; "I'm a Little Teapot"; "Clap Your Hands"

Predictable Book

Time for Bed

Literacy Skills

If Your Name Starts With [name a letter], Raise Your Hand; Those Words Rhyme!

Purposes

Recognizes letters in their name. Identifies the cover of a book and knows that the title, author, and illustrator of the book are on the cover. Recites songs, rhymes, chants, and poems, and engages in language and word play. Moves body with balance and control. Sings and listens to a variety of songs.

Suggested Sequence for Circle

1. "Five Green and Speckled Frogs"

2. If Your Name Starts With [name a letter], Raise Your Hand

3. "I'm a Little Teapot" (and Those Words Rhyme!)

4. *Time for Bed*

5. "Clap Your Hands"

Materials and Instructional Procedures

FIVE GREEN AND SPECKLED FROGS

Materials: CD Track 10, Song Lyrics p. 160, flannel board and flannel pieces

Vocabulary: green, speckled, log, delicious, cool, pool

Procedure

- Tell children that they will start today with "Five Green and Speckled Frogs." Ask children, *What's this?* as you place the log, pool, and bug pieces on the board. Add details as appropriate, such as, *Yes, a brown and speckled log!*

- As the frogs are placed, say something like, *Here's the first frog, and the second frog, and the third frog. . .fourth. . .fifth.*

- Pause for children to chime in with the number of frogs remaining, when there are 3, 2, 1, and none. When removing the frogs, you might say, *Let's make sure we have all the frogs: 1, 2, 3, 4, 5* (as each is picked up). *Yes, we have all five. I'm glad we didn't lose any in the cool, blue pool.*

IF YOUR NAME STARTS WITH [NAME A LETTER], RAISE YOUR HAND

Materials: children's name cards (with only the first letter capitalized), uppercase alphabet cards (all first letters and first letter combinations such as *Ch*, *Sh*, and *Th* found in children's names)

Vocabulary: letter, name, raise, starts with, touch

Procedure

- Tell children they are going to play a name game. Say, *I'll hold up a letter* (pick a letter). *If your name starts with* [name a letter], *raise your hand. Everyone will get a turn.*

- Play one round of the game, gently reminding any children who don't raise their hands when the first letter of their name is called and while holding up their name card. *I'm holding an S. Sarah, your name starts with S, so you can raise your hand.* (Point to *S* on Sarah's name card.)

- If time permits and children are enjoying the game, do a second round. Say, *This time, I'll have you do a different motion when I show the letter that begins your name. Instead of raising your hand, touch your nose.* Demonstrate touching your nose.

I'm a Little Teapot (and Those Words Rhyme!)

Materials: CD Track 8, Song Lyrics p. 160

Vocabulary: teapot, short, stout, handle, spout, tip, pour

Procedure

- Ask children to stand up. Sing the song as usual, leading them in the motions. If you like, sing it a second time.

- Ask children to sit again. You might say, *I heard many words that rhyme in that song and maybe you did too.* Shout *rhymes with* out. *Let's see if we can remember any other words in the song that end with the same sound.* Begin singing it to the children, slowly. Name the rhyming pair after the last word in each rhyming pair is said.

Time for Bed

Materials: book: *Time for Bed*

Vocabulary: bed, bee, bird, calf, cat, deer, fish, foal, goose, house, little, mouse, pup, sheep, snake, time

Procedure

- Hold up the book and tell children you will now read . . . (point to title) *Time for . . .* (pause to let children chime in) *Bed!*

- Point to the author and illustrator names on the cover and explain that these are the people who made up the words and painted the pictures they hear and see in the book.

- Read the book. Encourage children to chime in with the second word in each rhyming pair by slowing down as you pronounce it.

Clap Your Hands

Materials: CD Track 12, Song Lyrics p. 160

Vocabulary: clap, hands, together, stamp, feet

Procedure

- Sing one verse of the song slowly and do the clapping of hands as you sing. Children can join in, but many will just watch the first time.

- Say, *That was fun! Let's do that again.* This time, sing two verses, leading children in the motions (clapping hands and stamping feet).

Progress Monitoring

Note individual children's level of participation: no engagement, attentive but no participation, participating physically but not verbally, attempting verbal participation, or participating fully. Who recognizes the first letter of his or her name and who still needs prompting? Record your observations on copies of pages 155–156.

▶ Lunch/Quiet Time/Centers

This time is set aside for lunch, quiet time, and center activities. See pages 84–85 for suggested conversation topics during this time.

▶ Small Groups

For information on Small Groups, refer to pages 89–91.

▶ Let's Talk About It

Developing Self-Control: Turns List

Purposes

Follows rules and routines within the learning environment. Uses speech to communicate needs, wants, or thoughts.

Materials

turns list

Procedure

- Introduce the topic. For example, you might say, *It is disappointing when you don't get to do something you were looking forward to.* Explain that the Marbles Boxes and other activities in Center Time will be available for many days so that everyone will have several turns.

- Point to the turns list, and tell children that some children's names are still on the turns list from today, and that they will get a turn tomorrow. For example, *Clayton, Dontey, Jason, and Arabelle, your names are on the turns list for Marble Boxes, so I will call you tomorrow at Morning Meeting. Mei Lei, your turn is on the list for the blocks, so I will call your name for that during Morning Meeting tomorrow.*

- Sum up the discussion by telling children that everyone will have turns at the activities they want to try, and that the turns list helps everyone get turns.

- Ask children if there are other times they have had to wait for a turn to do something. For example, they might have to take turns at home or on a playground. Encourage discussion about those experiences, helping children clarify their stories by asking questions and restating their answers. If appropriate, highlight the value of having a system like a turns list so everyone gets a turn.

▶ End-the-Day Centers

Children spend time in Centers of their choice. As children leave for home, say something that will help each child look forward to the next day. For example, you might tell enthusiastic singers that tomorrow they will be singing a funny new song called "Five Little Ducks."

▶ **Start-the-Day Centers** (see pages 86–88)
Open two or three Centers for children as they arrive.

▶ **Morning Meeting** (see page 86)
Demonstrate center activities, then help children make a first choice.

▶ **Center Time** (see pages 86–88)
Children spend time in Centers of their choice.

▶ **Story Time: 2nd Reading**

Whistle for Willie

Author: Ezra Jack Keats

Purposes

Recalls some main events when asked, "What is happening in this story?" Links characters' basic emotions to their actions. Uses own experiences to understand characters' feelings and motivations. Expresses the main idea of a story or other text in a way that shows increasing understanding.

Read the Story

Reconstruct the story with children by asking questions like, *What is happening here? What did [Peter, his mother, or Willie] do next?* Point to pictures to support children's recall of events and characters' actions. Provide more information to deepen understanding of words. For example, mention a couple of errands that children performed recently for the class.

After reading, prompt discussion with the questions provided or with similar ones.

Suggested Vocabulary

Use these words during Story Time and throughout the day.

balance the ability to keep your body steady
dizzy likely to fall; unsteady
errand a trip to do something
practice do something again and again to learn to do it well
proud feeling good about yourself
quick as a wink very fast
raced ran fast
reflection a likeness in a mirror
scrambled moved quickly on hands and knees
shadow the shade made by blocking a beam of light
whistle make a shrill sound by blowing air past one's lips
wink a blink of an eye
wished desired; wanted

Extending the Book

Invite children who are ready for a challenge to read the name of the main character with you on some pages. Use your finger to underline the word *Peter* and read slowly with the children.

English Language Learners

When you read key words, say them slowly and clearly. Sometimes say them again or add a brief comment in which you use a story word. Look out at children to encourage them to say the words with you.

A MODEL FOR READING: *Be sure to read all the text on each page. When read, it will vary, depending on the flow of conversations with children.*

Cover

We know the name, or title, of this book because we read it a few days ago. It's . . . (Pause.) Yes, that's right. The title of this book is Whistle for Willie. *We are going to read this book again today, and you can help me remember what happens in the story.*

pp. 2–3

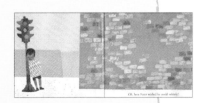

Point to Peter. *Here's Peter. It doesn't look as though he's doing anything right now, does it? And he looks a little sad. What does Peter want to do—what does he wish he could do?* (Children respond.)

*That's right, he **wishes** he could **whistle**.* (Read page 2.) *We know from last time that he finally learns, but it takes him a long time, doesn't it?*

pp. 4–5

Point to figures. *What is happening over here?* (Children respond.) *Yes, this older boy is playing with his dog.* Read text on page 4.

Read first line of text on page 5. *Then what did Peter do?* (Point to Peter on page 5. Children may say turned around or tried to **whistle**.) *Yes, Peter started turning himself around, after he gave up trying to **whistle**.*

What happened after Peter turned himself around and around very fast? (Children respond.) Finish reading page 5.

pp. 6–7

*Peter became **dizzy**.* (Read pages 6 and 7.) *He was spinning around and around so now everything seems to be moving. Peter looks like he might tip over, or lose his **balance**, doesn't he? What happened to Peter next?* Turn page to assist recall.

pp. 8–9

*Yes, Peter saw his dog, Willie, and hid in this empty **carton**, this big cardboard box right here.* Point to **carton**.

Read page 8, define **wink**, show children how to give a quick **wink**, and invite children to try winking themselves.

*A **wink** is very fast, isn't it? Why did Peter climb into the **carton** 'as quick as a wink'? That's right. He didn't want Willie to see him, so he had to move quickly.*

*Then what happened? What did Peter want to do once he was in the **carton**?* (He wanted to **whistle**.) *Yes, it says so right here in the book.* Read the top of page 9.

pp. 10–13

Read from page 10 to the first line on page 13. Point to the chalk line as you summarize what happened. *He started here after he got out of the **carton**, then he drew on the sidewalk around the corner, and then around these girls jumping rope.* (Turn the page.) *And then he went around this barbershop pole and right up to his front door.*

That's when he tried to **whistle** again, remember? He sure was trying hard, wasn't he? It says in the story, 'He stood there and tried . . . till his cheeks were tired.' And was he able to **whistle** this time? (Children respond.) No, it says here on page 13, 'But nothing happened.'

pp. 14-15

Read the first sentence on page 15, then point to Peter. *What is Peter doing here?* (Children respond.) *Yes, it looks as if Peter is trying to **whistle** again, and he's wearing an old hat of his father's. He wants to feel more grown up. Maybe he thinks if he looks more grown up, he'll be able to **whistle**. But is he able to **whistle** this time?* (No.) Read the rest of the page.

pp. 16-17

Oh, what is happening here? (After children offer their ideas, read the text to confirm.) *It says right here in the story that Peter pretended to be his father by wearing his hat and talking like him. Peter's mother played along with the game, didn't she? She pretended that he was his father, and she told him where she thought Peter would be playing. Then Peter decided he would go outside.*

pp. 18-19

Oh, what is Peter doing right here? (Point to Peter walking on the crack on page 18.) *See how he has his arms raised out by his sides? He's trying to keep his **balance**—to stay level so he doesn't tip over to one side or the other or fall off the crack.*

Point to Peter on page 19. *What's happening here?* (Children respond.)

*It looks as if Peter is running. Do you remember what that dark area on the wall is called? Yes, that's his **shadow**.* (Gesture to where the sun is.) *The sun must be over here and Peter's body is blocking some of the sunlight. That's why there is a **shadow** on the wall. Peter is trying to run away from his **shadow**, isn't he? I don't think he will ever get away from it, do you?* Read the text.

pp. 20-21

Oh, what's Peter doing here? Point to Peter on page 20 and pause as children respond. Then read the text.

pp. 22-23

*Next, Peter crawled under the **carton** on his hands and knees so he'd be hidden from Willie. Then what did he do?* (He whistled.) Read, *"Suddenly—out came a real **whistle**!"*

*Peter probably wasn't expecting a **whistle** to come out, because it didn't happen all the other times he tried. But he did it this time!*

Look at Willie. (Point to the dog.) *Do you think he is surprised too?* (Children respond.)

pp. 24-25

Read page 25. *Now Willie knows who **whistled**. Look at the smile on his face! Do you think he looks happy to find out that it's Peter?*

pp. 26–27

Read page 27. *So Peter raced home to show his mother and father that he could whistle. Why did he run home so fast?* (Children comment.)

And how do you think his parents—his mother and father—felt about his **whistling**? *How do you know that?* Guide children to notice the clues in the pictures.

Do you remember what happens next? (Children respond.)

pp. 28–29

Read pages 28 and 29. *That was fun when Peter could finally whistle, wasn't it?*

Story Discussion

Prompt discussion with questions like this: *Now, why do you think Peter kept on whistling at the end of the story?* Guide discussion. Peter wanted to do something he just learned, he wanted to practice, and he liked to whistle.

Okay, we need to stop reading for today. We'll read Whistle for Willie *again another day.*

Progress Monitoring

Notice whether children can name characters and objects in the pictures. Do some children recall Peter's motivations from the first reading? Do their responses and facial expressions show that they understand his desire to whistle and his frustration at being unable to? Copy pages 155–156 and use them to record your observations.

▶ Outdoor Play

Have children go to their cubbies and get ready for Outdoor Play when they match a family relationship you name. For example, *You may leave for Outdoor Play if you have no brothers or sisters, like Peter in this story . . . if you have a baby brother . . . a baby sister . . . a big brother . . . a big sister,* and so on. See pages 84–85 for suggested conversation topics during this time.

▶ Songs, Word Play, Letters

Today children will be playing word games, singing songs, and reciting poems. Add your favorite game, song, or poem to this collection.

Songs

"Five Little Ducks"; "Down by the Bay"; "The Wheels on the Bus"

Poems

"Ten Little Fingers"

Predictable Book

Brown Bear, Brown Bear, What Do You See?

Literacy Skills

Those Words Rhyme!; I'm Thinking of _____ Clue Game

Purposes

Segments the beginning sounds in words. Discriminates between sounds that are the same and sounds that are different. Understands that pictures, print, and other symbols carry meaning. Shows a steady increase in the number of words in listening vocabulary. Listens with increasing attention. Counts up to ten objects in a set using one-to-one correspondence.

Suggested Sequence for Today's Circle

1. "Five Little Ducks"
2. "Down by the Bay" (and Those Words Rhyme!)
3. "Ten Little Fingers"
4. I'm Thinking of _____ Clue Game (and *Noisy Nora* and *Whistle for Willie*)
5. "The Wheels on the Bus"
6. *Brown Bear, Brown Bear, What Do You See?*

Materials and Instructional Procedures

FIVE LITTLE DUCKS

Materials: CD Track 11, Song Lyrics p. 160

Vocabulary: out, over, far away, back

Procedure

- Hold up fingers of one hand and raise it. Ask children if they remember the song "Five Little Ducks." Say, *We're going to sing it again, so get your five ducks ready!* (Wiggle the fingers of your raised hand.)

- Sing the song, raising and lowering your hand to indicate hills and lowering fingers to your thumb to represent a beak that is quacking. Children should try the hand motions, and will enjoy saying, "quack, quack, quack."

- If you have time and the children enjoy it, sing the song again.

DOWN BY THE BAY (AND THOSE WORDS RHYME!)

Materials: CD Track 3, Song Lyrics p. 159, flannel board and flannel pieces

Vocabulary: bay, watermelons, pig, cow, hen

Procedure

- Use flannel board pieces as you did the last time while you sing. Use new ones for new verses.

- Place a pair of flannel pieces on the board whose names rhyme (e.g., snake and cake, or mouse and house). Say, *I'm going to put some pieces from that song back up. You tell me their names.* After children say the names, repeat them. Ask, *Do those words rhyme?* Confirm and add, *Yes,* mouse *and* house *rhyme. They sound the same at the end.*

- Repeat with a second pair of rhyming pieces.

TEN LITTLE FINGERS

Materials: Poetry Posters: Poem 1, CD Track 26

Vocabulary: fingers, fold, high, low, open, shut, tight, together, wide

Procedure

- Show children the poem and talk about the illustration.

- Present the poem as usual, looking at them, and modeling the finger movements.

- You might say, *Let's put our hands up again and count our ten fingers.*

I'm Thinking of ____ Clue Game (and *Noisy Nora* and *Whistle for Willie*)

Materials: books: *Noisy Nora, Whistle for Willie*; Picture Cards: shadow, shrub, wink

Vocabulary: shadow, shrub, wink

Procedure

- Introduce the game as usual. After children guess each answer, show the Picture Card. Provide more clues, or begin to pronounce the word, if children do not guess with the first few clues given.

- For *shadow*, use these clues: *When Peter played outside, he tried to run away from this, but he couldn't get away. This is something you see on the ground on a sunny day, when your body blocks the sun. We hear two parts* (clap two times) *when we say this word.*

- For *wink*, use these clues: *This is what we do when we close just one eye. The name of this motion starts with /w/. It rhymes with* sink.

- For *shrub*, use these clues: *When Noisy Nora's father was looking for her outside, he looked to see if she was hiding behind this bushy plant. Its name rhymes with* tub.

The Wheels on the Bus

Materials: CD Track 7, Song Lyrics p. 160

Vocabulary: wheels, bus, round, town, up, down, horn, money, box

Procedure

- Sing several verses slowly enough for children to sing with you.

- Model the motions (e.g., press nose three times for the horn's *toot, toot, toot* or *beep, beep, beep*).

- If time permits and children are enjoying it, add more verses and sing with sounds and/or motions.

Brown Bear, Brown Bear, What Do You See?

Materials: book: *Brown Bear, Brown Bear, What Do You See?*; flannel board and flannel pieces

Preparation: Make flannel board pieces: black sheep, blue horse, brown bear, goldfish, green frog, purple cat, red bird, white dog, yellow duck

Vocabulary: bear, black, goldfish, horse, purple, teacher

Procedure

- Read *Brown Bear, Brown Bear, What Do You See?* Keep the natural rhythm of the verse as you read. Point to the pictures to identify the objects named (e.g., brown bear, red bird).

- Each time a new animal is named, add that flannel piece to the board. Remove pieces as you go so that only two are there at once.

- When you're finished you might say, *We'll read this book another day.*

▶ **Lunch/Quiet Time/Centers**

This time is set aside for lunch, quiet time, and center activities. Refer to the Weekly Planner on pages 84–85 for suggested conversation topics during this time.

▶ Small Groups

For information on Small Groups, refer to pages 89–91.

▶ Let's Find Out About It

Birth Announcements and Birth Weight

Purposes

Understands that print carries meaning. Develops awareness of personal information. Develops beginning understanding of amounts (weight) using nonstandard units.

Materials

several birth announcements, paper, large-size flip calendar, bags, rice

Preparation

- If possible, obtain birth information for each child. Write children's names on their birth dates on a calendar. Also fill in half-sheets of paper on which you've printed the following:

  Name: _____, Date of Birth: _____

  Weight: _____, Height: _____

- Use an average weight and height if exact numbers are not available. Be sensitive to children who do not want to participate.

- Fill bags with rice to create bags with pound weights: 5 pounds, 6 pounds, 7 pounds, 8 pounds, and 9 pounds. Be sure each bag is labeled and secured tightly.

Suggested Vocabulary

Introduce these words and use them in the discussion: birth announcement, birth date, calendar book, day of the week, height, weight, month, pounds, inches, first name, middle name, last name, parents, grandparents

> **English Language Learners**
>
> Look through the calendar you have prepared and help children say the day of each child's birthday (*Friday, Monday, . . .*). Speak slowly and enunciate.

Procedure

- Bring in several birth announcements to show children. Read some of the information on each such as name, date of birth, weight, and height.

- Quickly read through the half-sheets you made for each child. Allow children to hold the prepared weight bags closest to their birth weights to give them an idea of how heavy they were.

- Invite observations and comparisons of the relative weights of the different bags. Use terms such as *lighter, heavier, heaviest* and standard measurement terminology such as *pounds* and *ounces* to introduce children to these terms.

- Explain to children that you have written all their birthdays on a calendar. Look through each month on the calendar book to show children where their birthdays are written.

- Give children the birth announcements you made to take home.

> **Extending the Activity**
>
> For children ready for a challenge, point to the day heading on the calendar for a birth date, and help them read the day and date with you (Friday, January 14th).

▶ End-the-Day Centers

Children spend time in Centers of their choice. As children leave for home, say something that will help each child look forward to coming to school tomorrow. For example, you might remind children they will be singing songs and reading *Noisy Nora*.

▶ **Start-the-Day Centers** (see pages 86–88)

Direct children to the open Centers as they arrive.

▶ **Morning Meeting** (see page 86)

Display and explain items from some of the Centers, then help children make a first choice.

▶ **Center Time** (see pages 86–88)

Children spend time in Centers of their choice.

▶ **Story Time: 4th Reading**

Noisy Nora

Author: Rosemary Wells

Read *Noisy Nora* Again

Have all children recite the part of Nora so that everyone can participate in the reading. Cue children when Nora's speeches are coming up, near the end of the book. You read the parts of Kate and her mother and father. It is okay if children chime in simultaneously with you on the other characters' parts.

Taking On the Roles of Story Characters

Nora: I'm leaving! And I'm never coming back! – p. 21

But I'm back again! – p. 28

Story Discussion

After reading, pose this question or a similar one for discussion: *If you have a baby brother or sister, you know that there are many things parents must do for a baby. What are some of those things?*

Other Book Suggestions

If you think *Noisy Nora* cannot easily sustain children's interest for a fourth reading, substitute *Where the Wild Things Are* (see page 7) or another theme-related book of your choice. *Where the Wild Things Are* is a story about a little boy who makes a lot of noise in his house. When he can't calm down and talks back to his mother, he is sent to bed without any supper.

Making Connections: *Ask children why they think Max was making noise at his house.* Guide children to notice that he seemed to have no one to play with, no brothers or sisters, and was making up games to have something to do. Ask children why Noisy Nora was making noise. Guide answers toward the idea that she was not getting attention and was a bit angry.

▶ **Outdoor Play**

Continue naming family relationships as you did yesterday to dismiss children for Outdoor Play. For example, *if you are the big sister in your family . . . if you are a little brother . . . if you have a grandmother,* and so on. See pages 84–85 for suggested conversation topics during this time.

▶ Songs, Word Play, Letters

Today children will be playing word games, singing songs, and reciting poems. Add your favorite game, song, or poem to this collection.

Songs

"If You're Happy"; "Head and Shoulders, Knees and Toes"; "I'm a Little Teapot"

Literacy Skills

If Your Name Starts With [name a sound], Raise Your Hand; Chiming In With Rhyming Words

Purposes

Finds words with the same beginning sound. Responds to their names and requests for action or information. Says the words that complete rhymes, poems, or lines from stories, individually or in a group. Continues to develop body flexibility. Sings and listens to a variety of songs.

Suggested Sequence for Today's Circle

1. "If You're Happy"
2. If Your Name Starts With [name a sound], Raise Your Hand
3. "Head and Shoulders, Knees and Toes"
4. "I'm a Little Teapot" (and Chiming In With Rhyming Words)

Materials and Instructional Procedures

IF YOU'RE HAPPY

Materials: CD Track 1, Song Lyrics p. 159

Vocabulary: clap, hands, stomp, feet

Procedure

- Sing two verses of the song using clapping hands and stomping feet as the motions.

- If you like, add new verses using different motions and/or feelings. For example, *If you're hungry and you know it, rub your tummy; If you're sleepy and you know it, yawn w-i-d-e; If you're thinking and you know it, tap your head.*

IF YOUR NAME STARTS WITH [NAME A SOUND], RAISE YOUR HAND

Vocabulary: starts with, hand, name, raise, sound

Procedure

- Tell children that today they are going to play the name game with sounds instead of letters. Explain that you are going to say a sound. Children think about their names. If their name starts with the sound you say, children raise their hands.

- Give an example, such as: *Here is a sound: /s/.* (Make the sound long—/sssssssss/—to give children a chance to think about it and compare it to their own names.) *Sam, your name starts with /s/, so you can raise your hand. Sarah, your name also starts with /s/, doesn't it?*

- Make sure you use all the initial sounds of children's names in the class, so that everyone gets a turn.

HEAD AND SHOULDERS, KNEES AND TOES

Materials: CD Track 4, Song Lyrics p. 159

Vocabulary: head, shoulders, knees, toes, eyes, ears, mouth, nose

Procedure

- Tell children to stand up so they can sing a song about the parts of our bodies. Say, *It's called "Head and Shoulders, Knees and Toes."*

- Sing the song once, touching the different parts of your body as you sing about them. Invite children to join in.

I'M A LITTLE TEAPOT (AND CHIMING IN WITH RHYMING WORDS)

Materials: CD Track 8, Song Lyrics p. 160

Vocabulary: teapot, short, stout, handle, spout, tip, pour

Procedure

- Sing the song as usual, leading children in the motions.

- Sing the song a second time, pausing a bit this time before the last word in each line (*stout, spout, shout, out*) to let the children chime in. Prompt with the first sounds of the word (*st . . .*) to help children join in.

Progress Monitoring

Continue to observe individual children's level of engagement during singing. Which children remember body motions from earlier days? Note children's responses to first sound in name activity. Which children need prompting? Which respond to prompting with recognition? (*Oh, that's right!*) Record your observations on copies of pages 155–156.

▶ **Lunch/Quiet Time/Centers**

This time is set aside for lunch, quiet time, and center activities. See pages 84–85 for suggested conversation topics during this time.

▶ **Small Groups**

For information on Small Groups, refer to pages 89–91.

▶ **Let's Find Out About It**

Birth Announcements and Birth Length

Purposes

Recognizes own name. Becomes familiar with standard units of measurement and terminology (tape measure). Compares objects of different lengths.

Materials

string, tape measure, hole punch, tag board, birth announcement

Preparation

If possible, obtain the birth length of each child from family members. Use an average length if exact length is not available.

Cut pieces of string to represent each child's length at birth plus a few extra inches. Punch a hole in the corner of a tag-board tag. Tie the string through the tag's hole, knot, and then adjust the string to correct length for each child. Write the child's name and length at birth on the tag.

Suggested Vocabulary

Introduce these words and use them in the discussion: birth date, birth announcement, weight, height, pounds, inches, first name, middle name, last name, parents, grandparents

Procedure

● Bring in a tape measure. Say, *A tape measure is used to measure how long something is.* Show children how big an inch is, then measure your arm. Talk about the measuring process. (For example, *I'll hold the end with 0 here with my thumb and finger, and stretch it to my shoulder.*) Read the number.

English Language Learners

Help each child say his or her length at birth. Say, *I was ___ inches long.* Repeat slowly so the child can say it with you.

● Say, *When a baby is born, a nurse or doctor measures a baby's length with a tape measure. This information— how many inches long a baby is— is usually written by parents on a birth announcement.* Show an example.

● Show children the pieces of string you made. Explain that these pieces of string show how long each child was at birth. Read the label for each string and give children the strings with their names. Ask them to compare their lengths at birth to their lengths now. Allow children to take their strings home.

Extending the Activity

Invite children who are ready for a challenge to use the tape measure to double check the information on their string's tag.

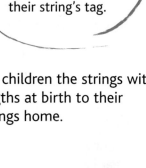

Progress Monitoring

Note if children show an interest in relative weights and lengths. Observe who is familiar with a measuring tape, and for whom measuring is a new concept. Listen to which children use comparative words (*bigger, longer, shorter, heavier*) in their spoken vocabulary. Record your observations on copies of pages 155–156.

▶ **End-the-Day Centers**

Children spend time in Centers of their choice. As children leave for home, say something to help each one look forward to the next school day. For example, you might mention you will be reading a brand new book about a little bear with green overalls who lives in the toy department of a big store.

Week 3 • Day 5

▶ **Start-the-Day Centers** (see pages 86–88)
Show children which Centers are open.

▶ **Morning Meeting** (see page 86)
Help children choose their first center activity.

▶ **Center Time** (see pages 86–88)
Children spend time in Centers of their choice.

▶ **Story Time: 1st Reading**

Corduroy

Author: Don Freeman

Summary: A little girl wants to buy a teddy bear, but her mother says no. The girl uses money from her piggy bank. Meanwhile, the bear has adventures in the store.

Theme Link: Family—Families have to make decisions about how they spend their money. Children can suggest ideas and work with parents to find solutions to some situations.

Purposes

Listens to stories read aloud. Demonstrates increasing levels of sustained and focused engagement. Shows a steady increase in the number of words in listening vocabulary. Develops understanding of main events.

Read the Story

Help children identify the setting and characters, as well as track story events. Say, *A store can be busy in the daytime, but it's dark and quiet at night. This night watchman's job is to keep the store safe.* Explain quickly so as not to interrupt the flow of the story.

Suggested Vocabulary

Use these words in Story Time and throughout the day.

admiring looking with enjoyment or approval

blinked opened and closed the eyes quickly

escalator a set of stairs that move

evening the time between sunset and bedtime

flashlight a small light you can carry around

furniture department part of a store that sells things like chairs and sofas

overalls loose pants with a piece covering the chest

palace a very large house, usually belonging to a king or queen

searching looking for something

shoulder where an arm is attached to the body

sighed let out a deep breath when tired or sad

thread a fine string used to sew things

Extending the Book

For children who are ready for a challenge, have them help you read the title of the book, *Corduroy*. Use your finger to underline the title letter by letter and sound it out to children.

English Language Learners

Repeat multi-syllabic key words (*escalator, furniture, department*) slowly and carefully to help children learn to say them.

Progress Monitoring

Note whether children show an interest in this new storybook. Do they show curiosity about the contents? Are they able to focus on the reading from the beginning? Are they able to focus on the story from beginning to end, or does their attention waver? Use copies of pages 155–156 to record your observations.

A MODEL FOR READING: *Use the following to help you plan your book reading.*

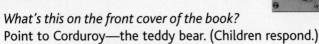

The title of this book is Corduroy. *The author of this book, the person who wrote the story, is Don Freeman.*

What's this on the front cover of the book? Point to Corduroy—the teddy bear. (Children respond.)

Yes, this is a picture of a teddy bear, a stuffed bear, whose name is Corduroy. This story is about some things that happen to Corduroy. The story is also about a little girl named Lisa and her mother. We don't see them on the cover. We'll find out all about them when we read the story.

p. 1 (Read page 1.)
Point to the teddy bear as you read.

Here's Corduroy, on the shelf with the other toys.

pp. 2–3 (Read pages 2 and 3.)
Point to the bear and his overalls on page 2.

After you read, "her mother **sighed**," on page 3, sigh to show the meaning of the word.

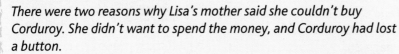

There were two reasons why Lisa's mother said she couldn't buy Corduroy. She didn't want to spend the money, and Corduroy had lost a button.

*We can see that they do have some bags that are full of packages. I guess they bought some other things. (Point to picture.) And, yes, we can see that this strap, which goes over Corduroy's **shoulder**—this part of our body—is not buttoned. (Point to strap and **shoulder**.) There's no button down here on his overalls for that shoulder strap. So Lisa's mommy had two very good reasons for saying no.*

pp. 4–5 (Read page 4.)
After reading page 4, ask, *How do you think Lisa is feeling about having to leave Corduroy at the store?* (Children respond.)

Now read page 5. Then say, *Oh, Corduroy is just now noticing that he's missing a button. He hadn't realized that until Lisa's mother mentioned it.*

pp. 6–7 (Read pages 6 and 7.)
So that night, when the shoppers weren't there, and it was kind of dark in the store, Corduroy started looking for his button.

pp. 8–9 (Read pages 8 and 9.)
As you read, explain **escalator** by saying it is a set of stairs that move; people move on them.

Corduroy is a little confused, isn't he? Mountains are tall, but they don't look like this, do they? (Children respond.)

pp. 10–11 (Read pages 10 and 11.)
Explain **palace** quickly when you come to it in the text.

*He's a little confused again, isn't he? He's not in a king or queen's **palace**; he's in the **furniture department** of the store, in the place where they sell beds and sofas and tables and chairs.*

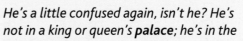

pp. 12–13 (Read pages 12 and 13.)

Define **admiring** quickly by saying, *He really liked all the furniture he saw.*

*Corduroy thought he could just pick up the button he saw, but it was attached to the mattress with a **thread**, which is a kind of string we use to sew things.* Point to the thread.

pp. 14–15 (Read pages 14 and 15.)

Why do you think Corduroy is covering his ears with his paws? (Children respond.) Link his action to the loud crash of the lamp falling.

pp. 16–17 (Read page 16.)

After reading page 16, ask, *What does the night watchman have in his hand?* (**flashlight**) *And why does he have a **flashlight**?* (Children respond.) Guide children toward the fact that it is night and very dark in much of the store. The night watchman needs some light to search for the source of the loud noise that he heard.

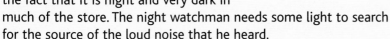

Now read page 17. Ask, *What did he notice that was out of the ordinary, or not as it usually is?* (Point to the fallen lamp.) *Yes, he noticed that the lamp was not standing up, and he wondered who knocked it down.*

pp. 18–19 (Read pages 18 and 19.)

Point to the two ears on page 18. *Who's there?* (Children respond.) *Does the night watchman know who it is?* (Children respond.) Reread the text if necessary.

pp. 20–21 (Read pages 20 and 21.)

Move finger in a downward motion along the escalator as you read page 20.

*Now he's back in the toy **department**, where he started.*

pp. 22–23 (Read pages 22 and 23.)

What's a piggy bank? Does anyone know? Guide comments toward a child's bank, often in the shape of a pig, for saving coins. Have one to show, if you can.

So Lisa had been putting money in her bank little by little, saving it, and she found out that she had enough to buy Corduroy. Her mother didn't have enough money to buy him, but Lisa had saved some money of her own.

pp. 24–25 (Read pages 24 and 25.)

Four flights of stairs is a lot, and Lisa ran up all the way. Lisa was very excited about bringing Corduroy home, wasn't she? (Children respond.) Move on quickly.

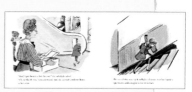

pp. 26–27 (Read page 26.)

After reading, "Corduroy **blinked**," say, *He opened and closed his eyes quickly several times.* Demonstrate **blinking**. Then finish reading page 26.

Does Corduroy like it here better than at the toy store? (Children respond.)

Now read page 27. Point to the **overalls** again when you read this page.

*It is rather uncomfortable if a **shoulder** strap is flopping around because there's no button to hold it down. Lisa likes Corduroy no matter what, but she thinks he'll feel a little better with his strap fastened. She's using a needle and **thread** to sew on a button.* Point to the illustration and have a needle and thread to show, if possible.

p. 28 (Read page 28.)

Have you ever wanted something a lot and your mom or dad or maybe your grandma said, "No, you can't have it. It costs too much money"? As children respond, guide them toward the realization that families some-

times have other important needs, so toys must wait. Help them to see that families often wait for special occasions to buy big things.

Story Discussion

Prompt discussion with questions. For example:

Does anyone have a piggy bank like Lisa? (Children respond.) Guide discussion toward the benefit of saving a little at a time, which adds up over weeks and months.

Do you think Lisa has any brothers and sisters? (None show up in the story, so probably not.) *Maybe she's like Peter, in the story* Whistle for Willie, *before his baby sister was born. Lisa is the only child in this family, it seems. Do you think maybe she wanted to buy Corduroy so she'd have someone to play with?* Children comment.

▶ Outdoor Play

Use colors to call children for Outdoor Play, pointing to items in *Corduroy*. For example, dismiss children wearing something green like Corduroy's overalls, yellow like letters in the book title, red like the cover's background, white like the button, and so on. See pages 84–85 for suggested conversation topics during this time.

▶ Songs, Word Play, Letters

Today children will be playing word games, singing songs, and reciting poems. Add your favorite game, song, or poem to this collection.

Songs

"Bingo"; "Clap Your Hands"

Predictable Book

Over in the Meadow

Literacy Skills

We Can Change It and Rearrange It; Chiming In With Rhyming Words; Can You Think of Words That Rhyme With _____?

Purposes

Produces words that rhyme. Uses pictures to understand a book. Observes teacher's left to right scanning of print. Listens to/attends to a variety of genres read aloud. Says the words that complete rhymes, individually or in a group. Names many uppercase letters. Listens to and imitates sounds, sound patterns, or songs.

Suggested Sequence for Today's Circle

1. "Bingo" (and We Can Change It and Rearrange It)
2. *Over in the Meadow* (and Chiming In With Rhyming Words)
3. Can You Think of Words That Rhyme With _____? (and *Over in the Meadow*)
4. "Clap Your Hands"

Materials and Instructional Procedures

BINGO (AND WE CAN CHANGE IT AND REARRANGE IT)

Materials: CD Track 2, Song Lyrics p. 150, flannel board and flannel pieces; add *T, R, S, W, P*; mount letters on a square of felt

Vocabulary: farmer, dog, name, clap, letter, replace

Procedure

- Name each letter as you place it on the board and encourage children to help.

- When you finish, turn letters back over on the board. Tell children that the word says *Bingo.* You might say, *I'm going to replace* B *with* T, *and change this word to* /t/, /t/, *Tingo!*

- Replace *T* with *R,* and say, *I'm going to remove the* T *and replace it with* R. Say */rrrrr/* and ask children what the new word says. Continue replacing the first letter with others, as long as they're interested and engaged.

- As you put the letters away, say, *We can change letters to create a lot of different words.*

OVER IN THE MEADOW (AND CHIMING IN WITH RHYMING WORDS)

Materials: book: *Over in the Meadow*

Vocabulary: bask, crickets, dive, fireflies, lizard, muskrat, sand, shine, turtles

Procedure

- Point to the title and read it to children. Point to each word as you read it.

- Read the book once as usual, pointing to the pictures to show the children the animals and other objects as they're named.

- Tell children, *I'm going to read this book again, and this time you can help me with some of the words.* When you come to the second word in a rhyming pair, hang onto the first sound or two to encourage children to chime in.

CAN YOU THINK OF WORDS THAT RHYME WITH _____? (AND *OVER IN THE MEADOW*)

Materials: book: *Over in the Meadow*

Vocabulary: blue, gate, shine

Procedure

- Tell children that you've picked some words from *Over in the Meadow* to use for a rhyming game. Choose 2–3 words (e.g., *blue, gate, shine*).

- Start with *blue*. Ask children if they remember the blue stream in the book. You might say, Too *rhymes with* blue, *and so does* flew. *Can you think of some other words that rhyme with* blue *and* too?

- Let children who raise hands offer one idea at a time. You might need to offer words and ask if it rhymes with *blue*. *Does* bike *rhyme with* blue? (No.) *How about* shoe? (Yes.)

- Repeat the same game with one or two other words, being sure to introduce the word by saying something about its context in the book.

CLAP YOUR HANDS

Materials: CD Track 12, Song Lyrics p. 160

Vocabulary: clap, hands, together, feet, stamp

Procedure

- Tell children that they are going to sing the song, "Clap Your Hands." Sing the line, clapping your hands.

- Sing the song as before. If you like, add one or two more verses (e.g., "tap your toes," "blink your eyes").

▶ **Lunch/Quiet Time/Centers**

This time is set aside for lunch, quiet time, and center activities. See pages 84–85 for suggested conversation topics during this time.

▶ Small Groups

For information on Small Groups, refer to pages 89–91.

▶ Let's Talk About It

Social Skills Development: Compliments

Purposes

Interacts appropriately with other children. Interacts appropriately with familiar adults. Uses language to develop relationships.

Procedure

- Explain that sometimes people compliment each other. They tell each other that they did a good job at something or made something that is interesting or pretty. Ask, *How do you think people feel when they receive a compliment?* Agree that it feels good or makes people happy when others say nice things.

- Say, *I have a compliment for each one of you.* Give each child a compliment about something specific the child did yesterday or today.

- Ask, *Would anyone else like to give a compliment to someone in our classroom?* Encourage a few children to give a compliment to another child or teacher in the classroom. If children have trouble framing their compliments, support them in using specific language.

- If a child gives you a compliment, thank him or her. For example, *Thank you so much,* [Maria]. *It makes me happy to know that you liked the way I drew a fierce dragon during art time.*

Connect With Families

Tell parents children have been learning about compliments. Suggest they compliment their children about something they bring home from school, such as the bright colors in a painting or the letter-like marks they bring home from the Writing Center.

▶ End-the-Day Centers

Children spend time in Centers of their choice. As children leave for home, say something that will help each child look forward to Monday. For example, tell them that next week they will read *Whistle for Willie* and there will be some new activities in Center Time.

Notes to Teachers

Adapting Activities to Your Program

Here are some tips and suggestions for planning Centers and Outdoor Play activities. Adapt them for what works in your program setting.

Center Time

Blocks

Add small props, such as rectangles of felt or other fabric for use as blankets for block beds. Add small jewelry boxes for baby cribs. Small plastic models of dogs and cats can serve as family pets. You might purchase small, inexpensive baby dolls at a toy store to extend the number of family members available for play.

Art Area: Table

If Clay Dough With Baking Props and Recipe Cards is of high interest, keep it at the art table for four days rather than three. Offer Painting With Marbles for two days of the following week, and provide Drawing With Chalk for only three days.

Outdoor Play

Turn-Taking

If tricycles are few and interest is high, establish a system for turn-taking. Use a clipboard for a turns list, and limit a turn to 8–10 minutes per child.

Helping Individual Children Adjust to School

Children who show symptoms of separation anxiety may have a harder time during outdoor play than during indoor activities. Invite the child to join you in digging in the sandbox or go with the child to the climber, and stand nearby to encourage independent play.

Greeting and Parting

Lending Library

Consider creating a classroom lending library. Tape a small envelope inside the back cover of books to hold an index card with the book's title written on it. Draw several lines on both sides of the card where children can write their names when they check out a book. Prepare a poster board chart with a labeled pocket for each child to hold cards of books checked out. You can easily check cards to know which book a child has at home.

Weekly Planner

	Day 1	Day 2	Day 3
Start-the-Day Centers 30 Minutes **Morning Meeting** 15 Minutes **Center Time** 60 Minutes pp. 124–126	Greet children and open selected Centers. Introduce Center Time activities. **Sand and Water:** Playing With Water Wheels; **Book Area:** Exploring Books; **Art Area/Table:** Painting With Marbles; Drawing With Chalk; **Blocks:** Building Block Towers; **Puzzles and Manipulatives:** Exploring Alphabet Puzzles and Fabric Swatches; **Dramatic Play:** Bath Time and Dress Up; **Writing Center:** My Favorite Stuffed Animal Pictures		
Toileting and Snack 15 Minutes			
Story Time 20 Minutes	**3rd Reading** – *Whistle for Willie* p. 131	**2nd Reading** – *Corduroy* pp. 135–138	**4th Reading** – *Whistle for Willie* p. 142
Outdoor Play 35 Minutes	**Conversations:** Watch for persistence in mastering physical skills, and talk to children about the value of continuing to try.	**Conversations:** Provide comfort and any necessary care, and also talk with children about what happened when two children bump heads or have another accident.	**Conversations:** Encourage new sand activities by talking with children about tunnels, rivers, or something else in which they might be interested.
Songs, Word Play, Letters 20 Minutes	**Songs:** "Old MacDonald Had a Farm"; "Five Green and Speckled Frogs"; "Open, Shut Them" **Poems:** "Stand Up" **Predictable Book:** *Brown Bear, Brown Bear, What Do You See?* **Literacy Skills:** Interesting-Sounding Words; Alphabet Clue Game pp. 132–133	**Songs:** "Clap Your Hands"; "Down by the Bay" **Predictable Book:** *Time for Bed* **Literacy Skills:** Chiming In With Rhyming Words; Can You Think of Words That Rhyme With ____? pp. 139–140	**Songs:** "If You're Happy"; "Bingo"; "I'm a Little Teapot" **Poems:** "Hands"; "Ten Little Fingers" **Literacy Skills:** We Can Change It and Rearrange It; I'm Thinking of ____ Clue Game pp. 143–144
Handwashing/Toileting 10 Minutes			
Lunch/Quiet Time/ Center Time 90 Minutes	**Conversations:** *What colors do we see in our food today?* Support naming of colors and food, especially with English language learners.	**Conversations:** *Have you ever seen something you really wanted but had to wait to get?* Support retelling.	**Conversations:** *What did you find when you used the water wheel today?* Support efforts to explain.
Small Groups 25 Minutes pp. 127–129	**Writing:** The Animal Game **Language and Print Manipulatives:** Stringing Colored Beads; Making Names With Letter Tiles; Rhyming Word Pictures **Book Browsing:** Exploring Books	**Mathematics:** The Animal Game **Language and Print Manipulatives:** Stringing Colored Beads; Making Names With Letter Tiles; Rhyming Word Pictures **Book Browsing:** Exploring Books	**Mathematics:** The Animal Game **Language and Print Manipulatives:** Stringing Colored Beads; Making Names With Letter Tiles; Rhyming Word Pictures **Book Browsing:** Exploring Books
Let's Find Out About It/ Let's Talk About It 20 Minutes	**Exploring Chalk** p. 134	**Practicing to Learn New Things** p. 141	**Different Types of Fabrics** p. 145
End-the-Day Centers 20 Minutes	Open selected Centers and prepare children to go home.		

Day 4	Day 5
3rd Reading – *Corduroy* p. 146	**4th Reading** – *Corduroy* p. 150
Conversations: Observe and talk to children about how they made the swing go high.	**Conversations:** Accept and pretend to eat pretend pies and cakes made of sand. Ask what flavor they are or what filling they have.
Songs: "Head and Shoulders, Knees and Toes"; "The Wheels on the Bus" **Poems:** "Diddle, Diddle, Dumpling"; "Stand Up" **Literacy Skills:** First Sound Matching: Story Characters' and Children's Names pp. 147–148	**Songs:** "Five Green and Speckled Frogs"; "Open, Shut Them"; "Five Little Ducks" **Predictable Book:** *Over in the Meadow* **Literacy Skills:** Alphabet Memory Pocket Chart Game; Can You Think of Words That Begin With the Same Sound as ____? pp. 151–152
Conversations: *What do we do outside that helps make us strong?* Discuss and name specific actions.	**Conversations:** *During the last four weeks. we have done many activities and talked about families. What do you remember?* Guide recall.
Science: Boxes and Bands **Writing:** Writing Alphabet Letters and Names **Book Browsing:** Exploring Books	**Science:** Boxes and Bands **Writing:** Writing Alphabet Letters and Names **Book Browsing:** Exploring Books
Exploring Feelings: Talking With Toy Animals p. 149	**Piggy Banks** p. 153

Half-Day Program Schedule

2 hours 45 minutes
A half-day program includes two literacy circles.

10 min.	**Start-the-Day Centers** Writing Center, Book Area, Puzzles and Manipulatives
10 min.	**Morning Meeting**
60 min.	**Center Time** Continue to build small group work into Centers.
20 min.	**Story Time** Integrate topics from Let's Talk About It and Let's Find Out About It as discussion questions. Read a second book on some days.
35 min.	**Outdoor Play**
20 min.	**Songs, Word Play, Letters**
10 min.	**End-the-Day Centers** Writing Center, Book Area, Puzzles and Manipulatives

Connect With Families

- Suggest parents look through family photo albums with their children. They can point out children's baby pictures, as well as photos of other family members, and talk about them. Encourage them to use words that name relatives, such as *aunt*, *uncle*, *cousin*, and *grandmother*.

- Children will sing two counting songs—"Five Green and Speckled Frogs" and "Five Little Ducks." Suggest that children try practicing these songs at home. If they know the tunes, parents can sing them with their children. Children may also know the songs well enough to demonstrate the tunes to family members. Encourage parents to count up to five with their children—five fingers, five toes, five plates, five pennies, and so on.

Start-the-Day Centers

- Open two to three Centers for children to visit independently upon their arrival.

Morning Meeting

- Introduce children to Centers by showing some selected objects from each Center and briefly demonstrating activities to help them make a first choice.

- For example, on **Monday:** Demonstrate how a water wheel works by pouring water from cups over the wheel, first quickly, then slowly, and talk about the effects. Demonstrate drawing with chalk on paper and using your finger or a cotton swab to blend colors. Make a connection to Peter's chalk line in *Whistle for Willie.* **Tuesday:** Use blocks to build a tower as you talk about the importance of balancing big and small blocks. **Wednesday:** Show bath time and dress-up materials from Dramatic Play and talk about caring for babies and animals. Make a connection to the little girl's love for her bear in *Corduroy,* which has been added to the Book Area. On all mornings, show a finished example from My Favorite Stuffed Animal Pictures or demonstrate finished pieces from ongoing activities such as Painting With Marbles.

- Use the suggested vocabulary words and phrases in a manner so that their meanings are clear.

- You might want to modify or substitute an activity to meet your children's needs. For more information on organizing and adapting Center Time activities to your classroom, see the Notes to Teachers on page 154.

▲ Playing With Water Wheels

SAND AND WATER

Playing With Water Wheels

SCIENCE

Purposes: Asks questions about materials. Explores simple machines. Engages in conversation and uses language to play with others. Coordinates body movements to perform simple tasks. Thinks about events and experiences.

Materials: 4 water wheels, cups for dipping water, 2 tubs of water, smocks

Preparation: Place two water wheels at each end of the water table. Place the two tubs of water in center of table, within reach of children. Place cups for dipping water in the tubs. Have children wear smocks to avoid getting wet.

Suggested Vocabulary: cup, water wheel; faster, slower, less, more; dip, pour, spin, turn

- Observe children and comment as children play freely. For example, *Can you dip your cup and fill it all the way up with water, like this?*

- Provide information by prompting children with questions. You might say, *How can you make the water wheel go faster or slower? That's right, the more water you pour over the water wheel, the faster it spins. The less water you pour, the slower it spins.*

Exploring Books

Purposes: Chooses independently to read or pretend to read books in the Book Area.

Materials: Add *Corduroy* to the book collection.

- Have children explore books together or independently.

- Join children for brief periods. Talk with children about the books, or listen as children retell the stories. Prompt them with questions if they are unable to remember parts of the story. For example, *Do you remember what happened after the night watchman found Corduroy?*

ART AREA: TABLE

Painting With Marbles

- Continue the same activity from Week 3 (p. 87).

Drawing With Chalk

Purposes: Creates original artwork to express thoughts and feelings. Explores and experiments with chalk. Shares opinions and ideas about personal creative work. Engages in a variety of fine-motor tasks.

Materials: white or manila drawing paper (with texture), colored chalk, polystyrene foam trays, markers, cotton swabs (optional)

Preparation: Place three to four different colors of chalk on trays and a few cotton swabs within reach of each child. Place a piece of drawing paper at each space at the table. Place extra paper in center of the table.

Suggested Vocabulary: chalk, color names, cotton swab, marks; blend, cover, mix, share, smear, spread

- Observe children as they draw, and encourage experimentation by providing prompts. For example, *You can draw over one patch of chalk marks with another color and see what happens. Or, you can use your finger or a cotton swab to mix the colors together. You made a new color!*

- Make a connection to how Willie used chalk to draw a long line on the sidewalk in *Whistle for Willie* and to the Let's Find Out About It activity where they explored chalk.

- Have children write their names on their pictures with markers. Help if a child requests it. Display pictures on a bulletin board.

BLOCKS

Building Block Towers

Purposes: Moves body with balance and control. Builds finger dexterity. Describes the physical properties of objects. Asks questions about materials. Uses language to describe observations. Supports dramatic play.

Materials: KAPLA© Blocks, small colored blocks, hard surfaces/bases for building towers (e.g. wooden bases, tile floor), KAPLA blocks design cards (optional)

Preparation: Divide blocks into sets for two children to share and place them in some kind of container. Place children far enough apart to be able to move around without bumping into each other's towers.

Suggested Vocabulary: base, block, board, bottom, foundation, middle, plank, stack, top, tower; flat, next to, on edge, on end, on top of, under, shaky, stable, sturdy; balance, build, topple

- Engage children in conversation about balancing blocks to create towers. You might say, *What do you think will happen if you put this big block on top of that small one?*

- Remind children how Peter built a tall tower of blocks that crashed when Willie ran into it in *Peter's Chair*.

- Caution children about bumping into towers. Explain that the activity is to build a tower, not to knock one down, and it wouldn't be fair to others to do that.

- Add simple level KAPLA block design cards if available, for children to use to guide construction of a specific kind of building.

- Take photographs of towers, label them with students' names, and display them on a bulletin board or in a photo album in the center.

PUZZLES AND MANIPULATIVES

Exploring Alphabet Puzzles and Fabric Swatches

- Continue the activity from Week 3 (p. 88).

DRAMATIC PLAY

Bath Time and Dress Up

Purposes: Engages in dramatic play. Includes events or characters from familiar stories in dramatic play. Uses play to explore social roles and emotions.

SOCIAL STUDIES

Continued on next page

Materials: Add to materials from Weeks 1–3 (pp. 14, 52, 88): plastic tub, sponge, towel, washcloth, dress up clothes, *Corduroy*.

Suggested Vocabulary: Add these words to those introduced in Weeks 1–3 (pp. 14, 52, 88): bath, clothes, soap, sponge, towel, washcloth, water; clean, dry, dress

- Observe children and engage them in conversation as they play freely with dolls and props. You might say, *I see you're giving the baby a bath. I'll bet he likes that. How will you dry the baby? With a towel. Yes, that's a good idea. Oh, I guess it's time now to get dressed! Is the baby going to take a nap now or go out with you somewhere?*

- Make connections to caring for babies and/or animals in *Peter's Chair, Oonga Boonga, Over in the Meadow,* and *Corduroy.* For example, *How did the little girl take care of Corduroy when she brought him home?*

WRITING CENTER

My Favorite Stuffed Animal Pictures

Purposes: Creates original artwork to express thoughts and feelings. Thinks about events and experiences. Shares opinions and ideas about personal creative work. Observes uses of print.

Materials: white sheets of photocopy paper, markers

Preparation: Print sheets of paper with the heading "My Favorite Stuffed Animal" at the top. Give one to each child. Have extra copies on hand.

Suggested Vocabulary: animal, animal names/body parts; favorite, stuffed; draw, write

- Talk with children about their stuffed animals or dolls as they make their drawings. You might ask, *Why is this tiger your favorite stuffed animal? Does he sleep with you at night?*

- Make a connection to *Corduroy* and the little girl in the story who loved him so much she brought him home from the store.

- Help children with drawings if they become frustrated, by asking them questions about what he/she looks like. For example, *What color is he/she? Does he/she have legs? How many? Show me with your hands how big he/she is.*

- Ask children to tell you something about their picture and if they'd like you to write it down for them. You might say, *Oh, this is a picture of your stuffed rabbit, Sniffy? That's a great name for a stuffed bunny. Should I just write "Sniffy" or should I write, "This is a picture of my stuffed animal, Sniffy?"*

Small Groups Overview

- There are three different Small Groups activities for each day. The same three activities are made available for three days, and each group of five or six children spends one of the three days in each activity. Small Groups work best when children are at tables.

- On Days 1, 2, and 3, children will compare sets of animals, string colored beads, make their names with letter tiles, match rhyming word pictures, and browse books.

- On Days 4 and 5, children will explore boxes and elastic bands, write their names, and browse books. These activities can be continued into a fifth and sixth week of programming. See Extending the Unit on pages 157 and 158.

- Use the suggested vocabulary words in a manner that makes their meanings clear.

▲ The Animal Game

MATHEMATICS

The Animal Game: Days 1, 2, 3

High support

Purpose: Uses one-to-one correspondence to compare two sets numerically. Determines whether two sets are equal or unequal numerically.

Materials: Activity Aid 6, craft sticks, dot stickers or stamps, round plastic chips, container for chips

Preparation: Make one set of the following for each pair of children in small group: a photocopy of Activity Aid 6, six craft sticks with one to six dots spaced to correspond to the sets of one to six animals on the game board, and a container holding 21 chips for the 21 animals on the game board.

Suggested Vocabulary: match; each dot gets an animal; each animal gets a dot

Procedure

- Use a 3-dot stick and game board to demonstrate the activity to children. Explain that they want to find the row of animals on the game board that matches a dot stick. This game is played without counting. Holding the 3-dot stick near the row of ponies, you might say, *Let's see if each pony gets a dot and each dot gets a pony.* Use two fingers to touch simultaneously the first pony-dot pair, then the second pair, and finally the third pair. Then say, *This row of ponies matches my dot stick. Now I will cover the ponies with chips to show that I found the stick that matched.*

- Pair children. Let one child select an unused stick and find the matching row of animals. When the children agree that they have found a match, the second child covers the animals in the matching row with chips. Then have them swap roles using a new stick. Play continues until all teams have found matches for all their sticks.

- *EXTRA SUPPORT* Assist children as needed. Remind children not to count in this game. If a child makes an error, help the child use two fingers to touch simultaneously the first animal-dot pair, and then the second animal-dot pair, and so forth to determine that the two sets do not match numerically. Say, *This animal doesn't get a dot* (or *this dot doesn't get an animal*), *so this family of __ (e.g., frogs) doesn't match your dot stick.*

- *EXTENDING THE ACTIVITY* For children who succeed in matching all six dot sticks, have them construct a row of chips (without counting) that numerically matches each dot stick. You might say, *Each dot gets a chip.*

Progress Monitoring

Note what the team did correctly. Record errors such as a team that incorrectly matched five dots and six animals, or difficulty a child had in using two fingers to touch corresponding pairs of objects. Record the name of any child who matched all six dot sticks. Record your observations on copies of pages 155–156.

LANGUAGE AND PRINT MANIPULATIVES

Stringing Colored Beads: Days 1, 2, 3

Medium support

Purposes: Uses eye-hand coordination to perform fine-motor tasks. Recognizes and extends simple patterns of repeating colors.

Continued on next page

Materials: beads (variety of colors), dishes for beads, shoelaces or pieces of yarn or heavy string with knots on the end; pattern cards (optional)

Suggested Vocabulary: bead, hole, string, tip; first, last, middle, next; pull, push

Procedure

- Show children a finished string of beads. Say, *You can use different kinds of strings and beads to make pretty things like this.* Demonstrate and explain how to string a bead. *I'm going to start with a red bead because red is my favorite color. Hold the tip of the string and find the hole inside the bead. Slowly push the tip of the string through the hole and pull it out the other side.*

- Give children dishes of beads and string. Review color names, if needed. Engage children in conversation. For example, *Look at all the pretty colors! Which colors are you going to use? What do you see in the middle of the beads? A hole, that's right.*

- *ELL* When they are done, ask children to show others their beads and name the colors of beads they used. For example, *What color is your first/second/next/last bead?*

- *EXTENDING THE ACTIVITY* Give pattern cards to children and have them copy and repeat the color patterns using their beads.

Making Names With Letter Tiles: Medium support
Days 1, 2, 3

Purposes: Recognizes his or her own name. Names letters in his or her own name. Experiments with making words by stringing letters together to look like words.

Materials: tag or poster board, printed name cards for each child, letter tiles for each letter of children's names (upper and lowercase), double-sided tape, dish for letter tiles, laminating machine (optional)

Preparation: Print and cut out name cards and letter tiles using a standard font. Laminate them if possible. Mount four names on a piece of tag or poster board. Prepare boxed strips to place below each name. (The number of boxes should match the number of letters in the name.) Place letter tiles in a dish and poster boards within easy reach of children.

Procedure

- Show children several name cards and a dish of letter tiles for one of them.

- Model and explain activity by selecting a name card and pointing to the first letter in the name. For example, *This name card says* David. *I am going to spell* David. *Point to the first letter. The first letter on the card is* D. *I need to find a letter that looks just like this one. Here it is. I will put the letter on the poster in the box under "D."* Keep going until all the boxes are filled up and the name is completely spelled.

- *EXTRA SUPPORT* Assist children who are having difficulty finding letters for their name card. Say, *That letter looks like an* F *but see? It has an extra line at the bottom, so it's an* E. *Let's keep looking.*

- *EXTENDING THE ACTIVITY* Challenge children to spell each other's names.

Rhyming Word Pictures: Medium support
Days 1, 2, 3

Purposes: Recognizes several highly familiar rhyming words. Produces words that rhyme.

Materials: picture cards made up of rhyming word pairs (ideally words from stories children have recently read or from rhyming activities in Songs, Word Play, Letters, such as: *snake/cake, frog/dog, mouse/house, chairs/stairs, cat/bat*).

Preparation: Make and illustrate 12 picture cards (6 rhyming pairs).

Procedure

- Choose four picture cards, two of which rhyme. Lay the cards face up on the table and help children identify them. You might say, *I heard two words that sound the same at the end:* snake *and* cake. *They both end with* -āk, *so they rhyme. I found a rhyming pair!*

- Place six picture cards (three rhyming pairs) on the table, and tell children to find the pairs that rhyme, and put them together on the table.

- *EXTRA SUPPORT* Help children identify words from pictures if they are having difficulty.

- *ELL* Repeat words several times if they are unfamiliar to children.

BOOK BROWSING

Exploring Books: Days 1, 2, 3; Medium support
Days 4, 5

Purposes: Chooses independently to read or pretend to read books. Uses and shares books in their play. Names the main character and recalls some main events when asked questions.

Materials: Add *Whistle for Willie* and *Corduroy* to the book collection on Day 1. Add other books that relate to the family theme on Day 4.

Procedure

- Encourage children to look at books together or independently.

- Observe children and ask questions to prompt discussion. For example, *What is that book called? Who is in this story? What happens in this story?*

SCIENCE

High support

Boxes and Bands: Days 4, 5

Purposes: Uses simple tools and equipment for investigation. Uses language to discuss, record, or describe observations. Makes comparisons among objects. Describes the physical properties of objects.

Materials: variety of boxes (e.g., shoe boxes, jewelry boxes, plastic storage tubs), variety of elastic bands (long, wide, short, narrow), guitar picks, guitar or other stringed instrument (e.g., zither, banjo, violin)

Suggested Vocabulary: elastic bands; high, loose, low, taut; pick, pluck, slack, stretch, strum, vibrate

Procedure

- Remind children that three of the books they've read talked about making sounds: *Oonga Boonga* (harmonica, baby crying), *Noisy Nora* (banging, slamming, dropping things on the floor), and *Whistle for Willie* (whistling). Also remind them that they made their own musical instruments (bottle shakers).

- Explain that they are going to learn about making sounds with a string stretched over an open box. If possible, demonstrate a real stringed instrument like a guitar. Say, *Listen for what happens when I strum the guitar strings with my fingers. That's right, the strings make music.* Let children take turns strumming while you hold the guitar.

- Show children a finished example of a box with elastic bands, strum it, and explain that they will make an instrument just like it. Provide a prompt like, *What is my instrument made of?*

- Give each child a box and elastic bands. Help them wrap the bands around the box. Invite each child to strum their instrument with their fingers for the rest of the group.

- *SOCIAL-EMOTIONAL SUPPORT* Warn children to be gentle with the elastic bands so they don't snap and hurt anyone.

- *EXTENDING THE ACTIVITY* Point out the differences in the number and widths of elastic bands, the size of boxes, and the type of sounds that are created. For example, *Sara's box is bigger than Jack's. It makes a louder sound, listen. Trevor used big elastic bands but Kathy used skinny ones. When Kathy strums her strings, it makes a high sound. When Trevor strums his, it makes a low sound.*

WRITING

Medium support

Writing Alphabet Letters and Names: Days 4, 5

Purposes: Experiments with letter forms by making mock letters and actual letters. Writes his or her own name, using approximations of letters needed.

Materials: two sets of printed name cards for all children (printed with uppercase first letter), hole puncher, metal binder ring, printed alphabet letters, tag board, paper, markers, alphabet chart cards, laminating machine (optional)

Preparation: Type and print out two name cards for each child in standard font, using conventional spelling with uppercase initial letter. Punch holes in cards and arrange them in sets of 3–4 secured by a metal binder ring. There should be a total of 6–8 sets, with two being duplicates. Print out six sets of alphabet letters, in rows, in alphabetical order. Attach them on six tag board charts, with three rows of letters on one side of the chart and three rows on the other side. Laminate the charts, if possible.

Procedure

- Show children the alphabet charts and name cards. Say, *Today you may use the letters from the chart and name cards to practice writing letters and your name.*

- Distribute paper and markers and position name cards and charts within easy view and reach.

- Encourage children to find their name card and copy it letter by letter on their paper. Remind them to use the alphabet charts to help them with their letters.

- *EXTRA SUPPORT* Distribute name cards to children who are unable to identify their names.

- *EXTRA SUPPORT* Assist children with letter formation if they ask for help.

- *ELL* Talk with children about their pictures. Ask them to share their pictures with another child.

- *SOCIAL-EMOTIONAL SUPPORT* Accept rudimentary marks and scribbles. For example, *I see four marks here for your name, Emma. That's great!*

SUGGESTED RESOURCES

Books

Brown, Margaret Wise. *Goodnight Moon*. New York: HarperTrophy, 1975.

Cox, Judy. *My Family Plays Music*. New York: Holiday House, 2003.

Potter, Beatrix. *The Tale of Peter Rabbit*. New York: Puffin Books, 1991.

Scott, Ann Herbert (author) and Glo Coalson (illustrator). *On Mother's Lap*. New York: Clarion Books, 1992.

Sendak, Maurice. *Where the Wild Things Are*. New York: HarperTrophy, 1963.

Developing Children's Language Through Conversation

In the first weeks of school, it is particularly important to have conversations that help you get to know each child. Try to learn about children's families and continue to encourage children to use traditional names for relationships, such as *aunt, brother,* and *grandmother.* Be aware that families have special names for relatives, such as *auntie* or *nana.* When possible, make links between the events in the stories and children's lives. You might find that encouraging children to tell stories about things that happened to them is a good way to learn about their families.

Talk About Resolving Conflicts

Watch for times when children show that they are striving to resolve a conflict. If they need help, intervene in a way that guides them through a problem-solving process. Help each child to recognize how the other is feeling and guide them toward a solution that is understood by both children. Later tell the full group about the event during Let's Talk About It. You might encourage children who were involved to tell about what happened, how they felt at first, and how the problem was solved.

Good Conversations

During mealtime conversations, listen carefully to the meaning of what a child is saying. Don't interrupt, but do ask questions after the child speaks, if you need clarification. Be sure to have conversations with more than one child at the table.

Model for Conversation

Outdoor Play Conversation: Resolving Conflicts

The teacher sees Jenny try to push Johnny off his tricycle. Johnny resists and yells at her and calls the teacher.

Johnny: No! It's mine. Teacher!

Jenny: Is not! (pushes again)

Teacher: (speaks quietly and calmly, gently putting a hand on Jenny's shoulder). *Hmm, it seems like you're having a problem. Can you tell me about it, Jenny?*

Jenny: I want a turn.

Teacher: *I see. You think Johnny has been on too long and you want a turn, right?*

Jenny: Yes. He's been on the whole time.

Teacher: *Okay, but you know we can't just push or hit. Johnny, we set the timer, and you have just a little while before it goes off.*

Johnny: But I want to ride some more.

Teacher: *I understand, but you know we only have three tricycles so we need to share. Jenny, do you remember we have a turns list for outdoor wheel toys? And it's just about time to change toys. Johnny, why don't you keep playing until it's time to change, okay?*

Johnny: Okay.

Jenny: No, I forgot. Can I put my name on now?

Teacher: *Sure. Let's see if there are other names. Oh, look! Yours is the only one, so you get the tricycle next. Just a little while longer, and the timer will ding.*

Good Conversations

Stay on a topic for multiple turns. Try to have at least five or six back-and-forth exchanges as you help the child develop ideas. Throughout the curriculum there are examples of conversations that show different ways teachers help children stay on a topic.

▶ **Start-the-Day Centers** (see pages 124–126)

Make available two or three Centers as you greet children and their families.

▶ **Morning Meeting** (see page 124)

Gather children and review plans for the day. Orient children to center activities and help them make a first choice. Create a turns list for Centers if necessary.

▶ **Center Time** (see pages 124–126)

Children spend time in Centers of their choice.

▶ **Story Time: 3rd Reading**

Whistle for Willie

Author: Ezra Jack Keats

Read the Story Again

Linger on the first sound as you read some of the words. Prompt children's recall by pointing to pictures. Purse your lips to prompt them to say *whistle* on page 3, and wink to demonstrate that word.

Story Discussion

After reading, use questions like the ones below to help children relate to Peter's actions, feelings, and reasons for them.

- *Are there things that you have learned to do, after trying, that you couldn't do when you were younger? For example, when you were a baby, you weren't able to put your own clothes on all by yourself, and now you can. What other things have you learned?*

- *How did you feel when you learned how to ____? Ask individual children based on answers to the first question. Guide children to express feelings.*

If there is time to read a second story, reread a book from this unit.

Words and Phrases for Chiming In

(Vocabulary words appear in **dark** type.)

wished – p. 3
whistle – pp. 3, 4, 22
whistled – pp. 4, 9
Willie – pp. 8, 17, 20
wink – p. 8
carton – p. 8
just walked on – p. 9
line – p. 10
whistle again – p. 13
tired – p. 13
nothing happened – p. 13
more grown-up – p. 15
mirror – p. 15
no **whistle** – p. 15
father – p. 16
dear – p. 16
shadow – pp. 19, 20
together again – p. 20
scrambled – p. 22
blew – p. 22
raced – p. 25
whistling – p. 27
errand – p. 28
all the way home – p. 29

Extending the Book

Ask children who are ready for a challenge to think about what kind of errand Peter was asked to run. Point out that Willie seems to have a list in his mouth. Ask where Peter's mother might have asked them to go.

English Language Learners

Ask children to repeat the word *pretended* with you. Point to the picture of Peter pretending to be his father. Explain that to *pretend* means to "make believe."

▶ **Outdoor Play**

To transition to Outdoor Play, name colors, pointing to items in the book *Whistle for Willie.* Dismiss children wearing those colors: *You may put your coat on if you are wearing green like the traffic signal . . . red like the light that means stop . . . yellow like this wall . . . blue like Peter's shorts and shoes,* and so on. See pages 122–123 for suggested conversation topics during this time.

▶ Songs, Word Play, Letters

Today children will be playing word games, singing songs, and reciting poems. Add your favorite game, song, or poem to this collection.

Songs

"Old MacDonald Had a Farm"; "Five Green and Speckled Frogs"; "Open, Shut Them"

Poems

"Stand Up"

Predictable Book

Brown Bear, Brown Bear, What Do You See?

Literacy Skills

Interesting-Sounding Words; Alphabet Clue Game

Purposes

Recites song, rhymes, chants, and poems, and engages in language and word play. Names many uppercase letters. Discriminates between sounds that are the same and sounds that are different. Listens with increasing attention. Communicates using verbal and nonverbal clues. Counts up to ten objects in a set using one-to-one correspondence.

Suggested Sequence for Today's Circle

1. "Old MacDonald Had a Farm"
2. "Five Green and Speckled Frogs"
3. Interesting-Sounding Words (and *Noisy Nora*)
4. "Open, Shut Them"
5. Alphabet Clue Game
6. *Brown Bear, Brown Bear, What Do You See?*
7. "Stand Up"

Materials and Instructional Procedures

OLD MACDONALD HAD A FARM

Materials: CD Track 6, Song Lyrics pp. 159–160, flannel board and flannel pieces

Vocabulary: duck, horse, goat, pig, sheep

Procedure

- Point out to children that it's been a long time since they sang "Old MacDonald Had a Farm." You might say, *We can sing about a lot of animals today. I'm going to put all of the animals down here* (place in a line in lower area of flannel board), *and then I'll move them one by one as we sing about them. Okay, let's do the duck first, and then the goat. Sing two verses. Okay, we need a third animal now. Which one should I pick?* Continue.

- Invite children to name animals as you remove them.

FIVE GREEN AND SPECKLED FROGS

Materials: CD Track 10, Song Lyrics p. 160, flannel board and flannel pieces

Vocabulary: green, speckled, log, delicious, jumped, cool, pool

Procedure

- Ask children something like, *How many frogs should you have for "Five Green and Speckled Frogs"?* (5 frogs) *Count with me as I put them on their log. They're all here, so let's sing.*

INTERESTING-SOUNDING WORDS (AND *NOISY NORA*)

Materials: book: *Noisy Nora,* easel and paper, marker

Vocabulary: hush, monumental, tralala

Procedure

- Explain to children that you've been reading the book, *Noisy Nora,* and there are some interesting-sounding words in that book. Tell them you are going to find a few that you think are interesting. Flip to page in the book.

- Say, *I think* hush *is an interesting-sounding word because it makes a quiet kind of sound.* Repeat the word, emphasizing /sh/. Nora's mother tells her to hush when she wants her to be quiet.

- Say, *I also think* tralala *is an interesting-sounding word because it sounds like a song. Nora's baby brother Jack says "tralala."* (Use a singsong voice.) Repeat *tra-la-la. I'll write that word to show you how it looks.* Write it, sound out /t/ at the beginning, and name the letters as you write each one. Then read the word, running your finger under it.

Say, *I also think* monumental *is interesting because it's such a long word. Let's say it.* Mon-u-men-tal. *Do you like how your tongue and lips feel when you say that word? It's fun to say interesting-sounding words, isn't it?*

OPEN, SHUT THEM

Materials: CD Track 9, Song Lyrics p. 160

Vocabulary: open, shut, clap, in, lap, creep, chin

Procedure

- Sing the song with children as before, modeling the hand gestures.

ALPHABET CLUE GAME

Materials: clip board or easel with paper, marker

Vocabulary: clue, guess, letter, vertical

Procedure

- Choose a letter that has more than one line (e.g., *F*).

- Tell children, *We are going to play a game. I'm going to think of a letter, give you one clue at a time, and you guess the letter. Here is the first clue.* Draw the first line of the letter, in this case the vertical line of *F. Any guesses about what letter I have in my mind?*

- Respond to each guess by talking about how that letter is made. Examples:

  H *is a good guess because it has a long vertical line, like this. But I'm not thinking about* H.

T *is a good guess. If I wanted to make a* T, *I'd add a line across the top. But I'm not thinking about* T.

- Add the next line, and ask children to guess. Children might guess *L* or *T.* Write those on the side, and point out how they differ. Add the last line to make *F.*

- You might say, *If I added one more line here, it would be an* E, *wouldn't it?*

- Tell children you will play the game again on another day, with a different letter.

BROWN BEAR, BROWN BEAR, WHAT DO YOU SEE?

Materials: book: *Brown Bear, Brown Bear, What Do You See?*; flannel board and flannel pieces

Vocabulary: bear, black, goldfish, horse, purple, teacher

Procedure

- Show children the cover of the book and ask what the title is. Confirm and then read the title slowly, pointing to the words. Tell children you are going to use the flannel pieces for this story today.

- As you put the flannel board pieces up, prompt children to join you in saying each animal's name and *What do you see?*

STAND UP

Materials: Poetry Posters: Poem 3, CD Track 28

Vocabulary: bend, bow, clap, hand, knees, stamp, stand, turn, wave

Procedure

- Display the poem, read the title, recite it, and model the motions.

▶ **Lunch/Quiet Time/Centers**

This time is set aside for lunch, quiet time, and center activities. See pages 122–123 for suggested conversation topics during this time.

▶ Small Groups

For information on Small Groups, refer to pages 127–129.

▶ Let's Find Out About It

Exploring Chalk

Purposes

Uses and develops background knowledge to understand story events. Observes and explores materials and objects in the environment. Makes comparisons among objects.

Materials

book: *Whistle for Willie*, colored pieces of chalk, crayons

Suggested Vocabulary

Introduce these words and use them in the discussion: chalk, crayon, dust/dusty, wax/waxy

Procedure

- Find the page in *Whistle for Willie* where Peter draws with chalk on the sidewalk. Tell children that many children like to draw and write. Chalk is something used for drawing or writing.

- Make marks with a colored piece of chalk on a large piece of paper mounted on a clipboard as children observe.

- Pass out pieces of chalk for children to hold and feel. Encourage children's observations. Have children inspect their fingers. Point out the chalk dust on them. Provide children with crayons to compare with the chalk. Support children's comparisons and expand with more details. For example, *The chalk and the crayons feel really different, don't they? My crayon has paper around it, but the crayon itself feels slick and waxy. The chalk leaves bits of dust on my fingers, but the crayon doesn't.*

> **English Language Learners**
>
> Repeat the words *chalk* and *crayon,* speaking carefully. Connect the words to the objects.

Center Time Connections

An art table activity is designed for use with chalk. If there is a classroom chalkboard positioned at a suitable height for children, provide children with chalk to draw on the board.

Outdoor Play Connections

If there is a suitable sidewalk or playground area, invite children to play with chalk outside.

> **Extending the Activity**
>
> Invite children to look at the words on a crayon or chalk box as you point to them and read the information.

▶ End-the-Day Centers

Children spend time in Centers of their choice. As children leave for home, say something to help each one look forward to the next school day. For example, say, *Tomorrow we will read about Corduroy again. I know you like that book about Lisa and Corduroy, Martina.*

▶ **Start-the-Day Centers** (see pages 124–126)

Direct children to choose among two or three open Centers as they arrive.

▶ **Morning Meeting** (see page 124)

Help children make a first choice in Centers after you orient them to the activities.

▶ **Center Time** (see pages 124–126)

Children spend time in Centers of their choice.

▶ **Story Time: 2nd Reading**

Corduroy

Author: Don Freeman

Purposes

Recalls some main events when asked, *What is happening in this story?* Links characters' basic emotions to their actions. Uses own experiences to understand characters' feelings and motivations. Expresses the main idea of a story or other text in a way that shows increasing understanding.

Read the Story

Reconstruct the story with children. Help them recall events and characters' actions by asking questions like, *What is happening here? What did Corduroy do next?*

If children need help with recall or constructing meaning, reread short portions of the text. Remind children that Corduroy is walking around the store at night because he is looking for his lost button.

Remember to use the key words as you discuss the story.

Suggested Vocabulary

Use these words during Story Time and throughout the day.

admiring looking with enjoyment or approval

blinked opened and closed the eyes quickly

escalator a set of stairs that move

evening the time between sunset and bedtime

flashlight a small light you can carry around

furniture department part of a store that sells things like chairs and sofas

overalls loose pants with a piece covering the chest

palace a very large house, usually belonging to a king or queen; sometimes called a castle

searching looking for something

shoulder where an arm is attached to the body

sighed let out a deep breath when tired or sad

thread a fine string used to sew things

Extending the Book

Remind children that Corduroy is in the toy department of a big store. Point to the sign that says *Toys* and read it with children. Use your finger to underline the word letter by letter and sound it out to them.

English Language Learners

Point to all the toys in the picture on page 2. Say the word *toys* clearly, then have children say it with you. Then name some of the toys on the shelves. Point to each one and say what it is. Children can say the names with you.

Progress Monitoring

Note how well individual children are able to remember and understand story events. Do pictures and a few prompts help them recall what happened? Notice expressions and nodding heads, as well as verbal answers. Record your observations on copies of pages 155–156.

A MODEL FOR READING: *Be sure to read all the text on each page. When you read it will vary, depending on the flow of conversations with children.*

Cover

We read this book once before, and you know that the title of the book is . . . Corduroy. Underline the word with your finger as you read the title.

We're going to read this story again today and talk about the things that happen.

p. 1

Read page 1.

pp. 2-3

Read page 2 and point to the **overalls**.

No one seemed to want Corduroy, but what happened one morning? (Lisa and her Mom stopped to look at a bear in the toy department; Lisa wanted to buy Corduroy.) *Yes.*

Read first four lines of page 3.

Did Lisa's mother say yes or no? (No.)

She said no, and what reasons did she give? (Children respond.) *Right, Lisa's mommy had spent too much money already, and she also didn't think Corduroy looked new because he'd lost a button.*

pp. 4-5

Read page 4 and the first sentence of page 5.

Corduroy has a plan for what he will do about the missing button. What is his plan? (He is going to look for it at night.)

Read the remainder of page 5.

pp. 6-7

Is it nighttime yet? (Children respond.) *It must be. The lights are low, and Corduroy is getting down from the toy shelf.*

Read pages 6 and 7.

pp. 8-9

Something happened that surprised Corduroy. What happened? (Children respond.) *Yes. He stepped on the* **escalator**, *and it started going up.*

Now read pages 8 and 9.

pp. 10-11

Read pages 10 and 11. *When Corduroy got to the* **furniture department**, *where did he think he was?* (in a **palace**) *A* **palace** *is a big house where kings and queens live.*

pp. 12–13

What's Corduroy doing here? Point to the bear climbing onto the mattress. (Children respond.) *And then what does he spy?* Point to a button on the mattress. (a button)

Read pages 12 and 13.

*What happened to the **thread** when Corduroy pulled hard on it?* Point to the picture. (It held tight at first, then broke.) Help children make connections between the broken string, Corduroy's tumble, and the crashing lamp.

pp. 14–15

Read pages 14 and 15.

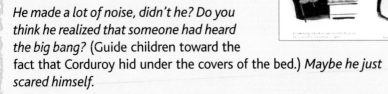

He made a lot of noise, didn't he? Do you think he realized that someone had heard the big bang? (Guide children toward the fact that Corduroy hid under the covers of the bed.) *Maybe he just scared himself.*

Did someone hear? Yes, the night watchman.

pp. 16–17

Read pages 16 and 17.

Where was Corduroy hiding? (under the covers) *Yes, but had he hidden himself completely? Was he all covered up, or was something sticking out?* (His ears stuck out.)

pp. 18–19

Read page 18.

What kind of light was the night watchman using so that he could see? (a **flashlight**)

*And did the night watchman know why Corduroy was upstairs in the store in the **furniture department**?* (Children respond.)

Now read page 19 to confirm children's answers or prompt recall. *No, he didn't know Corduroy was looking for his button. Maybe he thought that some child had carried Corduroy up to the **furniture department** during the day and had left him up there.*

pp. 20–21

Read pages 20 and 21.

pp. 22–23

*First thing in the morning when Corduroy woke up, who was looking at him in the toy **department**?* (Lisa) *And why was she back?* (She wanted to buy him.) *Right!*

Why had Lisa's mother changed her mind and said that Lisa could buy Corduroy? (Lisa was using her own money, money she had saved in a piggy bank.) *Yes.*

Read pages 22 and 23.

pp. 24-25

The saleslady asks Lisa something here. What is it? Point to the box in her hand. (Children respond.) *Right, and Lisa said no. She wanted to carry him.*

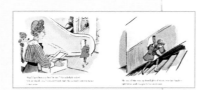

Read page 25.

How do you think Lisa is feeling right now? (happy, excited)

pp. 26-27

Corduroy saw something for him right next to Lisa's bed. Point to the tiny bed. *What is it?* (a little bed)

*He was thinking to himself that this was not a **palace** like at the store, but someplace else. What did he call this place?* (home) Give the first sound to prompt the word.

p. 28

Read page 28.

What did Corduroy say to Lisa when she hugged him? ("You must be a friend.")

Storybook Discussion

Prompt discussion with questions like these:

Do you think Corduroy really said "You must be a friend," to Lisa, or do you think she imagined that he said it? Guide children toward the idea that Lisa imagined it. Discuss how children pretend stuffed animals and dolls are real people when they play with them.

▶ Outdoor Play

Have children match beginning letters in their names to people and items in *Corduroy* to go to Outdoor Play. For example, hold up the letter L, saying, *If your name starts with L like Lisa [C like Corduroy, F like flashlight, P like palace, and so on], you may go outside to play.* See pages 122–123 for suggested conversation topics during this time.

▶ Songs, Word Play, Letters

Today children will be playing word games, singing songs, and reciting poems. Add your favorite game, song, or poem to this collection.

Songs
"Clap Your Hands"; "Down by the Bay"

Predictable Book
Time for Bed

Literacy Skills
Chiming In With Rhyming Words; Can You Think of Words That Rhyme With ____?

Purposes
Produces words that rhyme. Uses pictures to understand a book. Identifies the cover of a book and knows that the title, author, and illustrator are listed on the cover. Listens to/attends to a variety of genres read aloud. Says the words that complete rhymes, poems, and lines from stories, individually or in a group.

Suggested Sequence for Today's Circle
1. "Clap Your Hands"
2. *Time for Bed* (and Chiming In With Rhyming Words)
3. Can You Think of Words That Rhyme With ____? (and *Time for Bed*)
4. "Down by the Bay"

Materials and Instructional Procedures

CLAP YOUR HANDS

Materials: CD Track 12, Song Lyrics p. 160

Vocabulary: clap, hands, together, stamp, feet

Procedure
- Tell children that you are going to start today with "Clap Your Hands."
- Sing slowly enough for children to follow, modeling the motions.
- The second time, use motions and whisper the words.

TIME FOR BED (AND CHIMING IN WITH RHYMING WORDS)

Materials: book: *Time for Bed*

Vocabulary: bed, bee, bird, calf, cat, deer, fish, foal, goose, house, little, mouse, pup, sheep, snake, time

Procedure
- Point to the title on the cover of the book and ask children if they remember what the book is called. If needed, prompt them by saying, *Time for . . ..*
- Point to the pictures to show children the baby animals as they're named in the book. Hold onto the first sound longer than usual to encourage children to chime in with you.
- When you come to the second word in a rhyming pair, hold onto the first sound longer than usual to let the children chime in.

CAN YOU THINK OF WORDS THAT RHYME WITH ____? (AND TIME FOR BED)

Materials: book: *Time for Bed*

Vocabulary: bee, cat, sheep

Procedure
- Choose two to three words from *Time for Bed* for making rhymes (e.g., *cat, sheep, bee*). Tell children they are going to play a rhyming game with words from the story.
- Turn to the page with the cat. Say, *Here is the little cat.* Cat *and* that *rhyme—they both end in the same sound,* -at. *Can you think of other words that rhyme with* cat?
- Go around the circle, letting each child who has an idea offer it. If anyone suggests a nonsense word, accept it. For example, Jat *might not be a real word, but it does rhyme with* cat. Rhyming is still new to children, so be ready to add an idea or two of your own.
- When you've finished rhyming a word, review. You might say, *We thought of lots of words that rhyme with* cat: flat, mat, sat, bat, fat.
- Find another word in the book and repeat if time permits and children are having fun.

DOWN BY THE BAY

Materials: CD Track 3, Song Lyrics p. 159, flannel board and flannel pieces

Vocabulary: bay, watermelons, snake, frog, mouse

Procedure

- Sing the song as usual, placing the appropriate flannel pieces on the board for each verse. Remove the pieces for each verse before putting on the new ones.

- If time permits, sing the song a second time.

Progress Monitoring

Notice which children engage quickly with known songs and which ones need prompting to remember words or motions. Note which children can discriminate rhyming sounds, which attempt to chime in with rhyming words, and which ones are attentive but not yet able to distinguish rhyming from non-rhyming sounds. Record your observations on copies of pages 155–156.

▶ Lunch/Quiet Time/Centers

This time is set aside for lunch, quiet time, and center activities. See pages 122–123 for suggested conversation topics during this time.

▶ **Small Groups**

For information on Small Groups, refer to pages 127–129.

▶ **Let's Talk About It**

Practicing to Learn New Things

Purposes

Shows beginning understanding of persistence. Speaks clearly using appropriate volume so that words can be understood by peers and adults.

Procedure

- Remind children that in the story *Whistle for Willie*, Peter wanted to whistle, but he had to practice for a long time to learn how. Ask, *Is there something you really wish you could do, but you don't know how to do it very well yet? Something you may have to practice for a while to learn?* Children may give examples such as tying shoes, cutting meat at lunch, whistling, or making a letter in their name look the way they want it to look.

- Encourage children to keep trying. For example:

  Mercedes: I can't jump rope.

  Teacher: *Jumping rope is hard because the rope keeps coming around pretty fast.*

  Mercedes: My sister Tanya can do it, but not me.

  Teacher: *Well, Tanya is older than you, and I bet when she was your age, she had to practice before she could do it. You have to try it many, many times before you learn how to jump rope. Then, one of these days, you will be able to jump rope just like Willie could whistle.*

- Sum up the discussion. For example, you might say, *It takes a lot of practice to learn how to do new things well, and it feels really good when you learn to do something after practicing so long.*

▶ **End-the-Day Centers**

Children spend time in Centers of their choice. As children leave for home, say something to help each one look forward to the next school day. For example, tell them that tomorrow you'll be singing songs again, and that one of them might be their favorite.

▶ **Start-the-Day Centers** (see pages 124–126)

Open two or three Centers for children to go to as they arrive.

▶ **Morning Meeting** (see page 124)

Demonstrate some of the center activities, then help children make a first choice.

▶ **Center Time** (see pages 124–126)

Children spend time in Centers of their choice.

▶ **Story Time: 4th Reading**

Whistle for Willie

Author: Ezra Jack Keats

Read *Whistle for Willie* Again

Ask all children to speak the part of Peter. This includes lines where Peter had a thought, but did not speak out loud. Participating in this way gives children another chance to say new words and connect to Peter's feelings as he learns to whistle. Prompt children to get ready for dialogue by saying the first sound of a word or first word or two in a phrase.

Taking On the Roles of Story Characters

Peter: Wouldn't it be funny if I **whistled**? Willie would stop and look all around to see who it was. – p. 9; I've come home early today, dear. Is Peter here? – p. 16; Well, I'll go out and look for them. – p. 17; It's me! – p. 25

Story Discussion

Ask questions to prompt discussion. For example: *So Peter would try to whistle, and when it didn't work, he would play something else. Why do you think he did those other things?* Guide discussion toward the idea that when people are trying to learn something new, they can get frustrated.

Other Book Suggestions

You might want to substitute *On Mother's Lap* (see page 7) or another theme-related book for the fourth reading of *Whistle for Willie*. *On Mother's Lap* is a story about an older brother who is worried that his baby brother will get to sit in his mother's lap, and there won't be room for him.

Introduce the book by reminding children that they've been listening to some stories recently about children who don't get as much attention as they would like because of a baby in the house. Name Nora and Peter as examples. Tell children that, in this story, there's a big brother who has the same worries, but that his mother finds a good solution.

Making Connections: Ask how Mother solved the problem of attention to children in this family. Follow up with some comments that help children understand that a parent cannot always deal with both children at once, but that parents try to when they can.

▶ **Outdoor Play**

Dismiss children to Outdoor Play using information about pets. For example, *Go to your cubby if you have a pet dog . . . a pet cat . . . a fish . . . no pet . . . wish you had a pet,* and so on. See pages 122–123 for suggested conversation topics during this time.

▶ Songs, Word Play, Letters

Today children will be playing word games, singing songs, and reciting poems. Add your favorite game, song, or poem to this collection.

Songs

"If You're Happy"; "Bingo"; "I'm a Little Teapot"

Poems

"Hands"; "Ten Little Fingers"

Literacy Skills

We Can Change It and Rearrange It; I'm Thinking of _____ Clue Game

Purposes

Separates words into syllables. Substitutes one sound for another to create new words. Names many uppercase letters. Asks and answers questions and gives directions. Sings and listens to a variety of songs.

Suggested Sequence for Today's Circle

1. "If You're Happy"
2. "Bingo" (and We Can Change It and Rearrange It)
3. "Hands"
4. "Ten Little Fingers"
5. I'm Thinking of _____ Clue Game (and *Corduroy*)
6. "I'm a Little Teapot"

Materials and Instructional Procedures

IF YOU'RE HAPPY

Materials: CD Track 1, Song Lyrics p. 159

Vocabulary: clap, hands, stamp, feet

Procedure

- Lead the children in singing two verses of the song in the usual way, using *clap hands* and *stamp feet* as the motions.

- Add new verses using different motions for feelings. Examples:

  If you're frightened and you know it, hide your eyes.

  If you're funny and you know it, laugh, Ha ha!

  If you're grouchy and you know it, growl, Grrrrrrrrr!

BINGO (AND WE CAN CHANGE IT AND REARRANGE IT)

Materials: CD Track 2, Song Lyrics p. 159, flannel board and flannel pieces, plus the letters *T, R, S, W, P*

Vocabulary: farmer, dog, clap, name

Procedure

- Ask children to name letters as you place *B, I, N, G, O* on the board. Tell children, *We're going to sing "Bingo" the way we always do and then we're going to play around with the letters again like we did last week.*

- Put the letters back on the board. Change the first letter several times, each time sounding the letter, asking the children what they think the new word says, and then reading it (e.g., *Tingo, Singo, Ringo*).

- Tell children you're going to take away all the letters except *G* and *O*. Read the new word: *go*. Make the words *no*, *bin*, and *in*, if time permits and children are still attentive and interested.

- As you put the letters away, you might say, *We can change and rearrange letters to create a lot of different words.*

HANDS

Materials: Poetry Posters: Poem 4, CD Track 29

Vocabulary: chin, fingers, hands, nose, toes

Procedure

- Recite the poem the first time without referring to the poster. Do all the motions, pausing briefly between lines to allow children to follow along.

- Show the poster to children. Talk about the illustration and point out that the words of the poem are printed on the page.

TEN LITTLE FINGERS

Materials: Poetry Posters: Poem 1, CD Track 26

Vocabulary: fingers, fold, high, low, open, shut, tight, together, wide

Procedure

- Display the poster. Say something like, *The poem we just read was called* "Hands." Hold up your hands. *This poem is called "Ten Little Fingers."* Wiggle your fingers. Show children the illustration.

- Present the poem as usual, leading the children in the finger movements. If they enjoy it and time permits, perform it again.

I'M THINKING OF _____ CLUE GAME (AND CORDUROY)

Materials: book: *Corduroy*; Picture Cards: escalator, overalls

Vocabulary: escalator, overalls, thread, palace, flashlight

Procedure

- Show children the *Corduroy* book cover and tell them they are going to play a guessing game about some words in this story. Remind them to listen to the clues, think about them, and raise their hands when they think they know the word.

- For *escalator,* use these clues: *Corduroy rode one of these in the store. It has moving steps. When we say this word, we hear four parts* (clap four times).

- For *overalls,* use these clues: *Corduroy was wearing these when Lisa found him in the toy department. This piece of clothing has pants, shoulder straps, and buttons. The name of this item of clothing starts with the letter O.*

- After they guess each answer, show the picture card and point out features you gave as clues.

I'M A LITTLE TEAPOT

Materials: CD Track 8, Song Lyrics p. 160

Vocabulary: teapot, short, stout, handle, spout, tip, pour

Procedure

- Sing the song as usual, leading children in the motions.

- After singing the song, say something like, *I want to show you how to be a sugar bowl rather than a teapot. Put your hands on your hips, like this. That's it. Now you are sugar bowls with a handle on each side. That's kind of funny, isn't it?*

▶ **Lunch/Quiet Time/Centers**

This time is set aside for lunch, quiet time, and center activities. See pages 122–123 for suggested conversation topics during this time.

Small Groups

See pages 127–129 for information on Small Groups.

Let's Find Out About It

Different Types of Fabric

Purposes

Uses and develops background knowledge to understand story events. Listens with increasing attention. Uses new words as part of vocabulary in meaningful ways. Makes comparisons among objects.

Materials

book: *Corduroy*, swatches or items of clothing made from corduroy, denim, velvet, satin, cotton, and flannel

Suggested Vocabulary

Introduce these words and use them in the discussion: cloth, corduroy, fabric, ridges, denim, satin, velvet; smooth

Procedure

- Point out the ridges on the teddy bear's overalls in the book *Corduroy.* Explain that this kind of fabric is called corduroy. Point out that this is probably how Corduroy got his name.

- Pass out swatches of corduroy for children to hold and feel. Then pass out swatches of other types of material for children to contrast with the corduroy.

- Have children look at the clothes they are wearing. Ask them if they can describe how the material of their clothing feels—soft? Rough? Smooth? Ask if anyone is wearing corduroy. Denim? Velvet? Cotton? Flannel?

English Language Learners

Repeat the names of the fabric swatches several times, slowly and carefully, as you are discussing them, and allow children to touch them. Have children say the fabric names after you.

Extensions

Bring yarn to class and show children how people knit to make clothes (or ask a volunteer to do so). Show them a completed scarf or sweater.

Center Time Connections

Put swatches in a container and place it in Puzzles and Manipulatives for independent use. If available, place preemie-size infant sleepers in the Dramatic Play area for play with dolls.

Extending the Activity

Page through *Noisy Nora* or *Oonga Boonga* and ask children to help you name items of clothing the characters are wearing.

Small Groups Connections

Bring in stuffed animals. Tell how they are made, explaining that they are stuffed with soft material, like stuffing in a pillow. Talk about the difference between *alive* and *not alive*.

Progress Monitoring

Notice if children are able to repeat the names of fabric and use these new vocabulary words at other times. See if children can make comparisons among objects. Take notes on copies of pages 155–156.

End-the-Day Centers

Children spend time in Centers of their choice. As children leave for home, say something to help them look forward to the next school day. For example, tell a child who enjoys songs time that you will be singing "The Wheels on the Bus" and other songs.

▶ **Start-the-Day Centers** (see pages 124–126)
Open two to three Centers for children as they arrive.

▶ **Morning Meeting** (see page 124)
Display and explain items from some of the Centers, then help children make a first choice.

▶ **Center Time** (see pages 124–126)
Children spend time in Centers of their choice.

▶ **Story Time: 3rd Reading**

Corduroy

Author: Don Freeman

Read the Story Again

As you read *Corduroy*, slow down in some places to invite children to chime in. This gives them the opportunity to say many of the new words. Help their recall by saying the first sound of a word or first word in a phrase.

Story Discussion

After reading, use these or other questions to help children relate to the characters' actions and feelings, and the reasons for them:

● *Sometimes when mommies or daddies or grandmas say 'no,' children do things to show they are mad. Lisa seemed sad, but not mad when her mommy told her she couldn't buy Corduroy. What are some of the things that children do to show they are disappointed, or really sad, or really mad?*

● *I am thinking that Lisa is probably a little older than you are. Can you think of something in the story that might make me think that?* Guide children's answers toward

use of a needle to sew, and maybe doing chores and being paid an allowance.

If there is time to read another book, use any family story from Unit 1, *The Tale of Peter Rabbit*, or another theme-related book (see page 7).

Words and Phrases for Chiming In
(Vocabulary words appear in **dark** type.)

overalls – pp. 2, 27
sighed – p. 3
shoulder – p. 3
evening – p. 6
searching – p. 7
escalator – pp. 8, 10, 16, 20
palace – p. 11
admiring – p. 12
mattress – p. 12
yanked and pulled – p. 14
POP! – p. 14
crash – p. 15
fuzzy brown ears – p. 18
piggy bank – p. 23
blinked – p. 26
friend – p. 28

Extending the Book

Ask children who are ready for a challenge to describe Corduroy's ears on page 18. Invite them to read the story description with you. Hold up the book and underline "fuzzy brown ears" with your finger as you read the words slowly.

English Language Learners

Repeat some key words and phrases. Some children will chime in with you the second time, not the first. Add comments after some chiming in, to use key words again. For example, *This is how I look when I am searching.* Hold hand, palm down, above eyes and look around at the floor.

▶ **Outdoor Play**

Name items of clothing to call children to Outdoor Play: *You may walk to the door if you are wearing overalls like Corduroy . . . a dress like the doll . . . a bow like the rabbit . . . short sleeves like the doll,* and so on. See pages 122–123 for suggested conversation topics during this time.

▶ Songs, Word Play, Letters

Today children will be playing word games, singing songs, and reciting poems. Add your favorite game, song, or poem to this collection.

Songs

"Head and Shoulders, Knees and Toes"; "The Wheels on the Bus"

Poems

"Diddle, Diddle, Dumpling"; "Stand Up"

Literacy Skills

First Sound Matching: Story Characters' and Children's Names

Purposes

Finds words with the same beginning sound. Discriminates between sounds that are the same and sounds that are different. Responds to their names and requests for action or information. Asks and answers questions and gives directions.

Suggested Sequence for Today's Circle

1. "Head and Shoulders, Knees and Toes"
2. "Stand Up"
3. "The Wheels on the Bus"
4. First Sound Matching: Story Characters' and Children's Names (and *Peter's Chair*, *Noisy Nora*, and *Corduroy*)
5. "Diddle, Diddle, Dumpling"

Materials and Instructional Procedures

HEAD AND SHOULDERS, KNEES AND TOES

Materials: CD Track 4, Song Lyrics p. 159

Vocabulary: head, shoulders, knees, toes, eyes, ears, mouth, nose

Procedure

- Sing the song as usual, touching the different parts of your body as you sing about them.

- Continue the song, using only motions (no words) for one body part at a time, until the song is done quietly with only motions.

STAND UP

Materials: Poetry Posters: Poem 3, CD Track 28

Vocabulary: bend, bow, clap, hand, knees, stamp, stand, turn, wave

Procedure

- Display the poster, point to the title, and read it.

- Recite the poem with the children and model the motions.

THE WHEELS ON THE BUS

Materials: CD Track 7, Song Lyrics p. 160

Vocabulary: wheels, bus, round, town, up, down, horn, money, box, wiper, glass, driver, back

Procedure

- Sing the verses that the children already know, leading them in the appropriate motion for each verse.

- Introduce additional verses by singing them, modeling the motions, and inviting children to join in by singing slowly enough for them to follow along.

FIRST SOUND MATCHING: STORY CHARACTERS' AND CHILDREN'S NAMES (AND *PETER'S CHAIR*, *NOISY NORA*, AND *CORDUROY*)

Materials: books: *Peter's Chair*; *Noisy Nora*; *Corduroy*

Vocabulary: characters, first, name, sound, starts with

Procedure

- Show the children the books. Talk about the characters. You might say, *In* Noisy Nora, *there was Nora, her sister Kate, and baby Jack. In* Corduroy, *there was Corduroy, of course, and the girl Lisa. And in* Peter's Chair? (Children answer.) *Yes, there was Peter, his baby sister Susie, and someone else— Peter's dog, Willie!*

- Tell children they are going to play a game with some names from the stories. Explain that you'll say a name, and they think about the sound that name starts with. Then you'll go around the circle and everyone will say his or her name, and see if anyone has a name that begins with the same sound.

- When you play the game, you might say, Charles-Peter. *No, that's not a match. Charles' name doesn't begin with /p/, like* Peter. Larry-Peter. *Does* Larry *begin with the same sound as* Peter? *No. Okay,* Penelope-Peter. *What do you think? Yes,* Penelope *begins with /p/, just like* Peter.

- Choose character's names for which there is a first sound match with a child's name. Compare names quickly and move things along. Isolate the first sounds of the two names if needed: */n/ Nancy; /p/ Peter. No, not a match, they do not begin with the same sound.*

DIDDLE, DIDDLE, DUMPLING

Materials: Poetry Posters: Poem 2, CD Track 27

Vocabulary: off, on, son, stockings

Procedure

- Show the poster to children, talk with them about the illustration, then recite the poem.

- If you think the children would like to hear another poem, you could read "Good Morning." A source for this poem is provided on this page.

Progress Monitoring

Observe individual children's level of engagement or participation in song time. Note who can discriminate and match beginning sounds. Note which children are offering verbal answers, but also notice who is indicating understanding by nods or other positive responses. Record your observations on copies of pages 155–156.

SUGGESTED RESOURCE

Book

Sipe, Muriel. "Good Morning." *Sing a Song of Popcorn.* Beatrice Schenk de Regniers, et al. New York: Scholastic, 1988.

▶ **Lunch/Quiet Time/Centers**
This time is set aside for lunch, quiet time, and center activities. See pages 122–123 for suggested conversation topics during this time.

▶ Small Groups

For information on Small Groups, refer to pages 127–129.

▶ Let's Talk About It

Exploring Feelings: Talking With Toy Animals

Purposes

Recognizes and describes emotions such as happiness, surprise, anger, fear, or sadness. Tells a personal narrative.

Procedure

- Remind children that in the story *Corduroy,* Lisa treated Corduroy as a friend. She probably talked to Corduroy about things that were bothering her, such as missing her mommy when she was away, or having to go to bed at night before she was really sleepy.

- You might prompt children with, *It's nice to have a stuffed animal or doll to talk to like that when you're a little upset about something. Do any of you have a toy that you can talk to like a good friend when you're upset?* (Children will want to tell about their favorite toys).

- As each child shares about a special toy, support his or her feelings. For example:

  Kemal: I tell my kangaroo.

  Teacher: *What do you tell him?*

  Kemal: When I'm sad.

  Teacher: *It's nice to have a special friend to talk to, isn't it?*

  Kemal: I tell him when I'm mad at my brother, too.

  Teacher: *Sometimes it helps us feel better to talk about something that's bothering us.*

- Sum up the discussion by agreeing with the children that stuffed dolls and toys can sometimes seem like very caring friends.

- Thank individual children who shared stories about their special toys. Say for example, *Thank you, Kemal, for telling us today about your kangaroo.*

▶ End-the-Day Centers

Children spend time in Centers of their choice. As children leave for home, say something to help them look forward to the next school day. For example, tell children that tomorrow you will pick one of their favorite books to read and that it's going to be a surprise.

▶ **Start-the-Day Centers** (see pages 124–126)

As children arrive, show them which Centers are open.

▶ **Morning Meeting** (see page 124)

After orienting children to Center activities, help them make a first choice.

▶ **Center Time** (see pages 124–126)

Children spend time in Centers of their choice.

▶ **Story Time: 4th Reading**

Corduroy

Author: Don Freeman

Read *Corduroy* Again

Assign all children the part of Corduroy so that everyone can participate in the reading. Children usually need prompting to recall text. Provide the first sound of a word or the first word or two in a phrase. If children skip key words, say the words yourself, adding them as children say the lines.

Taking On the Roles of Story Characters

Corduroy: I didn't know I'd lost a button. Tonight I'll go and see if I can find it. – p. 5; Could this be a mountain? I think I've always wanted to climb a mountain. – p. 9; This must be a **palace**! I guess I've always wanted to live in a **palace**. – p. 11; This must be a bed. I've always wanted to sleep in a bed. – p. 12; Why, here's my button! – p. 13; This must be home. I *know* I've always wanted a home! – p. 26; You must be a friend. I've always wanted a friend. – p. 28

Story Discussion

Lead a short discussion, posing questions that help children uncover the main characters' feelings, thoughts, and actions. For example: *Last time we read* Corduroy, *we talked about what some children do when parents say no to them. Why you think Lisa did not do any of those things in the store?* Guide the discussion. Perhaps Lisa knew that was not a proper way to act, or perhaps she was already thinking about the money that she had saved.

Other Book Suggestions

Instead of a fourth reading, you might want to substitute a reading of *My Family Plays Music* (see page 7). Introduce the book by reminding children that Baby Louise's grandfather played the harmonica.

Making Connections: Point to instruments mentioned in the text as you read the book. Then, after reading, go back through and talk about some of the instruments. Compare and contrast instruments to the harmonica in *Oonga Boonga* and to the musical instruments (bottle shakers, boxes and elastic bands) that children have been making in Small Groups.

▶ **Outdoor Play**

Name clothing fasteners to call children a few at a time to Outdoor Play: *You may begin Outdoor Play time if you are wearing something with buttons . . . a buckle . . . a zipper . . . snaps . . . laces . . . something that slips on,* and so on. See pages 122–123 for suggested conversation topics during this time.

▶ Songs, Word Play, Letters

Today children will be playing word games, singing songs, and reciting poems. Add your favorite game, song, or poem to this collection.

Songs

"Five Green and Speckled Frogs"; "Open, Shut Them"; "Five Little Ducks"

Predictable Book

Over in the Meadow

Literacy Skills

Alphabet Memory Pocket Chart Game; Can You Think of Words That Begin With the Same Sound as _____?

Purposes

Finds words with the same beginning sound. Uses pictures to understand a book. Names many uppercase letters. Understands that pictures, print, and other symbols carry meaning. Listens to/attends to a variety of genres read aloud. Communicates using verbal and nonverbal cues. Uses sets of concrete objects to represent and decompose small numbers.

Suggested Sequence for Today's Circle

1. "Five Green and Speckled Frogs"
2. Alphabet Memory Pocket Chart Game
3. *Over in the Meadow* (and Can You Think of Words That Begin With the Same Sound as _____?)
4. "Open, Shut Them"
5. "Five Little Ducks"

Materials and Instructional Procedures

FIVE GREEN AND SPECKLED FROGS

Materials: CD Track 10, Song Lyrics p. 160, flannel board and flannel pieces

Vocabulary: green, speckled, log, delicious, cool, pool

Procedure

- Sing the song in the usual way, using the flannel pieces to show the motions and pausing to let children chime in with the number of frogs remaining.

- Take three frogs out of the pool together and then the other two, as you say, *Three frogs . . . four . . . , five frogs.*

ALPHABET MEMORY POCKET CHART GAME

Materials: two sets of uppercase alphabet cards (one letter per card), sheet of poster board with one pocket for each child in the class

Preparation: Glue three sides of paper rectangles to a sheet of poster board, leaving the top open. Number each pocket and post a sticker picture. Laminate, if possible, and slit pocket opening at the top with a mat knife.

Vocabulary: letters, matching, pair, pocket, uppercase

Procedure

- Choose as many letter pairs from the two sets of cards as there are children in the class. (e.g., if 12 children in the class, choose any 12 letters) Place one set of letters in the pockets on the chart; turn the cards backward, if needed, to hide the letters.

- Hand matching letters to the children, one per child. Say, *We are going to play a game to find a matching card for your letters.* Point to the pocket chart. *The cards in these pockets are the matches.*

- Read the numbers on the pockets (1, 2, 3 . . .) as you point to each one and name the picture on each pocket.

- Go around the circle, giving each child a turn to choose a pocket. Turn that card around for all to see. Give the matching card to the child to hold and say, *You found the other* B. *That was lucky!* If it is not a match, put it back in the pocket, and say, *Oh, the* F *doesn't match your* B. *It matches someone's card and maybe that someone will remember where it is. Okay, it's* [child's name] *turn to choose a pocket.* Play the game until all the children have found their match.

Over in the Meadow (and Can You Think of Words That Begin With the Same Sound as ____?)

Materials: book: *Over in the Meadow*

Vocabulary: meadow, mother

Procedure

- Show the book to children and remind them they read it in Story Time. Tell children that you are going to play a game using some of the words from this book.

- Tell children they are going to play a thinking game again. You will start with a word, and they will try to think of other words that begin with the same sound. Say, *Let's start with* meadow. *All the animals in this book lived "over in the meadow."*

- Explain that you are going to go around the circle to see if anybody has an idea for another word that begins with */m/* like meadow. You might say, *We've done this before, but it's still kind of hard to think of words that begin with the same sound.*

- Go around the circle, asking each child if they have an idea. If a child does not answer quickly, move on, saying, *Okay, you keep thinking. We'll see if* [child's name] *has an idea.* Few, if any, children may think of words on this first time of playing.

- After giving each child a chance to offer a word, suggest one yourself (e.g., *mother, milk*), and say, *I think* mother *starts like* meadow *with /m/. Does anyone have another idea? Raise your hand if you do.* Offer one more idea, if children do not offer any, then tell children, *We'll play this game again on another day.*

Open, Shut Them

Materials: CD Track 9, Song Lyrics p. 160

Vocabulary: open, shut, clap, in, lap, creep, chin

Procedure

- Sing the song as usual, modeling the hand motions.

Five Little Ducks

Materials: CD Track 11, Song Lyrics p. 160

Vocabulary: back, far away, out, over

Procedure

- Sing the song in the usual way, using hand motions to show the ducks, the hills, and the quacking. Encourage children to join in with the lyrics and the hand motions.

▶ **Lunch/Quiet Time/Centers**

This time is set aside for lunch, quiet time, and center activities. See pages 122–123 for suggested conversation topics during this time.

▶ Small Groups

See pages 127–129 for information on Small Groups.

▶ Let's Find Out About It

Piggy Banks

Purposes

Uses own experiences to understand story events and expository text. Refines and extends understanding of known words. Uses multiple-word sentences with at least five words.

Materials

book: *Corduroy*; piggy banks, plastic counters

Vocabulary

Introduce these words and use them in the discussion: piggy bank, slot; remove, save

Procedure

- Find the page in *Corduroy* where it says that Lisa counted out money she had saved in her piggy bank. Ask children if they know what a piggy bank is. Confirm that a piggy bank is a place to keep money.

- Bring in real piggy banks to show children. Point to the slot on top where coins can be dropped in and demonstrate, using plastic counters. Show how the piggy bank can be opened to remove money later.

- Discuss how people use piggy banks to save up their money for things they want to buy. Remind children that this practice allowed Lisa to buy Corduroy.

- Ask if anyone has a piggy bank at home. Give children a chance to tell about their banks.

> **English Language Learners**
>
> Invite children to count along with you as you drop counters into the bank. Pronounce the numbers slowly and clearly.

Center Time Connections

Place a few simple banks in Puzzles and Manipulatives along with small plastic counters to be used as coins. Children can play with them and practice putting in and removing counters.

Connect With Families

Tell parents you read a book this week called *Time for Bed* that had the names and pictures of many different animals. Suggest they say the names of any animals such as squirrels and birds that they see with their children over the weekend.

Also note that you have been talking about stuffed animals. Suggest to parents that if their children have stuffed animals, they can ask what kind of animal it is and talk about where the real animal is and what it eats.

> **Extending the Activity**
>
> Invite children who are ready for a challenge to name things that people might save up their money to buy.

▶ End-the-Day Centers

Children spend time in Centers of their choice. In the Book Area, children may enjoy looking for pictures in *Corduroy* that match items on the Picture Cards or playing the Picture Card Word Clue Game in pairs. As children leave for home, say something to help each child look forward to the next school day. For example, remind them that on Monday, there will be many new activities for Center Time.

notes to Teachers

Adapting Activities to Your Program

Here are some suggestions for adapting activities to meet the needs and interests of your children.

Story Time

Flexible Use of Storybooks

There are two third readings and two fourth readings of core story-books scheduled for this week. If you think your children will not sustain interest for four readings of a core storybook, read a suggested book for the family unit, or a related book that you like. You can find a list of suggested books on page 7.

Center Time

Blocks

Encourage Sustained Dramatic Play

If children are still interested in the family figures and in building houses and furniture for family play, keep the family figures in the Blocks area. The idea of towers might be introduced by suggesting that a family may live in a tall apartment building.

Exploring Balance

KAPLA blocks are suggested because their design prompts children to build towers. If you do not have KAPLA blocks, children can build towers with wooden unit blocks.

Art Area: Table

Extending Aesthetic Expression

If children still enjoy painting with marbles and you want to continue this activity, provide drawing with chalk at the easels rather than at the art table. Remove paint cups and put some pieces of chalk in the tray. Use manila or white drawing paper instead of newsprint paper.

Puzzles and Manipulatives

Accommodating Differences

There is usually a wide range of skills within any group of children. To ensure appropriate challenges for all, provide puzzles with a range of difficulty.

Teacher Support

When a child with beginning skills selects a puzzle that is too difficult, help the child learn strategies, such as looking for details. Avoid saying things like, *Oh, this puzzle is much too hard for you. Let's find an easier one.* When children are unable to assemble a puzzle and you can't provide help, tell them to place pieces in the puzzle frame rather than leaving them scattered on the tabletop. Tell children that they are "putting away" or "picking up" when they do that.

UNIT 1 Progress Monitoring Record

Child's Name _____

Observe each child as he or she engages in activities. Use this observation record to make notes of the child's accomplishments as he or she learns new skills and concepts. Include this in the child's assessment/portfolio folder along with work samples. Plan regularly for staff to discuss children's progress.

Story Time	Observation Notes
Shows interest in and enthusiasm toward a new book; reacts indifferently or negatively to a new book	
Focuses on the reading from beginning to end	
Demonstrates understanding of the story by responding to events with smiles, frowns, giggles, shaking heads, quizzical looks	
Participates in discussions	
Answers story questions at the end: • Yes/no to basic questions • Who is this? What is happening here? • What happened next?	
Understands why story characters behave as they do	
Shows understanding of new story vocabulary; indicates that words are new and unfamiliar	
Names characters and objects in the illustrations	
Remembers and understands story events; recalls what happened using pictures and a few prompts	
Songs, Word Play, Letters	
Participates actively when singing songs or reciting poems; participates physically, but not verbally	
Attempts hand/finger/body motions; remembers body motions and words to songs and poems	

	Observation Notes
Anticipates and chimes in with rhyming words; distinguishes rhyming from non-rhyming words	
Recognizes similar beginning sounds in words	
Responds to the first letter in the letter name activity without prompting; indicates that letter and letter name are unfamiliar; needs prompting to recognize first letter of their names	
Discriminates and matches beginning sounds	

Let's Find Out About It

Attends to explanations and information about musical instruments, fabrics, mixing paint	
Begins to use new vocabulary in discussions	
Uses color names in conversation	
Understands that print on objects is meaningful information	
Makes comparisons among objects (of fabrics and clothing; of musical instruments)	

Small Groups: Mathematics

Which sets did the child count correctly? (3, 7, 15, 30)	
Indicates that ordinal number words or color names are unfamiliar	
Shows an interest in relative weights and lengths; knows the purpose of a measuring tape	
Uses comparative words: *bigger, longer, shorter, heavier* in their spoken vocabulary	
Uses one-to-one correspondence to compare two sets numerically; determines whether two sets are equal or unequal numerically	

Unit 1 Extending the Unit

For each unit, suggestions are provided for ways you might extend the unit to five or six weeks. This will allow you to reinforce needed skills, continue activities children enjoy, and add your own favorite activities not included in the curriculum.

During these extensions you should try to retain the general flow of the day. Still, you might want to have one or two days that break from the classroom routine. For example, you may take a walk in the community, have community visitors, or do some other special activity.

Week 5

▶ Story Time

Continue to read other books already suggested for the theme, another book suggested here, or a theme-related book of your choice. To plan readings of the suggested or self-selected books, review models of core book readings (e.g., *Oonga Boonga* on pages 19–21, 31–33).

Suggested Book

- Meyrick, Kathryn. *The Musical Life of Gustav Mole.* Auburn, ME: Child's Play International, 1998.

▶ Songs, Word Play, Letters

Songs and Poems

Continue to sing familiar songs, recite poems, and play games. Use your own favorites as well.

Rhyme

Continue to develop children's sensitivity to rhyme, using Unit 1 games. (See Chiming In With Rhyming Words on page 28.)

Beginning Sounds

Continue to build children's sensitivity to beginning sounds in words using literacy-skill activities from Unit 1 [e.g., Those Words Begin With the Same Sound and Can You Think of Words That Begin With the Same Sound as ___? (pages 65 and 66)].

More Predictable-Book Suggestions

These books should be available through your local library.

- Bowie, C.W. (author) and Fred Willingbam (illustrator). *Busy Toes.* Watertown, MA: Charlesbridge, 2000.
- Dillon, Leo and Diane Dillon. *Rap a Tap Tap: Here's Bojangles—Think of That!* New York: Blue Sky Press, 2002.
- Falwell, Cathryn. *Feast for 10.* New York: Clarion Books, 1993.

▶ Center Time

Cooking Project: Apple Tarts

Read *Feast for 10* early in the week during Songs, Word Play, Letters in preparation for making an apple tart. Find a simple recipe. Prepare a written recipe chart, or cards representing each of the main steps. Organize work so that all children are doing something, most of the time. Remember: Children and adults must wash their hands before starting, and adults are responsible for putting items in the oven and removing them.

▶ Let's Find Out About It

Let's Make Music: Exploring Bottle Pipes

Turn to the last section in the book *Let's Make Music* (about bottle pipes), and read it to the children. Then, use three bottles you have prepared to demonstrate how sound varies with the water level.

▶ Small Groups

Bottle Pipes

Make several sets of bottle pipes that children can experiment with in Small Groups.

Science: Boxes and Bands

Continue the same activity from Week 4, page 129.

Week 6

 Story Time

Read a suggested book from Unit 1 or a theme-related book of your own.

Suggested Book (See page 7 for a description of the book.)

* Jennings, Sharon (author) and Ruth Ohi (illustrator). *Into My Mother's Arms*. Ontario, Canada: Fitzhenry and Whiteside, 2003.

Songs, Word Play, Letters

Songs and Poems

Continue to sing familiar songs and recite poems. Add your favorites to the collection.

Alphabet Letter Knowledge

Continue to develop children's ability to recognize and name uppercase letters, in their own names and others. If appropriate, write in list form all children's names that start with the same letter and comment about the other letters in the names that make them different from one another. Select appropriate activities from the previous weeks such as If Your Name Starts With [name a letter], Raise Your Hand (pages 22–23) .

Beginning Sounds

Continue to build children's sensitivity to the beginning sound in words by using activities from Unit 1 (e.g., Can You Think of Words That Start With the Same Sound as ___? and Those Words Begin With the Same Sound) pages 64 and 65.

Let's Find Out About It

Flashlight

Find the page in *Corduroy* where the night watchman uses a flashlight. Show children a flashlight, and flip the switch on and off. Take out the batteries. Now try it. Talk about what happened. Ask children when they have used flashlights.

Small Groups

Flashlight Exploration

Glue a random display of swatches (cardboard, shiny and dull paper, fabric) and jar lids to a sheet of poster board. Hold or prop up poster board, as children take turns shining a flashlight beam onto items you name.

Writing: Writing Alphabet Letters and Names

Continue the same activity from Week 4, page 129.

Center Time

Add new story and information books to the book area, do a favorite art activity such as leaf rubbings, and try cottage cheese water fountains at the water table.

Art Area: Easel

Leaf Rubbings In preparation, mount a collection of different kinds of leaves on large pieces of newspaper the size of the easel. Children put newsprint on the easel as usual. Before they begin, remove paper from the outside of crayons. Children use the sides of the crayons to rub them across the newsprint to make leaf rubbings. Outlines of the leaves will come through on the newsprint.

Sand and Water Table

Water Fountains Gather small cartons such as cottage cheese containers. Put four small holes in carton sides, starting halfway up. As children pour water in, it squirts out the holes.

IF YOU'RE HAPPY

1. If you're happy and you know it, clap your hands. *(clap twice)*
   If you're happy and you know it, clap your hands. *(clap twice)*
   If you're happy and you know it, then your face will surely show it.
   If you're happy and you know it, clap your hands. *(clap twice)*
2. . . . stomp your feet. *(stomp twice)* . . .
3. . . . shout, "Hurray!" *(Hurray!)* . . .
4. . . . *do all three. (Do all three motions.)* . . .

BINGO

1. There was a farmer had a dog,
   And Bingo was his name-o.
   B – I – N – G – O,
   B – I – N – G – O,
   B – I – N – G – O,
   And Bingo was his name-o.
2. . . . *(clap)* – I – N – G – O! . . .
3. . . . *(clap)* – *(clap)*– N – G – O! . . .
4. . . . *(clap)* – *(clap)* – *(clap)* – G – O! . . .
5. . . . *(clap)* – *(clap)* – *(clap)* – *(clap)* – O! . . .
6. . . . *(clap)* – *(clap)* – *(clap)* – *(clap)* – *(clap)* . . .

DOWN BY THE BAY

1. Down by the bay *(repeat)*
   Where the watermelons grow, *(repeat)*
   Back to my home, *(repeat)*
   I dare not go. *(repeat)*
   For if I do, *(repeat)*
   My mother will say, *(repeat)*
   "Did you ever see a snake baking a cake?"
   Down by the bay.
2. . . . "Did you ever see a frog walking a dog?" . . .
3. . . . "Did you ever see a mouse painting a house?" . . .

Suggestion:
Make up new rhyming verses *(a pig dancing a jig, a cow taking a bow, a hen counting to ten. . .)*

HEAD AND SHOULDERS, KNEES AND TOES

Head and shoulders, knees and toes, knees and toes,
Head and shoulders, knees and toes, knees and toes,
Eyes and ears and mouth and nose,
Head and shoulders, knees and toes, knees and toes.

Motion:
Touch each part of the body named as you sing.

Suggestion:
Sing the song four more times. The first time, leave out the word *head* and just do the action. Continue to drop body part words till you are just performing the actions.

EENTSY, WEENTSY SPIDER

The eentsy, weentsy spider went up the water spout.
Down came the rain and washed the spider out.
Out came the sun and dried up all the rain,
And the eentsy, weentsy spider went up the spout again.

Motions:
A. Make circles with thumbs and index fingers of both hands, close circles and twist upward.
B. Wiggle fingers and bring hands down.
C. Push hands out toward sides.
D. Make a circle with arms above your head.
E. Wiggle fingers and move hands up.

OLD MACDONALD HAD A FARM

1. Old MacDonald had a farm, E – I – E – I – O!
   And on his farm he had some chicks, E – I – E – I – O!
   With a chick, chick here, and a chick, chick there,
   Here a chick, there a chick, ev'rywhere a chick, chick,
   Old MacDonald had a farm, E – I – E – I – O!
2. And on his farm he had some ducks, E – I – E – I – O!
   With a quack, quack here, and a quack, quack there,
   Here a quack, there a quack, ev'rywhere a quack, quack,
   Chick, chick here, and a chick, chick there,
   Here a chick, there a chick, ev'rywhere a chick, chick,
   Old MacDonald had a farm, E – I – E – I – O!

3. . . . cow . . . a moo, moo here . . . (Repeat duck and chick sounds.)
4. . . . turkey . . . a gobble, gobble here . . . (Repeat cow, duck, and chick sounds.)

Motions:
A. Move head up and down.
B. Put thumbs under arms and flap elbows.
C. Close fists and motion as if milking a cow.
D. Hook thumbs together and wiggle fingers.

Suggestion:
Add more animals to continue the song. (Horse, neigh, neigh while lifting feet like a high-stepping steed; rooster, cock-a-doodle-doo while flapping hands against sides; goat, baaa-baaa while tossing head, index fingers held up for horns)

THE WHEELS ON THE BUS

1. The wheels on the bus go round and round,
   Round and round, round and round,
   The wheels on the bus go round and round,
   All through the town.
2. The people on the bus go up and down,
   Up and down, up and down,
   The people on the bus go up and down,
   All through the town.
3. The horn on the bus goes toot, toot, toot . . .
4. The money in the box goes ching, ching, ching . . .
5. The wiper on the glass goes swish, swish, swish . . .
6. The driver on the bus says, "Move on back" . . .

Motions:
A. Circle fists in a forward, round and round motion for a wheel.
B. Bounce up and down in seat.
C. Push palm outward as if pressing the horn.
D. Pretend to drop coin in a box.
E. Move forearms left to right like windshield wipers.
F. Gesture with thumb over shoulder.

I'M A LITTLE TEAPOT

I'm a little teapot, short and stout.
Here is my handle; here is my spout. (Place right hand at waist. Hold left elbow up with hand bent down.)
When I get all steamed up, hear me shout.
"Tip me over, and pour me out!" (Bend at waist to the left.)

OPEN, SHUT THEM

Open, shut them. (Open and shut fists.)
Open, shut them.
Give a little clap, clap, clap. (Clap three times.)
Open, shut them.
Open, shut them.
Put them in your lap, lap, lap. (Slap lap three times.)
Creep them, creep them. (Walk fingers up lap to chin.)
Slowly creep them
Right up to your chin.
Open up your mouth, (Open mouth wide.)
But do not let them in. (Bring hands down quickly.)

FIVE GREEN AND SPECKLED FROGS

Five green and speckled frogs
Sat on a speckled log,
Eating some most delicious bugs.
YUM! YUM! (spoken)
One jumped into the pool
Where it was nice and cool.
Then there were four green and speckled frogs.
GLUB! GLUB! (spoken)
Repeat the rhyme, losing one more frog each time until there are no frogs left on the log.

FIVE LITTLE DUCKS

Five little ducks went out one day,
Over the hill and far away.
Mother duck said, "Quack, quack, quack, quack."
But only four little ducks came back.
Repeat, losing one more duck each time until one duck is left. Have mother duck quack loudly and end with "And all five little ducks came back."

CLAP YOUR HANDS

1. Clap, clap, clap your hands, (clap)
   Clap your hands together. (clap)
   Clap, clap, clap your hands, (clap)
   Clap your hands together. (clap)
2. Stamp, stamp, stamp your feet . . . (stamp feet)
3. Shake, shake, shake your hips . . . (shake hips)
4. Bend, bend, bend your knees . . . (bend knees)

Glossary

alphabetic principle the concept that letters and letter combinations are used to represent phonemes

alphabet letter knowledge the knowledge of the names and shapes of letters

cardinal numbers numbers that tell how many

comprehension Listening comprehension refers to the ability to understand spoken language. Reading comprehension refers to the ability to understand what one reads.

comprehensive curriculum a curriculum that provides content reflective of standards across all domains: language and literacy, mathematics, science, social studies, social and emotional development, physical development, and the arts

concepts of print the growing understanding of how print functions and how books are used; concepts include the distinction between pictures and print, knowing that English is read left to right and top to bottom, and understanding that print is always read the same

consonant a speech sound or phoneme that is not a vowel and is formed with obstruction of the flow of air with the teeth, lips, or tongue

decoding the use of relationships between printed letters and the sounds they represent to translate print into words

early reading the initial phase of reading during which children develop a basic understanding of how to read. This phase includes children's early interactions with books and other print, pretend reading, growing familiarity with print, and initial ability to read selected words.

early writing the initial phase of writing during which children gain familiarity with and control of the elements of print. This phase includes scribble-writing, creation of letter-like forms, inventive spelling, playful uses of written forms, and writing of names and selected words.

expository text nonfiction; any text that is not fiction, such as an information book, map, chart, schedule, and game instructions

integrated curriculum a curriculum that addresses several domains of learning together and provides a broad range of experiences. An integrated curriculum is often organized around units of study.

literacy the term used to refer to reading, writing, and the creative and analytical acts involved in producing and comprehending texts

nonstandard measurement measurement done with objects, such as craft sticks or string, rather than with standard tools, such as a ruler or tape measure

observational assessment the gathering of information about children by watching them, usually in the context of typical, ongoing classroom activities

one-to-one correspondence the pairing of items from one set with the items in a second set

onset the consonant(s) at the start of a syllable. The remainder of the syllable is called its rime. In *pail*, *p* is the onset and *ail* is the rime.

ordinal numbers numbers that designate the place of an item in a series, such as *first, second, third*

patterns regularities that occur systematically, such as two red blocks, three blue blocks; two red blocks, three blue blocks, two red blocks, three blue blocks

phonemes the smallest units of sound that combine to form syllables and words. For example, *pond* has four phonemes: /p/ /o/ /n/ /d/.

phonemic awareness the conscious awareness that words are made up of segments of speech that are represented with letters and the ability to focus on and manipulate individual phonemes; for example, *Brad* without /b/ is *rad*. This competence requires attending to sounds, rather than to their meaning.

phonological awareness the awareness of the sounds of speech apart from meaning. It includes attending to syllables, onsets and rimes, and phonemes. This is a more encompassing term than *phonemic awareness*.

print awareness growing recognition of the conventions and characteristics of written language, such as print carries meaning, a book is held upright, and pages are turned from front to back. It also includes understanding the concept of a letter and the concept of a word.

predictable-text book books that use rhyme, alliteration, repetition of a sentence pattern, and other devices that make a text relatively easy for children to recall

rational counting matching a number word in order to each item in a set; understanding that the last number word tells how many items are in the set

retelling process of recounting, or telling what happened; a personal narrative or story heard from a book

rime the portion of a syllable that follows the onset. In *pail*, *p* is the onset and *ail* is the rime.

rote counting recitation of the number words used for the counting sequence; done from memory, without enumerating anything

rubrics sets of descriptive behaviors that are used to describe the abilities individuals are developing in selected areas. Teachers use rubrics to help determine a child's developmental status and plan instruction.

scaffolding instructional support that teachers provide to enable a child to complete a task. That support is carefully reduced over time as the child is more able to work independently.

self-regulation the ability to control one's behavior in ways that enable one to engage in social interactions in an acceptable manner

social skills behaviors used for initiating and sustaining interactions with others

standard measurement measurement done with standard tools, such as a ruler, tape measure, or scale

standard units of measurement conventionally recognized units, such as inches, feet, pounds, ounces, and miles

syllable a unit of pronunciation that is organized around a vowel. It may or may not have consonants before or after the vowel. For example, the word *baby* has two syllables: *ba* and *by*.

vocabulary words a person understands and can use

vowel an open phoneme that is the nucleus of every syllable (*a, e, i, o, u,* and sometimes *y*)

Index